RITUAL AND CHRISTIAN BEGINNINGS

# Ritual and Christian Beginnings

*A Socio-Cognitive Analysis*

RISTO URO

# OXFORD
UNIVERSITY PRESS

Great Clarendon Street, Oxford, OX2 6DP,
United Kingdom

Oxford University Press is a department of the University of Oxford.
It furthers the University's objective of excellence in research, scholarship,
and education by publishing worldwide. Oxford is a registered trade mark of
Oxford University Press in the UK and in certain other countries

© Risto Uro 2016

The moral rights of the author have been asserted

First published 2016
First published in paperback 2018

All rights reserved. No part of this publication may be reproduced, stored in
a retrieval system, or transmitted, in any form or by any means, without the
prior permission in writing of Oxford University Press, or as expressly permitted
by law, by licence or under terms agreed with the appropriate reprographics
rights organization. Enquiries concerning reproduction outside the scope of the
above should be sent to the Rights Department, Oxford University Press, at the
address above

You must not circulate this work in any other form
and you must impose this same condition on any acquirer

Published in the United States of America by Oxford University Press
198 Madison Avenue, New York, NY 10016, United States of America

British Library Cataloguing in Publication Data
Data available

Library of Congress Cataloging in Publication Data
Data available

ISBN 978-0-19-966117-6 (Hbk.)
ISBN 978-0-19-883322-2 (Pbk.)

Links to third party websites are provided by Oxford in good faith and
for information only. Oxford disclaims any responsibility for the materials
contained in any third party website referenced in this work.

Revised Standard Version of the Bible, copyright 1952 [2nd edition, 1971]
by the Division of Christian Education of the National Council of the Churches of
Christ in the United States of America. Used by permission. All rights reserved.

# Acknowledgements

This book would not have been possible without the 'community of brains' from which it has emerged. I take this expression quite literally. My thinking has evolved as part of a network of scholars who have worked together intensively on developing ritual and cognitive approaches to the study of early Christianity and religion in general. I have been dependent on this cognitive web to such a degree that it is impossible to think of the completion of any individual part without this collaboration, although I am, of course, alone fully responsible for the final result.

This book is part of a larger collective research project entitled 'Ritual and the Emergence of Early Christian Religion: A Socio-Cognitive Analysis' (REECR), funded by the Academy of Finland (project #1266452) and based at the University of Helsinki. I have had the privilege of working with three brilliant younger colleagues, Anne Katrine Gudme, Vojtěch Kaše, and Rikard Roitto, with whom I have been able to discuss most parts of this book in the inspiring project meetings held in many cities and countries. The external advisors of the REECR project, Joseph Bulbulia, István Czachesz, Douglas Davies, and Armin Geertz, have supported the work of the collective project, as well as my own book project, in many significant ways. With István I have been collaborating for many years in developing cognitive approaches to Biblical Studies. His profound knowledge of cognitive research and his sharp thinking have been invaluable assets to my work. Of vital importance to me have also been the support and encouragement that I have received from two central pioneers of new methods in my home discipline, Gerd Theissen and Philip Esler.

The initial idea of writing a book on ritual and Christian beginnings was born at the Helsinki Collegium for Advanced Studies, where I was working 2004–2005 together with Petri Luomanen, Ilkka Pyysiäinen, Petri Ylikoski, and others. It was Ilkka who introduced me to the Cognitive Science of Religion, and his guidance and enthusiasm have been crucial for my learning about this new field. After several years of intensive engagement in teaching and administration, I was able to concentrate on completing my book project as a visiting fellow at Clare Hall, University of Cambridge, for the academic year 2014–2015. The fellowship was funded by the Osk. Huttunen Foundation. I am grateful for this opportunity, and for all the assistance provided by the staff of Clare Hall to me and my wife during our stay in Cambridge. I also wish to thank my colleagues in Cambridge, Judith Lieu for supporting my application and Simon Gathercole for being my 'mentor'.

I am deeply indebted to the many collaborators and colleagues who have given me important feedback on my work in progress at numerous conferences, workshops, and seminars, and in personal communications, over the years. These include—but are not limited to—Veikko Anttonen, Johan Bastubacka, Tamas Biró, Juliette Day, Richard DeMaris, Jutta Jokiranta, Thomas Kazen, Thomas Lawson, Liv Ingeborg Lied, Luther Martin, Dietmar Neufeld, Ronit Nikolsky, Outi Pohjanheimo, Colleen Shantz, Edward Slingerland, Fred Tappenden, Terhi Utriainen, Cecilia Wassen, Hanne von Weissenberg, and Harvey Whitehouse. The students in Ritual Studies courses in Helsinki, Makumira (Tanzania) and Reykjavik have also greatly helped me to develop my ideas and thinking.

I warmly thank Ellen Valle for editing the language of the book, the staff at the Oxford University Press, Tom Perridge, Liza Robottom, Karen Raith, Anzil Steephan, Kim Allen, and Carolyn McAndrew, for their support and professional assistance, and my son Ilkka for helping me in preparing the indices.

Finally, I wish to thank my wife Marjatta, who has been there for me and has understood the importance of this project to me. In real life she has always had a better sense of ritual than I do.

*June 2015*
*Clare Hall, Cambridge, UK*

# Contents

| | |
|---|---:|
| Introduction | 1 |
| 1. Ritual Theory and Early Christian Studies | 7 |
| 2. Ritual, Culture, and the Human Mind: A Socio-cognitive Approach | 41 |
| 3. 'I Baptize You With Water': Ritual and the Rise of Religious Movements | 71 |
| 4. 'Are Any Among You Sick?': Ritual, Possession, and Healing | 99 |
| 5. 'When You Come Together': Ritual and Cooperation | 128 |
| 6. 'Baptizing... and Teaching': Ritual and Religious Knowledge | 154 |
| Concluding Remarks | 178 |
| *References* | 183 |
| *Index of Modern Authors* | 221 |
| *General Index* | 227 |

# Introduction

Why did Christianity happen? Ever since the rise of the historical-critical study of Christian beginnings, scholars have tried to identify reasons for the emergence and success of the early Christian movement. Among the aspects to which this success has been attributed have been the resurrection experiences of the first followers, the miracles performed by Jesus and the apostles, socio-political factors, organizational structures, and early Christians' willingness to suffer martyrdom—to mention but a few. The focus in this book is on one explanatory factor which has largely been ignored by scholars: the role of ritual in the emergence of the movement.[1]

From the viewpoint of the history of religion—which is the perspective of this study—the failure to include ritual in the story of Christian origins is striking. New religious movements often start with ritual innovations; the success of a movement depends, among other things, on its ability to get people engaged in ritual practices that consolidate the ideology and moral values of the movement. Without a ritual system of some sort, the core beliefs would not be remembered; nor would they be transmitted to the next generation.

This book attempts to fill this gap in the scholarship by giving pride of place in the study of Christian beginnings to ritual. It is not the only

---

[1] Throughout this study, 'ritual' is used as a general family-resemblance term for the kind of behaviours studied in the field of Ritual Studies, just as 'religion' is used to refer to the kind of phenomena that are studied in the academic discipline of Religious Studies. 'A ritual' is used as a synonym for 'rite', and denotes particular ritual enactments located at specific times and places (cf. Grimes 2014: 192). The various ritual theories employed in this study narrow the analytical focus and provide more specific definitions of ritual, or at least a framework within which actions that might be referred to as rituals can be examined.

study of its kind; certain other scholars, introduced in Chapter One, have felt the same need to apply ritual theory to the study of early Judaism and early Christianity. The particular contribution of this book is to combine insights from three fields of study: New Testament/Early Christian Studies (the home discipline), Ritual Studies (an interdisciplinary field focusing on ritual behaviour), *and* the Cognitive Science of Religion (a research programme in Religious Studies which seeks to explain religious phenomena by applying concepts and findings derived from the cognitive and evolutionary sciences).

Such an interdisciplinary enterprise involves challenges. Ritual Studies and the Cognitive Science of Religion, about which we will learn more in subsequent chapters, are highly interdisciplinary in themselves. A biblical scholar employing theories and perspectives from these fields has to digest knowledge from a host of new disciplines, and to apply it to test cases which are often quite different from the empirical data used in the original studies. He or she cannot have the same mastery of the auxiliary disciplines as of the home discipline—although we should keep in mind that Biblical Studies has always been an interdisciplinary field, absorbing ideas and theories from different disciplines in the humanities and the social sciences.

The task is even more demanding if an interdisciplinary study is intended to be a contribution to several disciplines, as is the case with this book. A critical reader representing any of the three disciplines will easily be able to say that this study does not go deep enough into the specific questions of one particular field: for example, into historical sources or the subtleties of ritual theory or cognitive science. New knowledge is often acquired by delving deeper and deeper into theoretical and historical (empirical) issues, but this comes with a price: it means that interdisciplinary dialogue between highly specialized fields becomes more difficult. Interdisciplinarity requires that specialization be kept at a moderate level, so that scholars representing different disciplines can interact and communicate with one another. In a successful case, the interacting contributions together become something more than the sum of the individual parts.

The challenges and difficulties involved in this study make it experimental (rather than advancing a fully developed theory of ritual) and its analyses illustrative (rather than presenting a systematic examination of the emerging early Christian rituals). The book opens with two chapters introducing the general research setting and central theoretical questions, followed by four chapters focusing on a particular test case each. The study does not attempt a full story of ritual and Christian beginnings, but offers a prolegomenon to its theme. It aims at providing building blocks, theoretical tools, and stimuli for further studies on the role played by ritual in the rise of Christianity.[2]

In Chapter One (Ritual Theory and Early Christian Studies), I ask why ritual has been a largely neglected theme in the study of Christian beginnings. The chapter also surveys earlier studies in which ritual *has* been in focus, most importantly among the members of the so-called History of Religion School and historians of early Christian liturgy. The chapter gives an account of the impact now being made by the field of Ritual Studies in the study of early Christianity and in the study of the Bible, and makes a case for the view that the emerging new approach employing ritual theory can be fruitfully extended toward the use of cognitive theories of ritual.

Chapter Two (Ritual, Culture and the Human Mind: A Sociocognitive Approach) introduces the reader to the Cognitive Science of Religion (CSR), especially to those aspects of this new field that are relevant for a deeper understanding of the cognitive theories used in this study. CSR is a research programme within Religious Studies which draws on a growing body of knowledge from the cognitive and evolutionary sciences to explain human religiosity. It is a pluralistic movement, comprising different schools and currents; what they have in common is the effort to achieve explanatory and testable theories, as well as a multilevel analysis of religious phenomena (operating across the traditional hierarchies of science). CSR is about 'sciencing up' the study of religion, but it also creates an arena

---

[2] This study is part of a larger collective research project 'Ritual and the Emergence of Early Christian Religion: A Socio-Cognitive Analysis' (REECR), based at the University of Helsinki and funded by the Academy of Finland for the period of 2013–2017. The work of the project focuses on three potentially relevant areas of ritual life in the Jewish and early Christian world: (1) practices related to death, burial, and the remembering of deceased family members (Anne Katrine Gudme); (2) rituals related to purification, conflict resolution, and forgiveness (Rikard Roitto); and (3) meal practices—the most important form of social gathering in antiquity (Vojtěch Kaše). See http://blogs.helsinki.fi/ritual-earlychristianity/. The REECR project is also engaged in producing the *Oxford Handbook of Early Christian Ritual*; this will consist of 42 chapters, written by ritual theorists, historians of early Judaism and early Christianity, and liturgical scholars, and will provide a manifold account of the ritual world of early Christianity from the beginning of the movement up to the end of the sixth century (Uro et al. forthcoming).

for mutual interaction between the natural and the human sciences. The survey of the schools and currents in CSR provides a basis for suggesting a 'socio-cognitive approach' to early Christian rituals, relying on cognitive theories of ritual that operate at both a social and a cognitive level. Three perspectives on ritual emerge from the discussion, described by the keywords 'action', 'cooperation', and 'religious knowledge'. These perspectives form the cornerstones of the study of early Christian rituals in the subsequent chapters.

In Chapter Three ('I Baptize You with Water': Ritual and the Rise of Religious Movements), the focus is on our first test case, John the Baptist: a charismatic figure and ritual entrepreneur, whose movement is seen by most early Christian scholars as one that had a significant impact on Jesus and his movement. It is usually recognized that John's immersion rite was a ritual innovation of some kind, but scholars of early Judaism and early Christianity have seldom seen this fact as an important piece of evidence. Nor has the issue of ritual innovation been a central theme in ritual theory. Some cognitive theories of ritual, nevertheless, prove to be helpful in analysing the role of ritual innovation in the emergence of the Baptist movement and its offshoot, the Jesus movement. Cognitive theory also allows comparisons between movements revolving around a ritual invention, such as John the Baptist and the famous contemporary Indian guru, Mata Amritanandayami or Amma ('Mother'), even when they come from quite different cultures and times. In addition to the question of ritual innovation, Chapter Three looks at how John's immersion rite facilitated the transmission of his teaching, and how the rite could signal commitment and mobilize adherents.

Chapter Four ('Are Any Among You Sick?' Ritual, Possession and Healing) examines Jesus' and the early Christians' healing activities from the perspective of ritual. In addition to problems related to the historical reliability of the sources, the analysis of Jesus' curative actions raises the question of whether such actions can fruitfully be studied as 'rituals'. The chapter argues that a ritual approach to Jesus' healing is a meaningful project: the topic converges with many issues that anthropologists of shamanism and spirit possession have discussed under the general rubric of 'ritual healing'. Insights and theories from such studies shed light on Jesus' healing activity, as well as on the rites of healing and exorcism in the early Church. The chapter takes issue with certain social-scientific interpretations of Jesus as a spirit-possessed healer (which show a bias toward cultural relativism), and makes use of recent cognitive research into spirit possession. Jesus' healings, spirit possession and more institutionalized forms of ritual healing cannot be lumped together under a single theory of ritual, but the cognitive analysis is helpful in pointing out aspects of ritual healing that have not been recognized in earlier studies.

Chapter Five ('When You Come Together': Ritual and Cooperation) delves into the question of how ritual facilitates social life and cooperation, leading back as far as Durkheim's functionalist theory. While the analyses of the two preceding test cases, John's baptism and ritual healing in early Christianity, largely relied on a definition of ritual as 'action bringing about changes', the 'cooperation perspective' shifts the analytical focus somewhat. Singing, dancing, or praying together are actions, but not the kind of actions in which a ritual agent is acting upon a ritual patient or patients. Changing the focus from the action perspective to one of cooperation enables the investigation of the third test case: the ritual life of the Pauline assemblies. Chapter Five discusses the Durkheimian tradition in ritual theory, in particular its passionate defence by Rappaport in *Ritual and Religion the Making of Humanity*, and situates the Commitment Signalling Theory, briefly introduced in Chapter Two, in this wider context. Commitment Signalling has been developed by evolutionary anthropologists to analyse and predict how religious practices motivate cooperation. The theory involves problems—for example, it is not clear whether it is being presented as a theory of ritual or of religious behaviour in general—but Commitment Signalling is nevertheless helpful in enriching the social-scientific interpretation of the Pauline rituals. The mechanisms of social dynamics suggested by signalling theorists shed light on issues tackled by New Testament scholars, for example by providing a corrective to overly idealistic descriptions of the social life of the Pauline groups.

Chapter Six ('Baptizing... and Teaching': Ritual and Religious Knowledge) highlights the third focal point of the study: the role of ritual in generating and conveying religious knowledge. This perspective is unfolded in the context of three kinds of knowledge related to ritual: embodied, common (shared), and extended knowledge. The chapter explores how these three approaches to ritual knowledge shed light on early Christian baptismal practices. In particular, it draws on the branch of cognitive science dubbed 'embodied' or 'extended' ('situated') cognition. Researchers promoting embodied cognition argue that cognition is fundamentally grounded in bodily actions and in the body interacting with the environment. Findings and insights from embodied cognition research are potentially highly relevant for the study of ritual, but very little work has been done along these lines so far. Finally, in Chapter Six I develop a hypothesis as to how early Christian baptismal practices accommodated implicit knowledge about power relations (this has been a theme in Ritual Studies, but without an input from research into embodied cognition). The chapter also shows how extensive symbolic technologies and systems of knowledge grew up around early Christian baptism, including the Catechumenate (baptismal teaching), credal formulae and creeds, and stories and pictorial representations, as well as physical structures and architecture. All these embeddings and technologies can be analysed as 'cognitive tools', interacting with and influencing religious cognition.

To put it as simply and briefly as possible: in this book I argue that ritual theory is indispensable for the study of Christian beginnings, and that the ritual approach to early Christianity is greatly enhanced by the application of cognitive theories of ritual.

# 1

# Ritual Theory and Early Christian Studies

In 2008, Richard DeMaris published a book, entitled *The New Testament in Its Ritual World*, in which he argued vigorously for the use of ritual theory in the study of Christian beginnings. At the same time, however, he stressed 'how new and, consequently, how experimental the approach is' (DeMaris 2008: 2). 'We are', DeMaris writes, 'probably several years away from being ready to conduct a comprehensive critical study of rites in the New Testament' (2008: 5). I would still argue the same.

Although a few new studies using ritual theory as a tool for analysing and interpreting New Testament and early Christian texts have appeared since the publication of DeMaris' book (Taussig 2009; Lamoreaux 2013; Turley 2015), it is still striking how little attention ritual theory, and the role of ritual in the emergence of the early Christian movement, have received in the field. In the past few decades, the range of different approaches applied by New Testament/early Christian scholars has been broad, including historical, literary, culturalist, feminist, poststructuralist, psychological, social-scientific perspectives along with many others, but ritual, either as part of any particular method or as a theoretical perspective in its own right, has been—in the grand scheme of things—a marginal topic among scholars. Perhaps the most striking fact is that even Social-Scientific Criticism, a subfield in Biblical Studies promoting the use of theories originating in the social sciences, has given surprisingly little consideration to the role of ritual in the formation of the early Christian movement and in the social life of early communities, even though the study of ritual has a long history in anthropology and in social theory in general.

Ritual was ubiquitous in the world in which Christianity was born, as it is in the world in which we live. No human society or culture, past or present, has ever been identified in which rituals are not practised and people could escape them. We cannot simply avoid encountering rituals. As Ilkka Pyysiäinen puts it, '[o]ne may quit smoking, stop drinking, and even adopt a celibate life, but rarely have we heard of a person totally refusing to participate in rituals' (Pyysiäinen 2004b: 135). Anthropologists and ritual theorists have long tried to explain the human compulsion to ritual, and a myriad of theories and explanations have been advanced. One important development over the three past decades or so has been the emergence of Ritual Studies, as a nameable and interdisciplinary field, with the aim of systematizing and developing approaches to this omnipresent aspect of human behaviour and social life (Grimes 1995, 2014; Bell 2007; Stephenson 2015). One relevant question is why resources from Ritual Studies have been so sparsely applied in the study of Christian beginnings, and only relatively recently in a theoretically reflective way. My overview in this chapter seeks to find some answers to this question, although a full account of the issue would require a much more detailed analysis of the history of the discipline than is possible here. A related and equally important task is to describe how early Christian ritual practices have been approached in those studies in which rituals *have* been in focus. Although rituals have been an under-researched topic in New Testament Studies in general, the topic has not, of course, been totally ignored. There was a period in the history of the discipline when ritual received more attention among members of the so-called History of Religion School, and in an adjacent theological subdiscipline, that of Liturgical Studies, the historical roots of Christian worship have naturally been a topic of interest. A few scholars making use of social-scientific theories have also paid attention to ritual practices in their explorations of the social world of the first Christians.

In addition to surveying previous studies, it is imperative to ask why knowledge concerning ritual is often achieved by way of theory, and to explain why so much emphasis in this book is given to theoretical reflections. Finally, it is necessary to give my reasons for choosing *the kinds* of ritual theories applied in this book, that is, cognitive theories of ritual.

## 1.1 HISTORY OF RELIGION SCHOOL

Two traditional domains in the study of early Christianity have held interest in ritual. One, the History of Religion School, belongs to a limited time and a specific group of scholars in the history of the discipline, although the school's legacy has exerted influence over many areas of more recent scholarship. The other domain is the study of early Christian liturgy; this in turn is part of the larger field of Liturgical Studies, studying the forms of Christian worship from historical and contemporary perspectives (Chupungco 1998; J. Day and Gordon-Taylor 2013).

The History of Religion School (*Religionsgeschichliche Schule*)[1] is the name attached to a group of biblical scholars and theologians who studied and taught at the University of Göttingen in the 1880s and 1890s, and who during the decades around the turn of the twentieth century championed a thoroughly historical approach to the study of biblical traditions. The members of the group included William Wrede, Johannes Weiss, Herman Gunkel, Albert Eichorn, Wilhelm Heitmüller, Ernst Troelsch, and Wilhelm Bousset (for biographical information about the group members, see Lüdemann and Schröder 1987). William Baird summarizes their main emphases and results as follows: 'a focus on religion rather than theology, a concern to view the history of Christianity with the course of the larger history of religion, an emphasis on the history of tradition rather than literary criticism, and a conviction that Christianity was decisively shaped by the impact of foreign religions' (Baird 2003: 222). Despite their interest in locating early Christianity within the larger frame of ancient religions and cults, the History of Religion School was mainly concerned with the history of *one* religion, Christianity, or, as Gunkel puts it, 'the history of religion of the Bible' (Gunkel 1927). The significance of the school may thus be seen more within the development of Biblical Studies and theology than in that of the field of Comparative Religion (Sharpe 1986: 149–51). The somewhat limited focus of the *Religionsgeschichliche Schule* should not, however, undermine the fact that the members of the school were determined to

---

[1] The plural 'History of Religions' is also often used, but this probably represents a misunderstanding of the 's' in the German word 'Religionsgeschichte' (Baird 2003: 222).

carry out their research as a matter of the history of religion (which at that time meant historical-philological analysis of *texts*), not as theology (Betz 2011a). The heyday of the History of Religion School overlapped with the formative period of the academic study of religion, and the aspirations of the members highlight what Jonathan Z. Smith has characterized as 'the deep interrelations of the two enterprises, the study of religion and biblical studies' (J. Z. Smith 2009: 6).

The focus on religion rather than on theological doctrine involved an interest in the ritual life of early Christians and its connections with the other cults of the Hellenistic world. The theologians belonging to the History of Religion movement argued for the priority of ritual over philosophical and theological articulations of faith. These scholars were united in their claim that the cult, as displayed in the religious actions of believers, is at the root of the theological ideas which can be found in the texts of the Bible (Lehmkühler 1996: 207–8), much in the same way as William Robertson Smith argued in his *Lectures on the Religion of the Semites* (W. R. Smith 2002 [orig. 1894]). In the preface to his celebrated *Kyrios Christos*, Wilhelm Bousset (1865–1920) pointed out that '[t]he present work... attempts to take its point of departure from the practice of the cultus and of the community's worship and to understand the way things developed from this perspective' (Bousset 1970: 11; [orig. 1921]).[2] For Bousset, the confession of Jesus as 'Lord' (*Kyrios*) represented a major Christological innovation among gentile Christians, who supposedly derived the title from pagan cults. The source of this doctrinal development is not, however, to be found in the theological reflections of the earliest Christian leaders, but in the 'Christ cult' of the Hellenistic Christian communities. Bousset describes the devotional life of these assemblies in vivid terms:

> What the *kyrios* signified for the first Hellenistic Christian congregations thus stands before us in bright and living colors. It is the Lord who

---

[2] The significance of Bousset's work is expressed by Larry Hurtado in the following words: 'In combined depth and scope, erudition, and influence, nothing equivalent has appeared in the nearly ninety years now since it was first published' (Hurtado 2003: 14). Hurtado's own monumental study, *Lord Jesus Christ*, attempts to describe the evolution of early Christian christology from the perspective of 'Christ-devotion', but the book as a whole gives relatively little space to ritual practices (cf. however, Hurtado 2003: 134–53) and shows no interest in the use of ritual theory.

holds sway over the Christian life of fellowship, in particular as it is unfolded in the community's worship, thus in the cultus. Around the *kyrios* the community is gathered in believing reverence, it confesses his name, under the invocation of his name it baptizes, it assembles around the table of the Lord Jesus; it sighs in the fervent cry 'Maranatha, come, Lord Jesus';... here in the gatherings of the fellowship, in worship and cult, there grew up for believers in Christ the consciousness of their unity and peculiar sociological exclusiveness (soziologischen Geschlossenheit). During the day scattered... they came together in the evening, probably as often as possible, for the common sacred meal. There they experienced the miracle of fellowship, the glow of the enthusiasm of a common faith and a common hope; there the spirit blazed high, and a world full of wonders surrounded them; prophets and those who speak in tongues, visionaries and ecstatic persons begin to speak; psalms, hymns, and spiritual songs sound through the room, the powers of brotherly kindness come alive in unexpected fashion... (Bousset 1970: 134–5; 1921: 88–9)

The cultic life of the Hellenistic Christian communities described by Bousset comes strikingly close to the 'effervescence' that according to Durkheim invigorated the collective rituals of the Australian aborigines (Durkheim 2001 [orig. 1912]).[3] Paul's 'Christ mysticism', according to Bousset, is also anchored in the worship and practical life of the community, although the apostle reorients the cultic experience to a 'personal' and 'spiritual-ethical' interpretation (1970: 156–7).

A central tenet of the History of Religion School was that early Christianity was decisively shaped by the impact of pagan religions. It was a 'syncretistic' religion. The members of the school were convinced that the genesis of Christianity was influenced by various ideas from Hellenistic and oriental religions (including Assyrian-Babylonian cosmology, Iranian dualism, Hellenistic syncretism, and the religions of Egypt). They were fascinated by the oriental-Hellenistic Redeemer myth, the idea that pre-Christian Gnosticism expresses the myth of primal man, the redeemer of all humanity (Reitzenstein 1921). When it came to the 'sacraments' of the early church, they identified the impact of syncretistic Gnosticism, of the Greek mysteries, and of Hellenistic religions in both baptism and the Lord's Supper (Eichorn 1898; Holtzmann 1897; Heitmüller 1903).

---

[3] There is, however, no direct reference in Bousset's work to *Les formes élémentaires de la vie religieuse*, which had appeared only a year before the first edition of *Kyrios Christos* (1913).

Issues of 'foreign' influence or 'syncretism' were of course theologically sensitive. Even the advocates of the history of religion method themselves were not always willing to follow their approach to its logical conclusion. Thus Bousset, for example, finds his heroes, Paul and Jesus, basically untouched by 'ecclesiasticizing Judaism and sacramentalizing Hellenism' (Baird 2003: 251).

The subsequent scholarship has levelled sharp criticism against many findings of the school. The arguments and debates about the 'syncretic nature' of early Christianity were for the most part misleading; lurking in the background were theological ideas of 'pure' or 'authentic' origins (King 2003). As Kurt Rudolph notes, 'there has never been a "pure religion"; this would be an ahistorical construct. Indeed, every religion is a syncretistic phenomenon' (Rudolph 1991: 17–18; see also L. H. Martin 2000). The hunt for religious historical parallels of early Christian ideas and practices was not always methodologically sound, ignoring as it did chronology and concrete historical complexes and processes (Bianchi 1975: 152). Suggestions that certain central early Christian ideas, such as Paul's doctrine of union with Christ in baptism, were simply 'borrowed' from Greco-Roman mysteries have proven to be mistaken (Wedderburn 1987).

The members of the History of Religion School criticized the literary-critical method of the former generation of scholars, but source-critical and philological approaches continued to dominate the study of early Christian rituals. Hans Lietzmann's monumental *Mass and Lord's Supper* (1979 [orig. 1926]) is an illuminating example of what I have elsewhere referred to as the 'genealogical approach' (Uro 2010). Lietzmann (1875–1942) was an eminent philologist and early Christian scholar who was influenced by the history of religion approach, even if he did not identify himself as belonging to the inner core of the movement (Seelig 2001: 211–18). Although its main results remained controversial, *Mass and Lord's Supper* stimulated the study of the origins of the Eucharist for decades (Bradshaw 2002: 65–7).

Lietzmann approaches the history of the rite through various liturgical sources, to detect the origin and meaning of the eucharistic meal. Working backwards from later texts to earlier ones, he traces two basic types of eucharistic liturgy in the early Church, the Egyptian and the Roman (or Hippolytan). The Egyptian, the main representative of which is the liturgy of Sarapion (the fourth-century bishop of Thmuis), did not originally include the narrative of institution (i.e. Jesus' words in the Last Supper) or the idea that the meal is

## Ritual Theory and Early Christian Studies

celebrated in remembrance of Jesus. An early form of this tradition can be found in the *Didache* (9:1–10:6, 14:1–3), in which the symbolism of 'bread' is emphasized but no reference is made to the Last Supper. This tradition goes back to the 'breaking of the bread' (Acts 2:42) in the early community in Jerusalem, and to the meals shared by Jesus with his disciples. The second main tradition, the Roman form of the eucharistic liturgy, is represented by Hippolytus and derives ultimately from Paul, who received 'from the Lord' (1 Cor. 11:23) the understanding of the Supper as a rite of remembrance and as a replica of Jesus' last meal. This eucharistic tradition was characterized by Hellenistic sacrificial concepts, and became the dominant form of the Eucharist in the majority of churches.

Lietzmann analyses the sources meticulously, looking for seams, later additions and textual relationships between the liturgical texts. His source-critical method has much in common with the textual criticism used by philologists in classifying manuscripts into textual traditions ('families'), identifying scribal errors, glosses, and interpretations, so as to ultimately arrive at a form of the text that is as close as possible to the original. The genealogical approach to early Christian rituals analyses rituals as they are represented in liturgical *texts*, and is interested in the most *original* form of the liturgical tradition under investigation, a kind of 'autograph' of the ritual. Lietzmann's methodology is also indebted to the literary criticism of nineteenth-century Biblical Studies, which focused on the literary relationships between ancient texts and on various strata in them, as well as attempting to reconstruct hypothetical sources.

### 1.2 LITURGICAL HISTORY

Textual approaches have also prevailed in the study of the earliest Christian liturgy as a specialized subdiscipline of Liturgical Studies,[4] although liturgical scholars are nowadays much more careful in

---

[4] Liturgical Studies combines academic and practical (liturgical reformist and ecumenical) aims. According to the website of the largest professional association in the field ('Societas Liturgica: an international society for liturgical study and renewal'), the society was founded in 1967 to promote 'ecumenical dialogue on worship, based on solid research, with the perspective of renewal and unity' (http://societas-liturgica.org/about/history/, access date 27 April, 2015).

identifying surviving liturgical texts with actual practices in the early church. There has been relatively little discussion as to the methods and approaches used in the study of early liturgy (Bradshaw 2002: 1), and reviewing the research done in this area of scholarship is therefore not easy. In his authoritative textbook, *The Search for the Origins of Christian Worship*, Paul Bradshaw distinguishes between three traditional methods or approaches: the philological, the 'structural', and the 'organic' (2002: 1–20). My discussion in this section relies in part on Bradshaw's review of scholarship, supplemented with observations concerning a few more recent studies in the field.

With regard to the 'philological method', Bradshaw discusses the work of the pioneers of the study of early Christian liturgy, noting that they were employing 'philological rather than historical methods in their work'. 'They treated liturgical texts like other ancient manuscripts, comparing variant readings and trying to arrive at the original that lay beneath them all' (Bradshaw 2002: 3). This method comes close to what I have referred to as the genealogical approach.

The 'structural approach', in turn, was advanced by Gregory Dix (1901–52) in his highly influential book, *The Shape of the Liturgy* (2005 [orig. 1945]). Dix criticized attempts by earlier scholars to identify a single original eucharistic rite. According to Dix, 'the genuinely apostolic tradition' behind the centuries of development and widely scattered churches lie in the fourfold 'shape' of the eucharistic liturgy: the dominical acts of taking, giving thanks, breaking, and distributing. However, as Bradshaw notes, Dix's structural approach does not diverge radically from the philological method, since Dix still assumes a common origin underlying the various forms of the early Christian Eucharist (Bradshaw 2002: 6). This common origin is not a 'text', but rather a general outline or shape—something that form critics might call 'form' and memory researchers 'schema' or 'script'. Recent scholars of early liturgy have emphasized diversity rather than an original common shape of the eucharistic traditions or other early Christian rites (Bradshaw 2002: x, 6, 140; see also McGowan 1999), although some scholars still accept a modified version of Dix's thesis (McGowan 2014: 27).

The third approach distinguished by Bradshaw was prompted by another classic work in the field, *Liturgie comparée* by Anton Baumstark (1878–1948) (Baumstark 1953), translated into English under the title *Comparative Liturgy* (1958). Baumstark's comparative approach was inspired by the comparative study of language, and ultimately by early nineteenth-century theories of cultural evolution (West 1995). What is relevant to the present discussion is that it was also influenced by the comparative study of religion of Baumstark's day (Botte 1958: viii n. 2). Baumstark's approach was an ambitious attempt to analyse the history of liturgy as a matter of 'organic' development, by carrying out systematic comparison and classification and by identifying the universal principles or 'laws' that governed the process of the historical evolution of liturgical traditions. According to Baumstark, these laws are fundamentally two in number: the 'Law of Organic Development', according to which new additions to the liturgy tend at first to take their place alongside more primitive elements, and the law that 'primitive conditions are maintained with greater tenacity in the more sacred seasons of the Liturgical Year' (Baumstark 1958: 23, 27).

The discussion of Baumstark's legacy among liturgical scholars has been characterized on the one hand by engagement with the 'positivism' of his approach, on the other by attempts to develop, in more probabilistic terms, further laws and tendencies in the evolution of liturgical rites (West 1995; Taft 2001). Comparative Liturgy has exerted a continuing influence on the philological and historical study of liturgical sources (Taft and Winkler 2001).[5] In spite of its early roots in the comparative methodologies of the late nineteenth and early twentieth centuries, the comparative approach has not led scholars of liturgy to consider insights from ritual theory or to develop their work toward genuinely cross-cultural approaches. Comparative liturgists have mainly focused on the various forms of the Christian liturgy (or its assumed roots in Jewish synagogue worship), understood as an organic whole.[6]

Bradshaw discusses his own desiderata for the study of early liturgy under the term 'hermeneutics of suspicion'. He notes that '[h]istorians of early liturgy have traditionally tended to show a greater degree of naiveté in relation to their primary sources than have their counterparts in biblical studies' (Bradshaw 2002: 14). Bradshaw argues for an awareness of the rhetorical nature of the sources, and for the

---

[5] To my knowledge, no liturgical scholar has attempted to develop Comparative Liturgy using recent theories of cultural evolution (see 2.2 in this volume), although Baumstark's original ideas may be suggestive of such developments.

[6] According to Baumstark, the 'vocation of the historian of Liturgy' is 'to investigate and describe the origins and variations of the changing form of this enduring substance of eternal value'. Liturgy is 'the living heart of the Church'. (1958: 1–2).

recognition that 'authoritative-sounding statements are not always genuinely authoritative' (2002: 17). He also warns that liturgical legislation does not provide direct access to actual practices, and that explanations propounded by early Christian writers are not necessarily helpful in determining the origin of a practice (2002: 18–20).

In the first two decades of the new millennium, many historians of liturgy have shifted from mere textual comparisons toward an analysis of the *cultural and social contexts* of early Christian rituals. This trend is in line with approaches in mainstream New Testament and Early Christian Studies, in which the importance of studying the 'social world' of early Christianity (its social institutions, social structures, cultural norms, economy, etc.) is often emphasized. This shift has also brought liturgical scholars into closer interaction with early Christian scholars and social historians of early Christianity. A particularly fruitful area has been the study of the early Christian ritual meal in the light of Greco-Roman banquet customs and the culture of food in antiquity (McGowan 1999; D. E. Smith 2003; Taussig 2009; Stringer 2011; D. E. Smith and Taussig 2012; Spinks 2013, esp. 1–29). Many of these works actually belong to the group of studies discussed under the section 'Social Science Approaches' below.

A massive three-volume work, *Ablution, Initiation, and Baptism: Late Antiquity, Early Judaism, and Early Christianity*, with contributions by fifty-eight specialists, examines extensively and in detail water rituals and baptismal practices in the cultural and religious milieus of early Christianity as well as in various early Christian texts and groups (Hellholm et al. 2011). While this volume includes a few articles that make use of ritual theories (Petersen 2011; Strecker 2011), most of the chapters focus on historical and theological issues, with no consideration of ritual theory, and the compendium as a whole lacks an overarching theoretical perspective—as such collections often do. This last criticism can also be made about the 860-page single-authored volume *Baptism in the Early Church* by Everett Ferguson (Ferguson 2009; see my comments below in section 1.5).

The shift away from an emphasis on mere texts toward the cultural and social context has led liturgical scholars to incorporate research and insights from archaeology, art history, social theory, and other fields outside the traditional theological and philological disciplines. Robin Jensen, for example, has developed an innovative approach to baptism, in which she integrates the analysis of early Christian

## Ritual Theory and Early Christian Studies 17

literature with evidence from the visual arts and from the design and decoration of ritual spaces, to understand how the Christian initiation was experienced by early Christians (Jensen 2011, 2012). Martin Stringer, a liturgical scholar with a background in social anthropology, has advocated a 'sociological' approach to the history of Christian worship, drawing on Foucauldian discursive analysis and on the theory of practice articulated by Pierre Bourdieu (Stringer 2005).[7] Stringer's work clearly opens up new avenues for the history of Christian liturgy in general, but with regard to the study of early Christianity (chapter 1 of the book) his discursive/practice approach does not provide many new insights beyond the traditional historical and exegetical approaches. Notably, the book makes no reference to ritual theory, even though the use of practice theory is suggestive of such a link by virtue of Catherine Bell's work (Driver 2007).

In recent years the study of early Christian liturgy has become more pluralistic and interdisciplinary, adopting approaches derived from social history and to some degree from the social sciences, but insights and theories from Ritual Studies have been utilized so far surprisingly little.[8] This is remarkable, considering the conceptual overlap of the key terms, 'liturgy' and 'ritual', defining these fields. One explanation for this hesitation to incorporate ritual theory in the history of early liturgy is that Liturgical Studies has been intimately connected to theology, especially practical theology and homiletics (Taft 2001: 228). As Stringer notes, histories of Christian worship have often been written 'from within the tradition itself, for purposes that are closely related to the needs of the church' (Stringer 2005: 5). The theological emphasis may have caused some inertia in employing perspectives from Ritual Studies, which expressly promote cross-cultural and etic approaches. But this is probably only a partial

---

[7] Stringer was not the first to apply social science approaches in the field of Liturgical Studies generally. See especially N. D. Mitchell 1999.

[8] This situation, however, may be rapidly changing. A recent introductory book on the study of liturgy and worship (J. Day and Gordon-Taylor 2013) includes contributions from historians of liturgy using analytical tools from Ritual Studies (see especially Bradshaw and Harmon 2013 and Johnson 2013). Bradshaw and Harmon gives a concise introduction to Ritual Studies as a 'multidimensional field', in which 'ritual could be identified as a basic behavioural act for human societies' (2013: 24). Johnson analyses Christian initiation as a ritual process, drawing on Victor Turner. Moreover, the forthcoming *Oxford Handbook of Early Christian Ritual* relies on collaboration among biblical scholars, ritual theorists, and historians of liturgy (Uro et al. forthcoming).

explanation. Scholars of early Christianity applying social-scientific approaches, often drawing on cross-cultural studies and perspectives, have also been slow to employ ritual theory.

## 1.3 SOCIAL SCIENCE APPROACHES

In Biblical Studies, social-scientific approaches started to become popular during the 1970s and the 1980s.[9] Early studies in this mode of interpretation included the use of the sociology of knowledge developed by Peter Berger and Thomas Luckmann. This approach was applied, for example, in exploring ways in which early Christian christologies functioned as 'symbolic universities' to legitimate the social situation of the communities (Meeks 1972); other research included the application of sociological studies of millenarian movements and Melanesian cargo cults to early Christianity (Gager 1975), and functionalist sociological analyses of the 'Jesus Movement' and Pauline Christianity (Theissen 1979; Meeks 1983). In North America, one particularly influential work was Bruce Malina's book, *The New Testament World: Insights from Cultural Anthropology* (1981), in which he outlined a model for analysing biblical texts vis-à-vis the 'pivotal values' of the ancient Mediterranean world. These values were elaborated in chapters on honour and shame in the Mediterranean culture, on the dyadic vs. the individualistic personality, on the perception of limited good, on distinctive norms of kinship and marriage, and on a set of rules to distinguish clean and unclean. Malina's concern was to guide his readers to appreciate the 'strangeness' of the New Testament world and its difference from the modern North American culture, thus enabling them to avoid an 'ethnocentric' reading of biblical texts.

Social-Scientific Criticism developed into a subdiscipline of biblical exegesis (Elliott 1993), and a wide variety of social-scientific ideas, perspectives, and models were harnessed to shed light on biblical texts and their cultural contexts. Typical topics examined by the

---

[9] Note, however, that in the early twentieth century several important contributions to the social history of early Christianity were made by such scholars as Adolf Deissman, Ernst Troelsch, and Shirley Jackson Case.

practitioners of social-science approaches have been cultural values, economic systems, group formations, leadership roles, gender, purity, ethnic categories, and social identity (see, for example, Esler 1995b; Rohrbaugh 1996; Blasi et al. 2002; Neyrey and Stewart 2008). Except for the study of purity issues, which usually relies heavily on the work of Mary Douglas (Malina 1986; Neyrey 1986a, 1986b; Williams 2010), themes related to ritual and the use of ritual theory have been rare (note, however, the work of DeMaris 1999, 2002, 2008).

The research trend building on the programmatic work of Malina, and of other early pioneers collaborating with him (Elliott 1981, 1986; Neyrey 1988) focused on the cultural values of the New Testament world (in particular as defined by honour and shame), and utilized, among other things, a field referred to as 'Mediterranean anthropology' (for a review, see Albera 2006).[10] These biblical scholars operated with a very general concept of culture, often spanning the whole ancient Mediterranean circuit; this culture was seen as having been passed on from generation to generation, down to the present day (Uro 2012). Such an approach reflects a style of cultural anthropology that was widely practised in the United States in the twentieth century, especially the kind of anthropology that stressed the construction of culture around 'key symbols' or 'core values' (Ortner 1973; Bloch 2012: 35-43). While cultural key symbols can certainly include rituals (cf. Ortner 1973: 1341), the social-scientific interpretation of New Testament and other early Christian texts centring around honour and shame mostly ignored ritual, possibly because ritual practices did not offer the best possible test cases for emphasizing the cultural gap between the ancient Mediterranean and the present-day North American world.

Other scholars applying approaches from the social sciences to early Christianity did occasionally embrace ritual theory and ritual themes in their work. Wayne Meeks' groundbreaking work, *The First Urban Christians: The Social World of the Apostle Paul* (1983), for example, includes a major chapter on ritual in the Pauline

---

[10] Much of such research has been carried out by scholars organized as the 'Context Group', founded in 1986 as a 'working group of scholars committed to the use of social sciences in biblical interpretation' (http://www.contextgroup.org/, access date 27 April, 2015; see also Horrell 2002: 11). A typical emphasis among scholars associating themselves with the Context Group is the use of clearly articulated models and theories, a method I myself support wholeheartedly.

communities, in which he discusses baptism and the Lord's Supper as well as what he refers to as 'minor rituals' (see also MacDonald 1988). Meeks is well informed about the various theoretical approaches to ritual in the anthropology of the time and applies insights from ritual theory in an eclectic manner. His approach is palpable in a passage in which he contrasts the analysis of origin or theological content to the approach that considers the social function of baptism:

> These passages [i.e., allusions to baptisms in Paul] have often been analyzed for their ideational content and for their parallels, connections, and possible antecedents in the history of religions. Our purpose is different; we are trying to see what baptism did for ordinary Christians, disregarding the question of where its elements may have come from and even the profounder theological beliefs that Paul and the other early leaders associated with it... (Meeks 1983: 154)

Meeks furthermore argues that Paul uses the symbolism of the Supper ritual 'to enhance the internal coherence, unity, and equality of the Christian group' as well as 'to protect its boundaries vis-à-vis other kinds of cultic association' (1983: 160). In addition to his moderate functionalist stance, Meeks draws on Victor Turner's famous theory in which Van Gennep's structural approach to rites of passage is extended to an analysis of societies as dialectical processes between structure and antistructure (van Gennep 1960; V. Turner 1969). Meeks points out that 'the dialectic between "structure and anti-structure" that Turner describes appears again and again in the tensions addressed by the Pauline letters' (Meeks 1983: 89). Meeks' functionalist account is discussed in more detail in Chapter Five (5.5).

Gerd Theissen is also among those scholars who developed social-scientific approaches to early Christianity independently of Malina's style of applying cultural anthropology. The use of ritual theory is prominent in Theissen's work, *A Theory of Primitive Christian Religion* (1999), where he analyses early Christianity as 'a semiotic cathedral' consisting of three elements: myth, ritual, and ethics. Theissen's approach integrates many different strands of the social sciences (for example, functionalism, sociology of knowledge, and Clifford Geertz' semiotic approach) and psychology. In many significant ways, it builds on the tradition of the History of Religion School. This is signalled not only by the frequent use of the terms 'religion', 'ritual', and 'myth', but by Theissen's overall goal of offering a constructive theological synthesis based on an analysis framed within the history of religion.[11]

Theissen's analysis of ritual, comprising a lengthy chapter in the book, mingles functionalist, semiotic, and psychoanalytic perspectives. Similarly to Meeks, he sees the Eucharist as a rite of integration renewing the cohesion of the group. At the same time, in Theissen's semiotic interpretation, both baptism and the Eucharist form a 'ritual sign language' loaded heavily with symbolic meanings. In contrast to the ritual sacrifices of antiquity, Christian rituals contain 'a consistent reduction of violence'. In Theissen's psychoanalytic reading, this reduction takes place through a kind of sublimation. 'The rites express in an unacknowledged way the hidden anti-social nature of human beings' (Theissen 1999: 135). In symbolic terms, baptism represents 'a symbolic suicide' and the Eucharist 'symbolic cannibalism'. The problem with this particular interpretation is the same as with the symbolist approach in general (see below, section 2.6): it is difficult to know to what extent such unconscious negative impulses motivated the performance of rituals among the earliest Christians.

A third example running against the general tendency to downplay ritual in the social-scientific study of early Christianity relates to a group of scholars committed to 'redescribing' Christian origins and relying particularly on the work of the theorist of religion Jonathan Z. Smith. The research of this group has largely been carried out under the programme units of the Society of Biblical Literature, 'Ancient Myths and Modern Theories of Christian Origins' and 'Redescribing Early Christianity' (Cameron and Miller 2004, 2011). Scholars associated with the group challenge the traditional histories of Christian origins, based on the canonical gospels and the 'myth-making' of the early communities, and propose that the beginnings of early Christianity can be understood as 'reflexive social experiments' (Cameron and Miller 2004). Although the emphasis of the 'redescribers' has been more on the side of myth than on that of ritual, the use of theories of religion (partly due to the influence of Jonathan

---

[11] Theissen has developed his ritual-theoretical perspective in several later works, drawing on various ritual theories (including cognitive ones) to form a hermeneutical synthesis. In his Lectiones Vagagginianae (2013), he advances a three-dimensional model, focusing on ritual as a visible side of religion (performative function), as repeated actions generating tradition, and as actions creating a liminal structure (taking participants beyond everyday reality). See also Theissen 2008 and 2010.

Z. Smith) gives their approach a special inflection. As Burton Mack, a prominent member of the group, writes in a programmatic article:

> New Testament studies are generally pursued without feeling the need for discussing theories of religion.... The historian of religion would say that New Testament scholars work with a concept of religion that is thoroughly and distinctly Christian in its derivation and definition. That may come as no surprise. Since we deal with Christian texts in the interest of understanding Christian origins, and since our discipline does not demand setting our work in the context of comparative religions, cultural anthropology, and religious studies, it has not seemed necessary to venture beyond the history of Christianity to develop a general theory of religion. Our familiarity with the Christian religion has taken the place of theoretical discussion, and Christianity has provided us with the categories we use to name and explain early Christian phenomena. (Mack 1996: 251–2)

Theory of religion, Comparative Religion, and Religious Studies are the keywords which connect Mack's approach to the field of History of Religion rather than to the style of social-scientific criticism conducted by Malina and his collaborators (despite the fact that cultural anthropology is mentioned in the above citation from Mack). This connection, I would argue, explains why Mack gives ritual an important place as part of his theses concerning social formation, myth, and ritual. Echoing Smith (J. Z. Smith 1987), he contends that 'rituals are the way humans have of concentrating attention on some activity or event of some significance to a group, and observing its performance apart from normal practice' (Mack 1996: 255). 'In the case of Christian origins, we need to know what activities were chosen for ritual performance, why they were chosen, how they were performed, and what such observation may have achieved for the group' (1996: 256). With regard to the early Christian meal tradition, Mack notes that 'we have a wonderfully elongated process of ritualization on our hands' (1996: 256).

Among the scholars close to the Redescribing programme, Stanley Stowers has in a number of publications examined topics related to evolving early Christian rituals in the context of Greek religion and Hellenistic philosophy (Stowers 1995, 1996, 2011a, 2011b). Stowers writes as a historian of religion and social theorist, drawing his theoretical inspiration in particular from Bourdieu and producing highly informative ethnographies of ancient practices. I discuss his analysis of Paul and the Corinthians in Chapter Five (especially section 5.3).

## 1.4 EMERGING RITUAL STUDIES

The studies on early Christian rituals referred to in the previous section represent exceptions to the general disregard of ritual in the study of Christian beginnings prior to the renewed interest in the most recent scholarship. It has been argued that the ideological roots of this dismissal can be traced back to the Protestant Reformation, with its emphasis on 'inner religious experience' and its openly 'anti-Judaistic and anti-Catholic stance', as well as to the Enlightenment's 'rational discourse on religion' (Gorman 1995: 14–18). There may be some truth to this claim, but the issue is far too complex to be discussed in detail in this study. In an insightful analysis of the 'repudiation of ritual in early modern Europe', Peter Burke argues that, rather than a straightforward anti-ritualistic movement, the Reformation was first of all 'a great debate, unparalleled in scale and intensity, about the meaning of ritual, its functions, and its proper forms' (Burke 1987: 226). According to Burke, one consequence of the long and intense debate over the meaning of both religious and secular rituals during the centuries following the Reformation was that they made 'western Europeans unusually self-conscious and articulate on the subject' (1987: 230). This would suggest that the academic study of ritual is in some respect a child of the Reformation and the Enlightenment (cf. also Muir 1997).

Be that as it may, the emergence, over recent decades, of Ritual Studies as a recognized academic enterprise has gradually begun to exert an influence on various fields in the humanities, including Biblical Studies and Early Christian Studies. In the study of biblical and cognate materials, this influence has given rise to studies in which ritual as a theoretical construct has become a major tool for the analysis of both texts and the communities that produced them. With the growing recognition of Ritual Studies as an emerging new discipline, some biblical scholars gave ritual theory a privileged position in their analyses; in other words, they began to examine biblical materials *from the perspective of ritual*. Pioneering studies appeared a little earlier in the field of Hebrew Bible and Ancient Near Eastern Studies, quite likely because their textual sources were rich in the instructions, descriptions, and reflections of cultic practices (see, for example, Gorman 1990; Klingbeil 1998, 2007; Gruenwald 2003; Gane 2004; Russell 2006). DeMaris' 2008 book was among the first in which ritual theory/Ritual Studies were used broadly as a primary tool for analysing New Testament and early Christian sources, but it was preceded by works in which various specific ritual-theoretical perspectives, such as Turner's theory of ritual process, were employed to early Christian materials (for example, McVann 1995; Petersen 1998; Strecker 1999; Estrada 2004; but see also Gruenwald 2003: 231–66).

This categorization of earlier studies does not mean that there is anything wrong in using ritual as just one perspective among many in the study of Christian beginnings (for example, as part of the broader analysis of the social world of Paul; cf. Meeks' work referred to above). There is even a danger that privileging ritual as a major analytical tool may narrow the focus, to the extent that other important explanatory factors (non-ritual practices, social structures, beliefs, and doctrines, etc.) will remain unexplored or underestimated. But digging a bit deeper into ritual aspects of the early Christian world has certain clear advantages.

First, as we have seen, previous scholarship has suffered from a bias that has caused a devaluing or even neglect of the role of ritual in the emergence of the early Christian movement. Since ritual aspects have not been very well researched, we need, in order to arrive at a more complete account of Christian beginnings, to focus on ritual, using the best possible knowledge of the subject available to us, that is, the knowledge obtained in Ritual Studies. The ritual approach to early Christianity, however, should not lead us to overestimate the topic, as a kind of magic bullet explanation for the rise of Christianity. A balanced view recognizes that a consideration of ritual factors can only provide a partial, yet relevant explanation. An overall understanding, as presumed in this study, is based on the idea that religious traditions spread as 'belief–ritual packages' which evolve under various selection pressures (cf. Henrich 2009). It would be a serious mistake to assume that religious representations circulate as some sort of 'pure ideas', in isolation from practices.

Second, a focus on ritual theory is helpful in developing the study of Christian beginnings toward genuinely cross-cultural and etic approaches (Petersen 1998). Our survey of scholarship has demonstrated that the comparative approaches applied in earlier studies have been limited in both aim and scope. The members of the History of Religion School did champion a comparative method, but their comparisons mainly concerned questions of how and to what degree biblical traditions were 'influenced' by various Hellenistic and Oriental religions. Scholars of Comparative Liturgy have promoted comparison, but this takes place within a single religious tradition and often in connection with the practical needs of Christian churches. Many scholars applying social-scientific approaches have focused on broad comparisons between the ancient Mediterranean culture and the modern western world, with the aim of providing culturally sensitive readings of biblical texts. Yet these scholars have not generally drawn on the tradition of Comparative Religion. These characterizations are not intended to belittle the aims of the earlier scholars, but to point out the direction in which ritual theory is taking us. We should not, of course, be too optimistic as to whether ritual theory, or any other form of theoretical reflection, provides a way to overcome the inside/outside problem in the study of Christian beginnings. But comparison is fundamental for understanding and for explaining. As Mack puts it, '[w]e can't do much with an absolutely unique phenomenon, one that is incomparable, one for which we know of nothing similar in any respect whatsoever' (Mack 1996: 257). Ritual theory opens up wider possibilities for the study of early Christian rituals, beyond the traditional comparisons between emerging Christian rituals and both Jewish and Hellenistic practices.

Third, while there is some truth to the argument that the study of early Christian rituals should not be carried out independently of other aspects of the social world, there is a value in studying ritual in its own right (Handelman and Lindquist 2005). From this perspective, rituals can be seen as 'autonomous expressions of the human mind', which do not translate into other human domains, such as music or the arts (Gruenwald 2003, 13–19; cf. Rappaport 1999). Ritual Studies is thus a field that studies a sufficiently autonomous domain of human behaviour, incorporating knowledge and methods from various disciplines in the humanities and the sciences; just as musicology or Musical Studies investigates music from a host of different perspectives, including among others the historical, the cultural, the psychological, and the performance-related. Before the emergence of Ritual Studies as a recognized interdisciplinary discipline, ritual was studied and theorized under a number of different disciplines, such as anthropology, Comparative Religion, psychology, and biology. Following the pioneering work of organizing, systematizing, and developing ritual theory and knowledge of ritual by such scholars as Ronald Grimes (1985, 1995, 2014), Tom Driver (1991), Catherine Bell (1992, 1997), the Collaborative Research Centre 'Ritual

Dynamics' (Kreinath et al. 2007, 2008b),[12] and others, a new discipline has begun to take shape in the academy—although the institutional forms are still much less developed than, for example, in the case of musicology. The central research question in this book is defined by the emergence of this new discipline: What light can Ritual Studies shed on the study of Christian beginnings? This question is similar to that posed in a few other studies in which ritual theory guides the examination of biblical rituals (Gruenwald 2003, esp. 19; cf. also Klingbeil 2007; DeMaris 2008). Naturally I have my own emphases and favourite theories, which will unfold in subsequent chapters. The important point is that the pay-off of ritual theory for the study of early Christianity does not come without sufficient attention to theoretical and epistemological issues. In such a task, cherry-picking eclecticism does not work.

## 1.5 WHY THEORY?

We need to dwell a little longer on this question. Why does knowledge of ritual come with theories and models?[13] Not all scholars in the guild of Biblical Studies would be too enthusiastic about the kind of theory-driven approach applied here. Even those who advocate

---

[12] The Centre 'Ritual Dynamics' (Ritualdynamik) was active during 2001–2013 at the University of Heidelberg, producing and facilitating a great amount of literature on ritual theory.

[13] Many early Christian scholars applying social-scientific approaches prefer to use the term 'model' instead of 'theory'. This may be at least partly due to Thomas Carney's influential work, *The Shape of the Past: Models and Antiquity*, in which he makes a distinction between these terms: 'a model is something less than a theory and something more than an analogy.... A theory is based on axiomatic laws and states general principles.... A model, by way of contrast, acts as a link between theories and observations' (Carney 1975: 8; for a preference of model, see Elliott 1993: 36–59). The idea that 'theory' is based on 'axiomatic laws', however, does not represent recent theories of explanation in the social sciences (see the discussion in 2.3). In the Cognitive Science of Religion, 'theory' is widely used as a general term for various explanatory frameworks and analytical tools, and a strict distinction between 'model' and 'theory' is not always made. Note, however, that 'modelling' is consistently used for the computational and network theory tools that have recently been developed for the study of religion and religious traditions in antiquity (Czachesz and Lisdorf 2013; Bainbridge 2014).

the use of social-science approaches disagree as to the role and function of models/theories in the study of the social history of early Christianity. While other scholars advocate more the rigorous employment and explication of cross-cultural models and theories, by way of theory-testing, others prefer to take historical sources as a point of departure and to use social-scientific models in a much more eclectic manner, avoiding an approach that tends to impose 'alien frameworks' on first-century data (for the debate, see Esler 1995a, 2000; Horrell 2000; D. B. Martin 1999; Meeks 2005). The usual response from the first group of scholars to the concern of the latter one is that all analytical work implies theories and models, whether or not they are made explicit. It is better to make models explicit than to use them unconsciously (Carney 1975: 5; Elliott 1993: 44–5; Esler 1995a: 4). This debate may somewhat obscure what is meant by the term 'model' (not all presuppositions, assumptions, perspectives, etc. are reasonably called 'models'; Horrell 2000: 85), but the main point of the 'model-users' is in my opinion valid. The explicit articulation of the theories, models, and hypotheses that guide our investigations is of utmost importance, although this does not mean that there is only one way to obtain the relevant knowledge (scholars may work in inductive or deductive order to achieve this goal; Grimes 2014: 169–70). But the bottom line is that a theory is needed. As Robert Taft puts it, '[k]nowledge is not the accumulation of data, not even new data, but the perception of relationships in the data, the creation of hypothetical frameworks to explain new data, or to explain in new ways the old' (Taft 2001: 221).

An example of a study on early Christian rituals which takes its point of departure from sources without a strong explanatory framework is the above-mentioned *Baptism in the Early Church* by Everett Ferguson (2009). This massive study examines a comprehensive amount of references to baptism in Christian writing (plus some archaeological evidence) from the first to the fifth century, organized mainly by geographical location and ancient author. In the course of his survey, Ferguson asks questions concerning the historical roots of baptismal practices as well as their theological and liturgical implications. The book offers an enormously rich compendium of references to baptisms and their interpretations, but some theoretical consideration of the approach adopted—in other words some sort of theory—would have made it more helpful for the study of early Christian ritual (J. Day 2011: 350).

There is one feature in the study of ritual that makes theoretical reflection and theory-forming particularly imperative. It is generally acknowledged that 'ritual' is a 'fuzzy-set' or 'family-resemblance' concept, not a natural kind (Snoek 2008; Sax 2010; Stephenson 2015: 70–73). As Grimes writes, 'defining "ritual" is like defining "jazz"' (Grimes 2014: 186)—or, for that matter, 'religion', we might add. If we want to undertake the task of studying early Christian rituals, starting inductively from texts or archaeological evidence, we thus inevitably face the problem of definition. Which early Christian practices would qualify as 'rituals'? We can of course rely on conventional (emic) views of 'sacraments', focusing, for example, on early Christian meal practices as rituals. But such an approach begs further questions. Which elements of various early Christian dining practices are the ones that make it 'ritual'? At which stage do we have a fully developed ritual meal on hand? What does the process of ritualization involve?[14] Definitions cannot be avoided; a definition, in fact, is a miniature theory (Franek 2014, for defining 'religion'; see also Guthrie 2007). Theories of ritual, on the other hand, often come with definitions, or at least with a focus on some particular aspect of the fuzzy-set category of ritual. This rationale supports the theory-driven approach adopted here (or a strong engagement in a dialogue between theory and data), as well as a general epistemological stance that I refer to as 'theory-dependent realism'. I elaborate further upon the latter concept in the next chapter. In short, theory-dependent realism argues that the category of ritual can serve as a helpful tool for analysing behavioural aspects of early Christianity (or human behaviour in general) only if it is anchored to a specific theory.

Such a position can be objected to by arguing that all definitions (of 'religion' or 'ritual', for example) are ultimately power structures that manipulate the content of the term to their own ideological benefit (cf. Franek 2014: 18). Theories and definitions are ultimately 'entrenched in unrecognized issues of discursive demarcation, power and control' (McCutcheon 1997: 191). Among theorists of ritual, it is Bell who most conspicuously represents a view that takes both the

---

[14] As part of his dissertation project at the University of Helsinki and Masaryk University (Brno), Vojtěch Kaše has developed a model that distinguishes various cognitive mechanisms operating in the ritualization of early Christian meal practices (see Kaše 2014). For a theoretically informed approach to the ritual elements of early Christian meal practices, see also Bormann 2015.

study of ritual and ritual practice as strategic means of exercising power (1992; see also Bell 1997, 2005). Inspired by practice theory (Bourdieu and others) and styles of post-modern (de)constructionism, Bell aims at dismantling 'ritual' as a 'theoretical construct' and as 'an intrinsic universal category or feature of human behaviour' (1992: ix). She suggests a focus on 'ritualization', both as a 'strategic way of acting' (1992: 7) and as a strategy for the 'construction of a limited and limiting power relationship' (1992: 8). Bell argues that

> theoretical discourse about ritual is organized as a coherent whole by virtue of a logic based on the opposition of thought and action. This argument suggests that, historically, the whole issue of ritual arose as a discrete phenomenon to the eyes of social observers in that period in which 'reason' and the scientific pursuit of knowledge were defining a particular hegemony in Western intellectual life. (Bell 1992: 6)

Bell's critique of the category of ritual and formal theories has been aptly responded to by Grimes (2008). Grimes notes that, in spite of her resistance to theories and definitions, 'Bell *acts as if* ritual exists: She writes almost six hundred pages on the topic. In addition she is sufficiently theoretical both to define ritual and to criticize other people's theories of it' (2008: 123; italics original). Bell's analysis is replete with descriptions that look like definitions, even though she may intend them to be merely descriptions. In reference to 'ritualization', she states that it is 'a way of acting that is designed and orchestrated to distinguish and privilege what is being done in comparison to other, usually more quotidian, activities' (Bell 1992: 74). Moreover, according to Bell, 'the most subtle and central quality of those actions that we tend to call ritual is the primacy of the body moving around within a specially constructed space, simultaneously defining (imposing) and experiencing (receiving) the values ordering the environment' (1992: 82). Whether descriptions or definitions, such statements in fact function as embryonic theories that define and restrict the analyst's perspective in her study of the behaviours that might be referred to as 'ritual' (note that a narrowing of the focus does not have to lead to the use of only one definition or theory; see the discussion on theoretical pluralism in section 2.5). Some of the issues that Bell raises, such as embodiment and power relationships, are relevant here too (see especially section 6.4). In the debate over theory, however, I side with Grimes, who contends that 'we scholars of rituals have little choice but to define and theorize about it. If we do not do it explicitly, it will happen tacitly' (Grimes 2008: 136).

It should be noted, however, that in scholarly use a theory can refer to many different kinds of ideas, approaches, and sets of principles. In relation to the study of religion, Michael Stausberg discusses different levels of generalization and explication in the discourse of 'theory', distinguishing between theoretical approaches, theoretical ideas, and fully-fledged theories (Stausberg 2009: 9). 'Theoretical approaches', Stausberg explains, refer to 'scholarly work based on or related to a corpus of shared theoretical or methodological assumptions or key problems'. As examples, he lists feminist, postcolonial, and cognitive approaches. Many theories used in the field of Ritual Studies are theoretical approaches, such as 'performance theory' (interested in rituals as public performance) and 'practice theory' (associated with the work of Bourdieu). 'Approach' is probably by far the most common type of theory referred to in the study of early Christianity. 'Theoretical ideas', in turn, are more explicit and specific than 'approaches'. According to Stausberg, theoretical ideas are 'embryonic theories or starting points for further theorizing that may or may not result in larger theoretical constructs' (i.e. 'theories') (2009: 9). It is difficult to determine exactly when a theoretical idea has reached the status of a theory, but as a general rule theories are more systematized and explicated as well as solidified by empirical testing. Theoretical approaches often encompass theoretical ideas or fully-fledged theories. For example, the performance approach involves analytical concepts (such as 'framing' or 'frame'[15]), as well as sets of categories which facilitate comparisons between forms of public performance (for example, Grimes 2014: 207-10).

There is more to 'theory' than can be conveyed by Stausberg's three-fold distinction. I return to this issue in the next chapter, where I discuss in more detail the approach and the specific theories used in this book. It is important to ask what different kinds of theories actually do—for example, whether their purpose is to describe

---

[15] In the study of ritual, 'frame' or 'framing' can refer to a way in which some activities are set up within a framework which separates them from ordinary activities (for example, the use of archaic speech, explicit statements announcing the beginning and end of the action, distinctive use of metaphor, stylized rhythms or vowel harmonies, and tempo or stress patterns; see Bell 1997: 72, relying on Goffmann). For a broader definition of 'framing' (including analyses of time, space, cultural domains, senses, ritual performance, and objects), see Stephenson 2010: 46-9.

phenomena or to explain them in some manner (cf. also Elliott 1993: 42–3)—and what kind of 'explanatory mechanism' (if any) they contain. At this point, suffice it to note that my general approach is cognitive (or more specifically 'socio-cognitive', a term which will be defined later). Several more or less fully-fledged theories of ritual have been advanced under the general umbrella of the cognitive study of religion.

## 1.6 WHY COGNITIVE THEORY?

In her contribution to the entry 'Ritual' in the second edition of the *Encyclopedia of Religion*, Bell gives '"a rough guide" to the current scene' of the study of ritual. She distinguishes between theories that 'remain heavily rooted in cultural explanation' and those that rely on 'naturalistic (or scientific) models of explanation' (Bell 2005: 7849). By the latter approach Bell is referring to cognitive theories of ritual, especially to that advanced by Thomas Lawson and Robert McCauley. In terms of Bell's big divide—which may still work today as a 'rough guide' to different styles and modes of ritual theorizing—the present book undoubtedly belongs to the latter camp. There is no reason, however, to create too sharp a dichotomy between cognitive and cultural theories of ritual. My motivation for employing cognitive theories does not arise from the assumption that theories relying, for example, on cultural performance, practice theory, or power relations are useless—I occasionally make use of these theories in the following chapters—but rather from the need to work with clearly articulated theories, designed for empirical testing. Taking this position, I follow the established style of social-scientific exegesis, but extend it to the use of knowledge from the cognitive and evolutionary sciences. This move, I believe, can be helpful in clarifying some of the unsettled debates among scholars practising social-scientific exegesis; for example, the above-mentioned issue of whether the use of models and explicit theories makes the analysis somehow deterministic by imposing 'alien frameworks' on the ancient world. The cognitive study of religion, exploring the cognitive and evolutionary underpinnings of religious phenomena, can provide a more solid ground for cross-cultural comparisons across space and time as well, by answering the question of why cross-cultural models, theories, and explanations are possible in the first place (Luomanen et al. 2007a: 19).

The Cognitive Science of Religion (CSR) emerged out of collaboration among religion scholars, anthropologists, philosophers, and psychologists in the 1990s. Today the movement spans a host of different research areas, approaches, and disciplines, of which more will be said in Chapter Two. The cognitive approach has aroused interest among historians of religion and archaeologists (Whitehouse and Martin 2004; L. H. Martin and Sørensen 2011; L. H. Martin 2011). Biblical scholars have also been active in developing cognitive approaches to the study of biblical texts and their religio-cultural contexts (Luomanen et al. 2007b; Shantz 2009; Kazen 2011; Czachesz and Uro 2013). Cognitive science has proved helpful in tackling some of the issues that have traditionally occupied the attention of biblical scholars, such as transmission (Czachesz 2013b), purity and contagion (Kazen 2002: 71–94; Uro 2013), and communal identity and ethics (Roitto 2011) as well as in opening up new kinds of questions and perspectives, related, for example, to the neuroscience of religious experience (Shantz 2009; Czachesz 2012a, 2013c) and to the spread of Christian ideas in antiquity, modelled by means of computer simulations or network theory (Czachesz 2012b; Czachesz and Lisdorf 2013). Ritual has been a central topic as well (Ketola 2007; Uro 2011a, 2011c, 2011d; Biró 2013; Gudme 2013; Jokiranta 2013). The cognitive approach can thus be seen as one driving force that is impelling ritual from the margin toward a more central place on the agenda of biblical scholarship.

Ritual theories have been an important part of the emerging cognitive movement within Religious Studies. Several theories of ritual have been advanced and subjected to empirical testing. These theories represent different schools and currents in the cognitive programme and deal with a variety of questions: for example how religious rituals are mentally represented in the minds of the participants, why people universally engage in seemingly counterproductive ritual behaviours, and how rituals support the transmission of religious traditions. CSR is rapidly expanding into new areas and developing novel hypotheses, but three theories stand out as having enjoyed considerable attention and having been subjected to extensive discussion, criticism, and further modification in the subsequent literature. These are, in the order in which they have been presented to the scholarly and scientific community, the Theory of Religious

Ritual Competence; the Modes of Religiosity Theory; and the Theory of Commitment (Costly) Signalling.

Thomas Lawson and Robert McCauley's *Rethinking Religion* introduced the *Theory of Religious Ritual Competence*, later also referred to as Ritual Form Theory (Lawson and McCauley 1990, 2002; McCauley and Lawson 2002). Their approach was inspired by Noam Chomsky's idea of 'universal grammar', according to which the ability to learn language is hard-wired in the human mind (although they distanced themselves from the modularity hypothesis that is usually associated with Chomsky's theory; more on this in section 2.4). Lawson and McCauley argue that people, irrespective of culture, social level, and learning, have some form of intuitive competence to draw inferences about religious rituals: 'With little, if any, explicit instruction, religious ritual participants are able to make judgements about various properties concerning both individual rituals and their ritual systems. These include inferences about religious ritual forms and relationships and about the efficacy of ritual actions' (McCauley and Lawson 2002: 5).

Lawson and McCauley's theory is based on the premise that religious rituals follow the general pattern of any action in which agents are doing something to somebody, often by using an instrument. The structural description of religious rituals thus includes three fundamental roles: agent, action/instrument, and patient. Religious rituals, however, differ from ordinary actions in one important respect: in religious rituals, 'culturally postulated superhuman agents' (CPS-agents) are associated with one of the three roles. In many forms of Christian baptism, for example, a CPS-agent is primarily associated with an agent, and in the Eucharist (or at least in some forms of it) with an act/instrument. Lawson and McCauley divide religious rituals into two profiles, 'special agent rituals' and 'special patient/instrument rituals', depending on which slot mainly includes references to CPS-agents. This dividing principle (the 'Principle of Superhuman Agency') signifies the fundamental difference that exists between the two ritual profiles (see Figure 1.1).[16]

---

[16] In addition to the action representation system, the theory includes another factor, the structural *depth* of ritual. This concept refers to the number of enabling rituals that need to be performed before a given ritual can be correctly performed. Just as any performance of actions presupposes certain earlier actions, rituals also normally presuppose the prior performance of another ritual action. A priest can baptize a child because he has been ordained by a bishop, the bishop can ordain the priest

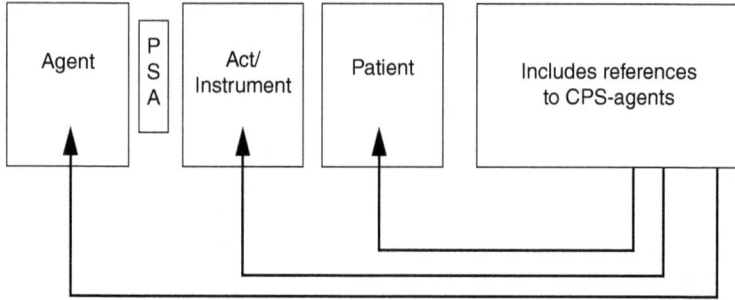

**Figure 1.1.** Illustration of the Principle of Superhuman Agency (PSA). In Lawson and McCauley's structural description, rituals in which CPS-agents (culturally postulated superhuman agents) are connected with the agent of a ritual are referred to as 'special agent rituals'. The other ritual structures or profiles are 'special instrument rituals' (CPS-agents are connected with the instrument of the ritual) and 'special patient rituals' (CPS-agents connected with the patient of the ritual). See McCauley and Lawson 2002: 26–7. Reproduced by courtesy of Cambridge University Press.

Central to Lawson and McCauley's theory are the predictions (hypotheses to be tested) based on the Principle of Superhuman Agency. These concern particularly the type of rituals they label special agent rituals, that is, those rituals in which CPS-agents are primarily associated with the agent of a ritual (for example in a Christian baptism with a priest or in shamanic healing ritual with a shaman). The theory predicts, for example, that special agent rituals typically involve elevated levels of sensory arousal and that they cannot be repeated, although they can be reversed.

To suggest such regularities for ritual practices in any given culture across space and time is a bold enterprise, running against the general aversion to 'universals' in cultural studies and in culturalist approaches to ritual (such as Bell's approach). We should keep in mind, however, that the theory's predictions (as also other cognitive hypotheses) are probabilistic; in other words, they suggest that, all else being equal, there is *some likelihood* that they will be materialized (cf. Boyer 2005: 7). They are not 'universal laws'. Moreover, the value of any testable theory is not limited to the validity of its predictions, but

because he himself has received ordination, etc. The concept of structural depth may be helpful in an analysis of entire ritual systems, but it remains less important for the purposes of the present study.

includes its ability to produce new knowledge and insights by means of theory-testing. To anticipate my conclusions in Chapter Three, I will argue that the predictions of the competence theory do not hold as such for my test case (John the Baptist); this conclusion leads me to suggest modifications to the predictions of the theory.

A notable feature of Lawson and McCauley's theory is their technical definition of 'religious rituals' as acts 'that bring about changes in the religious world' (McCauley and Lawson 2002: 14). This definition limits the scope of their work in two significant ways. First, it excludes many religious activities that most people intuitively regard as rituals, such as singing, dancing, or kneeling in religious contexts. This is not a flaw. As I have argued, definitions and theories are needed in order to narrow the focus of the analysis and to demarcate the object of the research from the broad set of phenomena typically associated with the category of ritual. But it is worth noting that the definition of ritual as 'an act that brings about a change' connects Lawson and McCauley's theory to a specific line of theorizing about ritual, one that privileges the *action dimension* of ritual activities over their communicative or expressive aspects (Laidlaw and Humphrey 2008). Moreover, the emphasis on 'bringing about changes' relates to the controversial issue of ritual efficacy (Sax et al. 2010). The use of Lawson and McCauley's theory thus takes us into the murky waters of magic and ritual.

The second point related to Lawson and McCauley's definition is that it refers to *religious* rituals that bring about changes in the *religious* world. Lawson and McCauley say nothing about non-religious rituals, or of 'ritualization' as a mode of behaviour not limited to the human species (Stephenson 2015: 5–20). Their first book, in particular, outlined 'a theory of ritual systems as well as a framework for a larger theory of religious systems' (Lawson and McCauley 1990: 171). It has, indeed, been viewed as a general theory of 'religion as superhuman agency' (Engler and Gardiner 2009), not merely as a theory of ritual alone.

In contrast to the Ritual Competence Theory, which is based on a theoretical and philosophical analysis, Harvey Whitehouse's *Modes of Religiosity Theory* grew out of his anthropological fieldwork in Papua New Guinea (Whitehouse 1995). His ethnography of a millenarian cult, known as the Pomio Kivung, provided a point of departure for the formation and further development of the theory in a series of subsequent publications (for example, Whitehouse 2000, 2002, 2004a,

2004b; Q. Atkinson and Whitehouse 2011). During his work among the adherents of the Pomio Kivung, Whitehouse became eyewitness to a fervent splinter group movement within the millenarian cult. The events associated with the rise and the decline of the splinter movement provided him with an opportunity to observe and analyse two different modes of religious activity, one (the mother movement) based on repetitive teaching and the faithful performance of an extensive set of rather boring rituals, the other (the splinter group) fuelled by a series of increasingly arousing and exciting rituals.

With reference to similar dichotomous theories of religious dynamics by earlier theorists (for example, Weber's routinized and charismatic religious forms or Turner's *'communitas'* and 'structure'), Whitehouse argues that all religious traditions tend to develop either towards large-scale organizations, characterized by orthodoxy and dry ritual routine (doctrinal mode), or towards small-scale communities with an emphasis on emotionally arousing rituals without any sanctioned interpretation of their meaning (imagistic mode). At the heart of the theory is the simple observation that religious traditions cannot emerge without two things taking place: first, people have to be able to remember the beliefs and rituals involved in the tradition, and second, they have to become motivated to pass on the beliefs and the rituals (Whitehouse 2002: 295). This entails that memory and motivation are the crucial constraining factors in the transmission of religious traditions. In the doctrinal mode, the motivation arises through the creation of 'a very repetitive regime of religious transmission' (2002: 295), and religious knowledge is codified primarily in semantic memory (a system in memory that relates to the retrieval of general knowledge). In the imagistic mode, adherents are motivated by highly arousing but less frequently performed rituals, which typically trigger vivid and enduring memories in episodic memory (a system related to the retrieval of specific life events).

What is crucial here is that people's political and ideological systems are influenced by the type of cognitive processing (memory systems). Whitehouse outlines twelve psychological and socio-political features that function as 'organizing principles for religious experience and action' (see Table 1.1). Doctrinal religions, for example, sustain dynamic leadership, large-scale communities, and centralized structure. Imagistic religions, in contrast, lack dynamic leadership and appear in small-scale non-centralized societies.

Table 1.1. Contrasting modes of religiosity: twelve psychological and socio-political features in Whitehouse's Modes of Religiosity Theory

| Variable | Doctrinal | Imagistic |
| --- | --- | --- |
| **Psychological features** | | |
| 1. Transmissive frequency | High | Low |
| 2. Level of arousal | Low | High |
| 3. Principal memory system | Semantic schemas and implicit scripts | Episodic/flashbulb memory |
| 4. Ritual meaning | Learned/acquired | Internally generated |
| 5. Techniques of revelation | Rhetoric, logical integration, narrative | Iconicity, multivocality, and multivalence |
| **Sociopolitical features** | | |
| 6. Social cohesion | Diffuse | Intense |
| 7. Leadership | Dynamic | Passive/absent |
| 8. Inclusivity/exclusivity | Inclusive | Exclusive |
| 9. Spread | Rapid, efficient | Slow, inefficient |
| 10. Scale | Large scale | Small scale |
| 11. Degree of uniformity | High | Low |
| 12. Structure | Centralized | Noncentralized |

Source: Whitehouse 2004b: 74. Reproduced by courtesy of Rowman & Littlefield.

Although both modes of religion are often present within a single religious tradition, this does not result in a simple fusion: 'Invariably, those aspects of a religious tradition associated with doctrinal and imagistic modes respectively, remain distinct from the viewpoints of both participants and observers' (2002: 309).

Whitehouse's theory has stimulated extensive theory-testing and discussion among anthropologists, religion scholars, archaeologists, and historians (Whitehouse and Laidlaw 2004; Whitehouse and Martin 2004; Whitehouse and McCauley 2005).[17] The theory, or some aspects of it, have also been applied to biblical and early Christian materials (Ketola 2007; Uro 2007; Jokiranta 2013). A particularly important element of Whitehouse's theory is that it introduced the issues of memory and transmission into the study of ritual. Biblical scholars have been exploring ways in which the findings of memory research can shed light on the study of ritual (Czachesz 2010; Uro 2011b) and on biblical transmission in general (Luomanen 2013; Czachesz 2013b).

---

[17] See also the thematic issue of *Method and Theory in the Study of Religion* 16 (3), 2004, on the Cognitive Science of Religion, in which many contributions focus on the modes theory.

The third theory that has gained currency in the broad field of the Cognitive Science of Religion is Commitment (Costly) Signalling (Sosis 2003, 2004, 2006; Sosis and Alcorta 2003; Bulbulia and Sosis 2011). This theory attempts to answer the question of why humans are universally engaged in performing actions that seem to be pointless, even harmful, from the point of view of practical life management.[18] Many rituals are indeed costly; they require apparently unnecessary expenditure of resources, such as time, material, and energetic costs, and they may also involve physiological or psychological pain. Traditional functionalist theories in anthropology and in the study of religion have answered this puzzle by suggesting that collective rituals enable societies to express and reaffirm their shared beliefs, norms, and values, and thus to maintain communal stability and group solidarity. The Commitment Signalling Theory recalls the traditional 'social solidarity theory' (Sosis and Alcorta 2003), but takes its point of departure in evolutionary theory, with the aim of formulating an empirically testable and falsifiable theory (classical functionalism has been criticized for being unfalsifiable). Signalling theorists argue that the primary adaptive value of religion—and hence also religious rituals—is its ability to foster cooperation and to overcome problems of collective enterprises that humans have faced throughout our evolutionary history. They contend that a central challenge of collective actions is free-riding; in other words, the fact that individuals can achieve the greatest gains by refraining from cooperation while others cooperate. If too many refrain, however, no one can benefit from the collective action. Groups therefore need social mechanisms that limit free-riding and enhance trust among the members that others will also cooperate. The key point of the theory is that religious behaviours that are too costly to fake can function as mechanisms facilitating cooperation in collective enterprises.

Taking a cue from ethologists, signalling theorists argue that religious rituals are a form of communication (cf. communication-related

---

[18] Commitment Signalling is not the only cognitive theory that seeks to answer the question of human compulsion for ritual. Pascal Boyer and Pierre Liénard, building on earlier work on connections between ritualized behaviour and Obsessive Compulsive Disorder (see e.g. Fiske and Haslam 1997), have suggested an evolved Hazard-Precaution System, specialized in the detection of and response to potential threats, which is activated in ritualized actions. Boyer and Liénard 2006; Liénard and Boyer 2006.

patterned behaviour among many species in mating, feeding, controlling territories, etc.). Costly rituals are signals that advertise an individual's level of commitment to a religious group (Sosis and Alcorta 2003: 267). As a reason why counterproductive religious behaviours have evolved in the human species, signalling theorists refer to the so-called Handicap Principle. This principle is intended to explain such puzzles of natural selection as peacock's tails (Zahavi and Zahavi 1997). Why has selection favoured a trait that is an obvious burden to the bird, making it slower, heavier, and less capable of moving readily? The Handicap Principle proposes that such traits have evolved exactly because they are handicaps. A costly trait signals that the animal is fit enough to afford to carry it—in other words, it is too costly to fake. Although costly religious practices and peacock's tails at first sight have little in common, according to Commitment Signalling Theory the character they share is that in both cases evolution has afforded a trait that is costly to its bearer, presumably because it works as an 'honest advertisement'.

Commitment Signalling highlights an important characteristic of the cognitive approach that will be elaborated upon more carefully in the next chapter. The cognitive study of religion does not merely draw on the various fields of cognitive science which focus on how mental processes, such as memory, language, and 'action representation', work in the human mind. It also employs findings from the fields of behavioural science, such as behavioural ecology and evolutionary psychology, that attempt to explain why and how the human mind and behaviour *have evolved* into their present state. Throughout this book, the Cognitive Science of Religion is defined broadly, as a field that explores the cognitive *and* evolutionary roots of human religious thinking and behaviour.

The three cognitive theories of ritual introduced in this chapter are not the only theories that will be made use of in this book. More than merely individual theories of ritual, these theories open up three perspectives on ritual that focus on different aspects of behaviours that might be deemed rituals, and thus help to narrow down the analytical scope. Depending on which theory we adopt as a clue, rituals can thus be analysed as actions that are designed to bring about changes (cf. Lawson and McCauley), as key mechanisms of religious transmission (cf. Whitehouse), or as cooperative cues (Commitment Signalling).

## 1.7 TOWARDS A NEW APPROACH

Our survey of earlier scholarship has shown that until quite recently, New Testament and early Christian scholars have not considered ritual as a central perspective or a theoretical tool for the study of Christian beginnings. Around the turn of the twentieth century, the members of the History of Religion School did emphasize the role of ritual in the emergence of early Christian religion, but their work focused mainly on the history of one religion (Christianity). Furthermore, due to the undeveloped stage of Comparative Religion at the time, they lacked the necessary methodological and theoretical apparatus to accomplish their vision. Their work, however, has exerted a continuing influence on later studies (including the present one) in which ritual has received attention. The other domain of Early Christian Studies in which ritual has played an important role is the study of early liturgy. In the past, liturgical scholars have conducted their work by and large independently of other branches of Early Christian Studies and without strong links to the study of religion and ritual theory. This pattern is now changing.

The most important reason for the growing interest in the use of ritual theory in the study of early Christianity is the emergence of Ritual Studies as a recognized interdisciplinary field. The application of social-scientific approaches as such did not provide New Testament and early Christian scholars with adequate means to account for the role of ritual in the rise of the early Christian movement. As part of Ritual Studies and the new field of Cognitive Science of Religion, cognitive theories of ritual represent a promising approach to early Christian rituals, developing the established tradition of Social-Scientific Criticism toward the incorporation of new findings from the cognitive and evolutionary sciences.

# 2

# Ritual, Culture, and the Human Mind

## *A Socio-cognitive Approach*

In the previous chapter, several references were made to cognitive theories of ritual and to the Cognitive Science of Religion in general. I now need to contextualize these references in the larger framework of the cognitive study of religion.

As defined above, the Cognitive Science of Religion (CSR) is an interdisciplinary research programme that draws on a growing body of knowledge from the cognitive and evolutionary sciences to explain religious thinking and behaviour. The cognitive programme spans numerous academic disciplines and subdisciplines, but as a current in Religious Studies it is nowadays commonly referred to as 'the Cognitive Science of Religion'. This title is used, for example, in the name of an international professional association founded to promote cognitive approaches to religion, and in the official journal of the same association.[1] Ritual has played a central role in the pioneering work of CSR, as well as in more recent theoretical and empirical studies emerging out of this programme. While a great deal of important work on ritual is taking place outside the sphere of the cognitive programme (Sax et al. 2010; Stephenson 2010; D. J. Davies 2011; Hüsken and Neubert 2012; Grimes 2014, to mention just a few examples), cognitive and evolutionary theories of ritual nevertheless represent a significant new development in both Religious Studies and Ritual Studies, reflecting broader integrative tendencies between the

---

[1] The International Association for the Cognitive Science of Religion (IACSR) was established in 2006. The first issue of the *Journal for the Cognitive Science of Religion*, published by Equinox, appeared in 2012. See http://www.iacsr.com/iacsr/Home.html.

natural sciences and the humanities (Slingerland 2008). Historians of religions and biblical scholars have begun to apply and develop cognitive approaches in their work (Whitehouse and Martin 2004; Luomanen et al. 2007b; L. H. Martin and Sørensen 2011; Czachesz and Uro 2013). It is a natural—if not inevitable—step to consider cognitive theories and perspectives in the context of the role of ritual in Christian beginnings.

In this chapter, I want to introduce those aspects of CSR that are relevant for understanding the socio-cognitive approach applied in the book. What were the key ideas of the pioneering work that gave rise to the cognitive movement? How are cognitive theories of ritual different from other approaches to the theorizing of ritual? It is now a quarter of a century since the publication of the book often seen as a landmark in the rise of the cognitive programme, Lawson and McCauley's *Rethinking Religion: Connecting Cognition and Culture* (1990); how to describe the field today? As we will see, the present state of CSR is characterized by multi- and cross-disciplinary approaches, methodological pluralism, and a variety of schools; it is not easy to define what is shared in common between the variegated studies and undertakings which have been carried out under the general rubric of CSR. However, some leading ideas important for the present work can be recognized, which in turn will help us to specify the approach adopted in the subsequent chapters.

## 2.1 THE COGNITIVE TURN IN THE STUDY OF RELIGION

In the 1990s, four studies appeared that played an important role in the development that led to the emergence of the Cognitive Science of Religion as a collaborative effort, approaching religion from cognitive and science-driven perspectives (J. L. Barrett 2011: 230). Lawson and McCauley's *Rethinking Religion* introduced a new cognitive framework for the study of religion, in particular a theory of how religious rituals are mentally represented in the minds of participants: the Theory of Religious Ritual Competence; in the later literature, this was also referred to as the Theory of Ritual Form. The title of the book echoes Dan Sperber's *Rethinking Symbolism* (1974), whose critique of symbolic anthropology can be seen as a significant harbinger of the cognitive programme. In his *Faces in the Clouds*, Stewart Guthrie advanced a theory of religion as 'a systematic anthropomorphism' (Guthrie 1993: 3), relying in part on cognitive science (in an earlier essay, he had given the epithet 'cognitive' to his theory, Guthrie 1980). Pascal Boyer's *The Naturalness of Religious Ideas* (1994a) introduced some of the central ideas of the cognitive programme, arguing that all religious representations are constrained by universal properties of the human mind, and that the regularities of religious ideas across different cultures can be explained by paying heed to the cognitive processes that generate these ideas in the first place. The last of the four works, *Inside the Cult* by Harvey Whitehouse (1995), presents a vivid ethnography of a millenarian cult (Pomio Kivung) in Papua New Guinea; here he anticipates the ideas that he later developed into a Theory of the Modes of Religiosity (Whitehouse 2000, 2004a).

While these four pioneering studies differ in many regards, they share the roughly common conviction that the striking regularities of religious ideas and behaviours across time and space can be explained by the human mental architecture, which 'canalizes' the spread of religious traditions (Pyysiäinen 2012b: 6). Importantly, they also agree that scholars of religion should focus on these pan-cultural features; this would allow them to theorize religious phenomena cross-culturally. These studies thus represent a significant shift away from the constructionist and culturalist views that had prevailed in Religious Studies and related fields for several decades—and to some degree still do.[2] Against the backdrop of psychological science, CSR can be seen as an aftershock of the so-called Cognitive Revolution, which in the 1950s and 1960s had begun to refashion behaviourism, the dominant paradigm of scientific psychology in the first half of the twentieth century (J. L. Barrett 2004a: 401). Since Cognitive Science (an outcome of the Cognitive Revolution movement) is a highly inter- and multidisciplinary field, the pioneers of the cognitive study of religion drew on a great variety of fields and theoretical resources, including generative linguistics (Lawson and McCauley),

---

[2] For a perceptive analysis and critique of social constructionism, see Hacking 1999. It is possible, however, to see the cognitive approach as complementary to the *original* constructionism advocated by Berger and Luckmann 1967. Cf. J. S. Jensen 2009: 131. For the relation between Berger and Luckmann's sociology of knowledge and the cognitive study of religion, see Luomanen 2007.

developmental and evolutionary psychology (Boyer), perception studies (Guthrie), and memory studies (Whitehouse). Later new fields and areas of study were accommodated, such as experimental psychology (here Justin L. Barrett has been a leading scholar), neuroscience (Aarhus MindLab section on 'Culture and Cognition'), archaeology (Mithen 1996), and various evolutionary sciences. What made possible the cumulative progress in the emerging field of CSR was this interdisciplinary collaboration between anthropologists, religion scholars, psychologists, philosophers, historians, and so on, leading eventually to the establishment of the IACSR.[3]

A central and probably the most provocative part of the cognitive programme has been its focus on the unconscious and intuitive cognitive mechanisms, or 'mental tools' (Barrett), that constrain religious thought and behaviour as well as the transmission of religious traditions. Much of our religious thinking and the motivation for religious behaviour is hidden from conscious inspection (Boyer 2002: 108). Many of the pioneering theories both build on and are intended to demonstrate this fundamental assumption: for example, the *Ritual Competence Theory* (Ritual Form Theory), discussed in detail in this book (Lawson and McCauley 1990; McCauley and Lawson 2002); the *Theory of Minimal Counterintuitiveness*, which predicts that minimally counterintuitive concepts have a selective advantage in transmission as compared to intuitive or massively counterintuitive ideas (Boyer 1994b; J. L. Barrett and Nyhof 2001; Boyer and Ramble 2001); the concept of *theological incorrectness*, which demonstrates that adults' religious views can function in markedly divergent ways depending on contextual demands (it has been shown, for instance, that abstract theological concepts are replaced by anthropomorphic ones in fast 'online' thinking; J. L. Barrett and Keil 1996; J. L. Barrett 1999;

---

[3] An event that launched this future collaboration was a small conference hosted by the Department of Comparative Religion at Western Michigan University in February 1996, under the title of 'Cognition, Culture, and Religion'. Along with Thomas Lawson (presiding) the speakers were Justin Barrett (a psychologist), Pascal Boyer (an anthropologist), Brian Malley (a religion scholar), Robert McCauley (a philosopher), and Harvey Whitehouse (an anthropologist). J. L. Barrett 2011: 230. A series of three conferences, held in Cambridge (UK), Burlington (University of Vermont), and Atlanta 2001–03 followed, focusing on the modes theory of Harvey Whitehouse and resulting in three conference volumes (Whitehouse and Laidlaw 2004; Whitehouse and Martin 2004; Whitehouse and McCauley 2005). The list of foundational conferences also has to include the one held in the Turku Archipelago, Finland, in the summer of 1999, the papers of which were published in Pyysiäinen and Anttonen 2002.

Slone 2004); and the hypothesis of the *hypersensitive agent detective device* (HADD), according to which the human mind has a strong bias towards interpreting ambiguous environmental stimuli as being caused by or being an agent (J. L. Barrett 2004b).[4]

Although the centrality of intuitive knowledge has been at the heart of the cognitive programme, this tenet has also been qualified or even challenged by cognitive scholars. For example, the idea of intuitive religious knowledge has been conceptualized and qualified by means of the dual-process approach in social psychology, neuropsychology, and cognitive science (Pyysiäinen 2004a, 2009: 6–8; 189–92, 2012b: 8; Tremlin 2005; see also Uro forthcoming). Alternative models have been presented as well (see below section 2.2).

During and since the first decade of the new millennium, CSR has become increasingly multidisciplinary, has taken new directions, and has become allied with other groups interested in 'sciencing up' (J. L. Barrett 2011: 230) the study of religion. The most influential trend in CSR has been the integration of various evolutionary and biological approaches, making the broadly defined field of CSR even more pluralistic. Early pioneers of cognitive approaches to religion did not unanimously rely on evolutionary approaches. Boyer, for example, has been keen on using evolutionary psychology in his work (Boyer 1994a: 291–4, 2002), whereas Lawson and McCauley's *Rethinking Religion* does not refer to biological or evolutionary factors in its account of panhuman ritual competence. The trend toward a greater integration of evolutionary science into CSR is reflected in two review articles by Justin Barrett, published in 2007 and 2011 respectively. In the former, Barrett regards evolutionary psychology and anthropology as a 'secondary project' rather than as 'intrinsic' or 'necessary to the field' (J. L. Barrett 2007: 768, 779). In the latter, however, he writes that the 'most natural growth area for CSR is to forge an even stronger alliance with evolutionary approaches' (J. L. Barrett 2011: 233). Today the evolutionary perspective is by and large seen as an important part of CSR, sometimes referred to more specifically as the 'Evolutionary Cognitive Science of Religion', ECSR (L. Turner 2014).

---

[4] Whitehouse's modes theory also relies on intuitive cognition, since we do not have direct access to our memory systems. Note, however, that Whitehouse also emphasizes the role of conscious, 'cognitively costly', religious concepts and practices in transmission; see Whitehouse 2004a: 49–59.

## 2.2 SCHOOLS AND CURRENTS IN CSR

The pluralism and complexity that define the present state of CSR can be illustrated by describing the different schools and currents in the field. These reflect the diverse disciplinary backgrounds of their proponents, as well as different strands in cognitive science at large.

One way of clarifying the complexity characterizing the cognitive programme is to refer to some of the central ideas and principles advanced by the pioneers in the 1990s and the early 2000s as the 'standard model in CSR' (J. S. Jensen 2009; Pyysiäinen 2012a: 242–6; L. Turner 2014: 3–4; cf. Boyer 2005).[5] Among the key notions of the 'standard model' (sometimes also called 'cognitivist') is the assumption that religious representations arise out of the normal operations of innate cognitive systems, in response to certain challenges faced universally by human beings (L. Turner 2014: 2). The idea that religion emerges from quite natural cognition has provided an important critical response to the phenomenological tradition in the study of religion, that is, to the idea that religion or the religious experience somehow constitute an autonomous sphere in human life (Pals 1996: 161–2). But the thesis about the 'naturalness' of religious ideas has also led to a debate *inside* the growing field of CSR, between those who regard religion as a by-product (mostly identifying themselves with the 'standard' model) and those who emphasize the adaptive nature of religious behaviour (Sosis 2009; see Pyysiäinen 2012b: 246–52, 2014: 23–5). The adaptionist vs. by-product debate is quite complicated, not least because 'religion' itself is a multi-faceted category. While I agree as to the critique of the phenomenological approach, and the claim that religious phenomena can be explained—bearing in mind that all explanations are partial—in terms of ordinary cognitive processes, for the purposes of this study it is not necessary to

---

[5] To my knowledge, the expression '"standard" model (of religious thought and behaviour)' was first used by Boyer 2005. He lists several theories and approaches that summarize the 'standard' model, including the selectionist view of human culture, memory optimum (cf. minimal counterintuitiveness), religious morality 'being parasitic upon evolved moral intuitions', and religious rituals being constrained by agency assumptions. More generally, he argues that all the propositions of the standard model are *general* (they can be applied to any cultural milieu), *probabilistic* (they predict likelihood), and *'experience distant'* (their explanations do not easily map on to people's own experience). These three points may describe the cognitive approach to religion more generally.

align oneself definitely with either party to the debate. My contention is that the theories and insights emerging from *both* the 'standard' model *and* other schools in CSR are helpful in the study of early Christian rituals.[6]

As already mentioned, some of the pioneers of CSR were subsequently influenced by a new approach, dubbed evolutionary psychology (see Boyer 2002; Atran 2002, in particular). As a specific research programme within the larger field of evolutionary approaches to human behaviour, evolutionary psychology argues that much of human behaviour can be explained by focusing on psychological adaptations that evolved to solve recurrent problems in the environment of our early human ancestors (Barkow et al. 1992; Buss 1999; Confer et al. 2010). For example, our inclination to interpret all kinds of cues in our environment as being caused by or being agents (the Hypersensitive Agent Detection Device, HADD, mentioned in section 2.1) can be supported by evolutionary reasoning: in Pleistocene conditions, it was much more advantageous to over-detect agency than to under-detect it (Boyer 2002: 165).

The 'standard' cognitive science of religion approach is closely associated with a particular understanding of the human cognitive architecture, usually referred to as the modularity hypothesis. The modularity of the mind is a hotly debated issue among cognitive scientists, and several different versions of it can be found in the literature (see H. C. Barrett and Kurzban 2006, for a review of the debate). The basic idea is that the human mind consists of modules, also called inference systems (Boyer) or mental tools (Barrett), that are relatively independent from each other and have specialized cognitive functions (Visala 2011: 34). I will have more to say about modularity in Chapter Six (6.2). At this point, suffice it to note that the reliance on the modularity hypothesis, particularly on a strong version of it, explains why Boyer and some other proponents of the standard model assume that much of our religious thinking is not 'accessible to conscious inspection' (Boyer 2005: 6; cf. also Atran 2002: 57–9; McCauley 2011: 59). The strong version of modularity, usually called 'massive modularity', suggests that modularity extends

---

[6] I use quotation marks for 'standard' throughout the chapter, to avoid the impression that the model currently represents the authoritative or dominant approach among the schools and currents in CSR (note that Boyer does not refer to *the* standard model in Boyer 2005 and also uses quotation marks).

to the central cognitive processes, that the modules are mostly automatic (thus unconscious), and that they come in great variety and numbers (Visala 2011: 38). The evolutionary psychologists have been keen advocates of the massive modularity hypothesis; they argue that the mental modules dominating human psychology each evolved in response to some specific challenge to our ancestors' survival (Tooby and Cosmides 1992; Pinker 2002; Carruthers 2006). A common analogy among advocates of the massive modularity is to compare the human mind to the Swiss Army Knife.

While evolutionary psychology has been important for the many proponents of the 'standard' model, it should be noted that evolutionary theory has been applied in recent CSR approaches in a number of different ways. One distinctive approach is represented by a group of religion scholars who have turned to co-evolutionary (dual inheritance) theory to develop models of religious and cultural transmission. Cultural co-evolution theory, often shortened to 'cultural evolution theory', argues that human behaviour is best explained as the product of two interacting forces: genetic selection and cultural selection. Theorists of cultural evolution typically draw on population genetics and use rather sophisticated mathematical models and quantitative methods (Boyd and Richerson 1985; see also Mesoudi 2011), but the approach was popularized for a larger public in *Not By Genes Alone*, by Peter Richerson and Robert Boyd (2005).[7]

Cultural evolution theorists of religion argue that the transmission of religious concepts is dependent on *both* intuitive cognitive biases *and* those of cultural learning. The approach is illustrated by a programmatic article by a group of researchers at the University of British Columbia (Gervais et al. 2011). The UBC writers contend that that the intuitive cognitive predispositions established in the cognitive 'standard' approach offer necessary but not sufficient explanations for the distribution of religious concepts among human populations. They argue that the cognitive approach has to be supplemented with models that explain how cultural learners acquire information from those around them. A full cognitive theory of religion should explain why some counterintuitive representations motivate commitment and faith, while others are treated merely as entertaining figures or stories (the so-called 'Mickey Mouse problem'; Atran 2002: 13; see

---

[7] For a different model of gene–culture interaction, see Jablonka and Lamb 2005.

also Gervais and Henrich 2010). According to the cultural evolution theorists, the answer to the question of why people come to believe in certain counterintuitive representations as religious truths and accept them as objects of devotion should be sought in both content and context biases, not merely in panhuman cognitive constraints. They distinguish three predilections which guide people's beliefs and behaviour in cultural learning (see also Richerson and Boyd 2005): (1) a conformist learning bias (people often adopt the views and behaviours of the majority); (2) a prestige-based learning bias (people often imitate those who are successful and exemplary); and (3) a deception avoidance bias (such as CREDs, credibility enhancing displays, discussed in more detail in Chapter Three).

Population thinking, or the 'selectionist' perspective, is central in the 'standard' model of CSR as well, but there are important differences. While theorists like Boyer emphasize that some characteristics of representations, such as minimal counterintuitiveness, give representations a relative probability of surviving in cultural transmission (Sperber 1996), the cultural evolution theorists focus on 'learning biases', which include both content biases (for example the memorability of a tradition) and context biases. In practice, they focus mainly on the context biases elaborated in the three cultural learning biases.[8]

Evolutionary psychology and the co-evolutionary (dual inheritance) approach represent two different ways to analyse human behaviour from the perspective of evolutionary theory. There is also a third approach, associated with the field known as 'behavioural ecology'. Behavioural ecology applies 'the theory of natural selection to the study of behavioural adaptation and design in an ecological setting' (Sosis and Bulbulia 2011: 343). The three approaches to the evolutionary analysis of human behaviour are best identified by their different research foci and explananda (objects of explanation) (E. A. Smith 2000). For evolutionary psychologists, the primary interest, as we have seen, is in the panhuman set of genetically evolved psychological predispositions (modules), which are argued to provide a link between evolution and behaviour. In co-evolutionary theory, the main interest is in culturally and genetically inherited information,

---

[8] The debate between theories of 'cultural learning' and 'content-based attraction' is conveniently summarized in Pyysiäinen 2012b: 248–9. These two approaches need not be seen as contradictory. The mind constrains possible cultural forms just as the environment constrains biological traits (Czachesz, oral communication).

and in the ways in which this information is transmitted. Human behavioural ecology, for its part, focuses on 'observable patterns of behaviour, with the goal of linking these patterns to environmental conditions . . . and to fitness-correlated payoffs' (E. A. Smith 2000: 34). In short, evolutionary psychologists are interested in panhuman cognitive predilections, co-evolutionary theorists in gene–culture interaction and transmission, and behavioural ecologists in adaptive behaviour in ecological contexts.

Behavioural ecologists have only recently begun to focus their research on religion (Sosis and Bulbulia 2011: 346). The most prominent theory of religion coming from this field is Commitment Signalling Theory, according to which religious behaviour evolved at least in part to support cooperation (Bulbulia and Sosis 2011: 363; see above, section 1.6). Since behavioural ecologists' major interest is in behavioural aspects of religion, Commitment Signalling has important implications for the study of religious rituals. Signalling theorists argue that rituals are often costly, that is, they require material, physiological, or psychological resources, and that the adaptive benefit of costly religious behaviours is their ability to function as honest signals and as an efficient mechanism for minimizing the presence of free-riders (Irons 2001; Bulbulia 2004; Sosis and Alcorta 2003; Sosis 2003, 2004, 2006). This version of the theory was originally called Costly Signalling. The signalling approach has generated considerable empirical testing and has inspired further research questions and hypotheses, such as Charismatic Signalling; I will have more to say about these in Chapters Three (3.8) and Five (5.2).

Cultural-learning and signalling theorists readily see each other's approaches as complementary, and some integration has indeed taken place between the two approaches (Bulbulia and Sosis 2011: 370). The gap is somewhat wider between behavioural ecology and evolutionary psychology, and hence between the forms they take in the study of religion, the 'standard' model of CSR and Signalling Theory. As Sosis and Bulbulia note, behavioural ecologists are largely agnostic with regard to the underlying cognitive mechanisms that produce adaptive responses in particular ecological contexts (Sosis and Bulbulia 2011: 344). Behavioural ecology takes a calculated 'black-box approach' to evolved cognitive mechanisms (E. A. Smith 2000: 30), and clearly differs thus from the 'standard' model's emphasis on panhuman cognitive capacities, which are used to explain cross-cultural regularities in religious thinking and behaviour (but compare Bulbulia 2013).

## Ritual, Culture, and the Human Mind    51

Among the schools and currents in CSR, we should finally note Armin Geertz' biocultural theory of religion (Geertz 2010). Geertz' theory is built on an expanded (embodied) view of cognition, in particular on Merlin Donald's theory of culture as 'a gigantic cognitive web' (Donald 2001: xiv). Merlin Donald is a psychologist and neuroscientist, known for his position that a decisive role in the development of homo sapiens cognition was played by the social environment, the 'community of brains'; the human mind evolved into a 'hybrid' mind, one whose uniqueness lies in its dependence on cultural storage systems.[9] Donald's view of the origin of human cognition can be seen as one version of the co-evolutionary approaches discussed above, but it also strongly resonates with a branch of cognitive science called 'embodied' (also 'extended' and 'situated') cognition. In accordance with the embodied cognition stance (Robbins and Aydede 2009b; Glenberg et al. 2013; see also sections 6.3 and 6.6), Geertz argues that cognition is both embrained and embodied, deeply dependent on culture, and distributed beyond the boundaries of individual brains. Cognition does not simply produce culture; in a reciprocal process, culture also 're-engineers' human cognition by means of 'cognitive tools' such as numbers, maps, writing and literacy, musical notation, etc. (M. Wilson 2010).

Geertz' biocultural theory extends the cognitive study of religion considerably beyond the original vision, to produce relatively narrow and testable theories about the cognitive constraints of religious concepts and behaviours. The perceived advantage of the biocultural approach is that it is able to deal with more complex relations between cognitive and cultural phenomena; the challenge, however, is to translate this general theory into further theories, hypotheses, and tests, as also noted by Geertz himself (2010: 305). Chapter Six takes steps towards drawing on insights from embodied cognition research to tackle the question of how ritual in fact conveys religious knowledge.[10]

---

[9] Donald strongly criticizes the 'hardliners' (i.e. those cognitive scientists who argue that human thinking is based largely on intuitive, 'hard-wired' mental modules) for their uncompromising belief in the irrelevance of the conscious mind and in the illusory nature of free will (Donald 2001: 28–31). This book takes the view that many of Donald's ideas as well as the embodied cognition stance in general are complementary to the approach that draws on the intuitive mental tools.

[10] Note that the 'Religion, Cognition and Culture' Research Unit (RCC) at Aarhus and the MIND*Lab* section 'Cognition and Culture', both directed by Geertz,

## 2.3 KEY PROPERTIES OF THE COGNITIVE APPROACH

Even this brief summary of the different schools and currents in CSR demonstrates the complex and manifold nature of the cognitive movement. The original vision, that of searching for the mental mechanisms underpinning religious concepts and behaviours, has grown into a diverse set of research programmes, applying various cognitive and evolutionary theories as well as experimental research. Yet a few unifying ideas and principles can be recognized. In what follows, I elaborate three key properties of CSR which contribute to the approach applied in this study. Cognitive research is (1) explanation-driven; (2) relies on testable theories; and (3) promotes a multilevel analysis of religious phenomena.

### 2.3.1 Explanation

There is no doubt that CSR champions an explanatory approach to religious phenomena, that is, it focuses on causal relationships. It is also obvious that various schools and trends in CSR are united in their commitment to seeking natural explanations for religious phenomena. This of course entails that they do not endorse transcendent or supernatural explanations; but there is more than that to naturalism, as we shall see in the following discussion. Both explanation and naturalism—often revolving around the issue of 'reduction'—are hotly debated issues in the philosophy of science, and a wide variety of approaches to them has been offered (Horst 2007; Pyysiäinen 2011a; Visala 2011). It is beyond the limits of this chapter to summarize this discussion in any detail. The two points I want to make here are that an explanatory approach can enrich a historical analysis, and that explanation should not be understood as being exclusive of interpretation, the traditional approach to culture in the humanities.

---

have been developing specific research hypotheses based on experimental research and neuroscience. See e.g. Schjødt et al. 2013. This work, however, does not make direct reference to the embodied or extended cognition perspectives elaborated in Geertz 2010.

This last point was emphasized already in the pioneering work by Lawson and McCauley, where they advocate an interactionist approach to the relationship between explanation and interpretation (1990: 14–31). Their position 'acknowledges the differences between interpretation and explanation and champions the positive values of each' (1990: 22). The scholar of religion applying explanatory approaches cannot dispense with interpretation, since 'explanation is riddled with interpretation' (1990: 23). This view can be contrasted with the approach that argues that scientific explanation and humanist interpretation are quite distinctive modes of research, which may at best live in 'peaceful coexistence' (Laidlaw 2007: 231), but it also differs from the position that calls for a radical unification of sciences (labelled 'explanatory fundamentalism' by Visala 2011: 102–11). The latter position is closely related to the issue of multilevel analysis discussed below in section 2.3.3.

The interactionism promoted by Lawson and McCauley is particularly applicable to Biblical Studies, in which much of scholarly activity centres on the interpretation of ancient texts and other historical artefacts. Here cognitive theories cannot be employed without the careful analysis and interpretation of texts (or archaeological evidence), providing the data for cognitive explanations. This does not mean that explanation is flawed by interpretative analysis. In contrast, a case can be made for the view that the study of biblical and related texts is considerably enriched by the introduction of cognitive explanatory approaches (Nikolsky et al. forthcoming).

Interpretation is indispensable, but explanatory approaches can enrich Biblical Studies and the study of ancient religions in a number of ways. They can generate interesting and novel research questions, which cannot be addressed with mere interpretative or descriptive analyses. A descriptive historical approach, for example, an analysis of the diverse forms of early Christian beliefs and doctrines (Räisänen 2010), cannot provide answers to explanation-seeking questions: why certain early Christian beliefs spread as effectively as they did, what role rituals played in the emergence of Christian beliefs, and so on. Moreover, the focus on explanation is a helpful tool in explicating the scope of the research. What is the explanandum (the thing to be explained) of the current task? What is the explanans (the thing that explains)? What is the 'explanatory mechanism' which links explanans and explanandum? Such questions, not often addressed in the humanities, can be helpful in finding new ways to analyse the available data. Lastly, a mechanism-based account (see the next subsection) can help scholars to identify the limits of explanation. Explanations are always about particular aspects of a phenomenon and are inspired by particular questions. As McCauley puts it, 'all explanations are partial explanations; all explanations are from some perspective, and all explanations are motivated by and respond to specific problems' (McCauley 2007: 150).

### 2.3.2 Testable Theories

From the outset, the aim of formulating testable, systematic, and clearly formulated theories has been central to the cognitive programme. Testability means that the theory makes falsifiable predictions, which can be empirically validated. To be sure, there has been some criticism among cognitive scholars themselves as to the dominance of theory over empirical testing in CSR. Barrett, for example, complains in an article published in 2008 that '[a]lthough one of the attractive promises of the Cognitive Science of Religion is to inject the study of religion with empirically testable theories, theoretical projects have outpaced empirical ones' (J. L. Barrett 2008b: 296). On the other hand, experimental research has been increasing during the second decade of the twenty-first century, experiment-oriented researchers not always showing much interest in the big theoretical issues that characterized the pioneering studies in CSR.[11]

In order to be empirically testable, a theory cannot be all-inclusive or overly general. The concept of the *middle-range theory* can help to illustrate the point. It was originally advanced by Robert Merton after the Second World War, and has been used in criticism of 'grand theorizing' in sociology, such as functionalism or conflict theory (Merton 1949, 1967; Boudon 1991). Advocates of the 'analytical (mechanistic) sociology' movement have placed considerable emphasis on middle-range theory (Hedström and Swedberg 1998b,

---

[11] The growing interest in experiments can be seen, for example, in the research carried out in the MindLab section 'Cognition and Culture' (University of Aarhus) directed by Armin Geertz (see note 10 above) and at the *LEVYNA: Laboratory for the Experimental Research of Religion*, Masaryk University, Brno. See http://www.levyna.cz/.

1998a; Hedström and Ylikoski 2010). Peter Hedström and Richard Swedberg contend that 'what often goes under the rubric of social theory, should more properly be viewed as conceptual or sensitizing schemes, not as explanatory theory proper' (Hedström and Swedberg 1998a: 1). The remedy they offer is middle-range sociology, which differs from taking on 'broad-sweeping and vague topics' or (unrealistic) attempts to establish universal social laws, but instead aims at 'explanations specifically tailored to a limited range of phenomena' (1998a: 24). Among the key elements of middle-range theory are its focus on 'social mechanisms' (referring roughly to a constellation of explanatory factors that is predicted to bring about a particular type of outcome) and 'the general reductionist strategy in science of opening black boxes' (1998a: 25). The mechanistic approach extends beyond sociology, and the discussion of explanatory mechanisms in neuroscience and the philosophy of mind is quite active and complex (see, for example, Craver 2007). It would probably not make sense to argue that a good theory in the study of religion always includes an explanatory mechanism; we have in fact seen that this is not always the case in the theories discussed in this chapter. Nevertheless, it is important to note that the tendency toward middle-range theory—with or without an emphasis on mechanisms—resonates with the common sentiment among ritual theorists that 'the age of "grand theories"... is over' (Kreinath et al. 2008a: xxiii; see also Grimes 2014: 336). Narrowing the focus of investigation by means of middle-range theory also generates a need for theoretical pluralism (more on this in the next section, 2.3.3).

A special challenge is to test cognitive theories against the historical evidence, such as early Christian sources. The issue is not so much whether theory-testing within the context of historical studies is possible in principle; the problem arises with the scarcity and haphazard nature of sources for New Testament/Early Christian scholars and with the relatively short historical time frames they usually deal with. Early Christian scholars cannot control or design the conditions of their research, in the way, for example, experimental psychologists can; nor are they used to collecting the kind of 'big data' needed to test cultural evolutionary theories (Mesoudi 2011). Much, however, depends on the particular task at hand. The opportunities and challenges of testing cognitive theories against the historical evidence are discussed in connection with each particular application of the theory in the coming chapters.

### 2.3.3 Multilevel Analysis

Cognitive approaches operate across the traditional hierarchies of disciplines or 'levels' of knowledge by using cognitive or biological science to explain religious phenomena. These are traditionally understood as taking place most conspicuously at a social level, and thus best analysed by means of social or cultural theories. Does the cognitive programme, then, assume that all religious institutions, movements, and collective behaviours can ultimately be reduced to the cognitive architecture of the human mind? Some theorists think that this indeed is the case, at least in the 'standard' model (Van Slyke 2011).

A typical objection to the integration of social and cognitive levels of analysis is that it involves a naturalistic approach; in other words, it presupposes the naturalization or re-conceptualization of the domain of social-cultural phenomena in terms of natural science. A religious experience, for example, is approached as an empirically measurable activity in the human brain.[12] Although cognitive scholars of religion sometimes express leanings toward a more or less straightforward naturalism (see examples in Visala 2011: 88–90), the cognitive movement as a whole is hardly committed to such an epistemological position. Much of the work done in CSR is in accord with what Visala describes as *broad naturalism*.

> Contrary to the strict naturalist view, we should not expect neat reductions of theories and explanations from higher levels to lower levels. Instead, disciplines on different levels should be considered as autonomous to the extent that their theories actually work and answer questions that the discipline is asking. Although seeking inter-level links is a useful research strategy, the lack of reduction does not lead to elimination. It follows from this that a unified and integrated natural, behavioural and socio-cultural science will be highly unlikely. (Visala 2011: 117)

Visala connects broad naturalism with *explanatory pluralism*, which holds that inter-level cooperation between the sciences is a goal

---

[12] For example Kelly Bulkeley, in a review of *Religion Explained* and *How Religion Works*, writes: 'Beliefs, doctrines, practices, rituals, mystical experiences, moral systems, communal structures—everything about religion can be explained, according to Boyer and Pyysiäinen, by using the latest advances in evolutionary theory and cognitive science'(Bulkeley 2003: 671).

worth striving for, but that it should not be understood as a form of reduction or elimination (the latter term refers to a version of reductionism in which reduced entities are eliminated in favour of reducing entities). McCauley, one of the founding fathers of CSR, is also a leading developer of explanatory pluralism in the philosophy of mind (McCauley 1996, 2013; McCauley and Bechtel 2001). Pyysiäinen too has elaborated upon explanatory pluralism in a number of publications (Pyysiäinen 2009: 201–4, 2011a,b). While the discussion embraces many philosophical and theoretical subtleties, the core issue is that explanatory pluralism regards biological and cognitive/psychological knowledge as *relevant* to an understanding of cultural or social processes (including religion), but does not claim that cultural or social phenomena are reducible to individual psychology or biological processes (Pyysiäinen 2011a: 28).

To sum up the key properties of CSR: we can conclude that the cognitive programme is best characterized by its work toward explanatory and testable theories, and by a multilevel analysis which seeks to bridge the gap between on the one hand the social and cultural level, the traditional domain of Religious Studies, and on the other the natural sciences. In these respects, the cognitive programme is essentially about 'sciencing up' the study of religion, as Barrett puts it. This may be a hard lesson for the scholar used to operating with approaches more typical of the humanities. On the other hand, our analysis shows that there are several 'softening' elements in the approaches applied by cognitive scholars of religion. Explanation and interpretation are not viewed as exclusive; rather, they complement one another (Lawson and McCauley 1990: 15). Cognitive scholars are well aware of the fact that all explanations are partial, and they prefer a piecemeal approach instead of promoting grand theories of religion (J. L. Barrett 2007). Their work should not generally be seen as representing a strict naturalist position; 'explanatory pluralism', as developed by McCauley and Pyysiäinen, may be a more appropriate label. It should also be noted that many cognitive scholars of religion come from different fields of social, historical, and theological studies, bringing with them a range of traditional methods and approaches which can supplement and enrich the cognitive methodology. From this perspective, CSR also contributes something from the humanities to the natural sciences (see also Slingerland and Collard 2012).

## 2.4 (SOCIO-)COGNITIVE THEORIES OF RITUAL

The pluralism that characterizes the cognitive approach as a whole is also conspicuous in the area of cognitive theories of ritual. Ritual theories, and theories relevant to analysis of ritual, derive from different schools and currents of the cognitive movement, and should therefore be viewed against the background of the particular cognitive or evolutionary theory each school draws upon. In the following, I discuss some of the central cognitive theories of ritual, already introduced in Chapter One, in the light of the above survey of the versions and properties of CSR.

Ritual Competence Theory was advanced by Lawson and McCauley in the earliest of the pioneering work that gave rise to CSR. Lawson and McCauley's fundamental proposition, that humans have a universal competence for making judgements about various properties of religious rituals, seems to be in full accord with the 'standard' model of CSR, which focuses on the innate cognitive mechanisms that constrain and canalize religious beliefs and behaviours. It should not, however, go unnoticed that Lawson and McCauley's interactionist position gives a rather different cast to their approach as compared to the 'standard' CSR—represented, for example, by the work of Boyer and Atran. This difference has rarely been emphasized in the literature (but see Engler and Gardiner 2009). Although Lawson and McCauley's approach was inspired by Chomsky's idea of a 'universal grammar' (an innate language module or capacity that explains the rapidity with which children learn a language), for them 'it is much less obvious that the commonalities that are characteristic of religious ritual systems require such a biological explanation' (Lawson and McCauley 1990: 181). Instead of the modularity theory or any other biology-based constraints, they look to *connections between cognition and culture* as explanatory factors for the universal ritual competence they suggest. Lawson and McCauley call their approach 'integrative' (1990: 180): they assert that 'ritual systems have both cultural *and cognitive* dimensions' (1990: 68, italics in the original), and maintain that 'analyses of these two domains will reflect and mutually inform one another' (1990: 42). The question of the precise nature of the mechanism that connects cognition and culture to produce the ritual competence in the participants does not find a full answer in *Rethinking Religion*; in their later book, (McCauley and Lawson 2002), they develop the theory by integrating it with Whitehouse's modes theory and memory studies.

The bottom line in their argument is that the cognitive approach is 'just a place to start' since it is 'only through our representations of... [cultural] systems that we have the sort of access to them which renders them at all tractable empirically. Symbolic-cultural *systems* have no way of being directly observed' (Lawson and McCauley 1990: 182–3, my italics).

In spite of their integrative approach, Lawson and McCauley present their Ritual Competence Theory as an explanatory and testable theory. The theory puts forward predictions—more systematically presented in McCauley and Lawson 2002—which, in principle at least, make it falsifiable. Lawson and McCauley's ritual theory has indeed been tested against historical, ethnographic and experimental evidence in a number of studies (Abbink 1995; Vial 1999; J. L. Barrett and Lawson 2001; Malley and Barrett 2003; Ketola 2007; Biró 2013). As is often the case, the theory is not simply proven false or true. For example, a study by Malley and Barrett, based on interviews with participants in the Hindu, Jewish, and Islamic traditions, found support for some of the major predictions of Lawson and McCauley's theory, but also raised questions as to the causal mechanism they propose. Biró examines the theory against mainstream rabbinic Judaism, and makes several critical observations as to its applicability to that religious tradition. But he also argues that Lawson and McCauley's theory is not falsified by rabbinic Judaism, and that it should be developed further 'by looking at additional problematic case studies' (Biró 2013: 142). Chapter Three in this volume offers another such case study, an analysis of John the Baptist's water ritual from the perspective of ritual innovation.

Whitehouse's Modes of Religiosity Theory is also among the pioneering theories in CSR, but its scope and scale are quite different (Whitehouse 2000, 2004a). While Ritual Competence Theory can be described as a middle-range theory, consisting of relatively few parameters and leaving out of consideration a great deal of what has usually been of interest to ritual scholars, the modes theory is in many regards the opposite. It starts with the 'big' question of why the world's religious traditions tend to coalesce around one of two contrasting types of religiosity. Scholars of religion have often suggested similar grand-scale dichotomies: distinguishing, for example, between 'charismatic' and 'routinized' forms (Weber), *'communitas'* and 'structure' (Turner) or literate and non-literate religions (Goody). In Whitehouse's model, the world's religious traditions are divided into the 'doctrinal' mode, accommodated by large-scale organizations sustaining orthodoxy and dry ritual routine, and the 'imagistic' mode, characterized by small-scale communities practising emotionally arousing rituals. The modes, or 'attractor positions', are described in terms of twelve psychological and socio-political variables, which can have either an imagistic or a doctrinal content (Whitehouse 2004a: 64–75; see also Table 1.1 in section 1.6). What makes the theory cognitive is its reference to two memory systems: episodic memory, which is central to the codification of imagistic traditions, and semantic memory, which dominates in the transmission of doctrinal traditions.

How testable is Whitehouse's modes theory? The theory is clearly meant to be tested against ethnographic and historical evidence (Whitehouse 2004a: 157–70), and it has attracted considerable attention from scholars across many fields (Whitehouse and Laidlaw 2004; Whitehouse and Martin 2004; Whitehouse and McCauley 2005). The testability of the theory, at least in its original form, is nevertheless weakened by its attempt to create a causative link between a host of different socio-political and psychological variables (explananda) and one single set of cognitive mechanisms, that is, the use of two retrieval systems in cognitive memory (for the use of memory studies in relation to ritual, see Czachesz 2010). This does not mean that Whitehouse's ethnography and theoretical reflections are of no relevance for the kind of analysis carried out in this book. Some parts of his theory, such as the idea of 'spontaneous exegesis' (spontaneous reflection of matters of ritual meaning), will be helpful in the subsequent analyses. Moreover, Whitehouse and his collaborators have over the years been developing the theory into more testable form, adding elements from other cognitive theories and using computational modelling to simulate its predictions (for example, Q. Atkinson and Whitehouse 2011; Whitehouse et al. 2012; see also Xygalatas 2013).

Although Modes of Religiosity Theory has often been compared to and associated with Ritual Competence Theory (most conspicuously in McCauley and Lawson 2002), among the schools of CSR Whitehouse's approach can also be linked to the cultural evolution approach. Modes of Religiosity focuses on the role of ritual in the transmission of religious traditions, and hence resonates with those CSR approaches that focus on the mechanisms of cultural learning. Since Ritual Competence Theory, in its original form, is a theory of tacit ritual competence, it does not have much to say about *explicit* religious knowledge transmitted via ritual practices.[13] Whitehouse's theory may be seen as an important groundwork for the study of ritual transmission, which earlier ritual theorists mainly analysed within the framework of symbolic anthropology.

As we have seen above (section 2.2), the approaches of both behavioural ecology (Commitment Signalling) and cultural evolution differ significantly from the 'standard' model of CSR, but the theories advanced in these currents meet the general properties of CSR already described. The advocates of these approaches develop explanatory theories, which are designed for empirical testing, and are in fact often subjected to data analysis. By combining biological and cultural evolution, these approaches also employ multilevel analysis and work across traditional disciplinary hierarchies. How exactly the direction of causation between the social/cultural level and the cognitive/biological one(s) is envisioned as going varies in each theory. In the social sciences, it is often assumed that the direction of causation is from the society to individual psychology: social structures exert influence over the minds of individuals (Sun 2012: 18). The 'standard' model of CSR provided a significant counter-balance to this one-sided view. More recent work in the field of CSR has emphasized the importance of two-way interaction between society and cognition, or between external and internal forms of religion (Bulbulia 2009a; Pyysiäinen 2012a); but interaction had been emphasized already in the pioneering writings, most explicitly in *Rethinking Religion*.

In the terminology of the present study, theories of ritual operating at both the social/cultural and the cognitive/biological level are referred to as *socio-cognitive*. All cognitive theories do this to some extent, but there are differences in the degree to which the explananda or predictions of a particular theory focus on the socio-cultural realm (Uro 2011c). The approach applied in this study is interactionist; it assumes that causation between the social and the cognitive occurs in both directions. It should also be noted that each theory employs 'explanatory pluralism', that is, non-reductive cross-fertilization between different levels of analysis, in its own particular way. As a

---

[13] Chapter 6 of *Rethinking Religions* does contain a discussion of the semantics of religious rituals, but I have difficulty in seeing how this discussion is related to their Theory of Ritual Competence. Cf. Engler and Gardiner 2009, according to whom Lawson and McCauley's argument for 'reflexive holism' in fact 'cuts the ground out from under their theory', although the 'false start continues to set an exemplary precedent' (2009: 34).

general rule, the analyses put forward in the following chapters move from an emphasis on upward causation (from the cognitive to the social) in Chapters Three and Four (ritual intuitions) to more interactionist explanation in Chapters Five and Six (cooperation, embodied cognition).

## 2.5 THEORETICAL PLURALISM

In the present work, I adopt an approach of theoretical pluralism, subscribing to the view that '[i]n modern scholarly practice of the study of ritual, one will... need to refer to more than one theory' (Kreinath et al. 2008a: xxiii). In *scientific* practice, theoretical pluralism is not so obvious. Science typically fosters competition between different theories and explanations. For an analysis of early Christian rituals as well, it would be quite possible to select a single theory or theoretical perspective. An approach based on theoretical pluralism, however, affords a number of advantages in the kind of multilevel analysis carried out in this study.

First, as we have seen above, CSR does not provide a uniform or coherent methodology for the study of early Christian rituals. CSR is a complex and pluralistic movement, consisting of different schools and currents which draw on a host of different fields and theoretical backgrounds. Taking sides between the schools would set limits to the scope of the investigation. By applying several different cognitive theories of ritual, however, the biblical scholar is in a position to overcome the limitations of any one such theory, and to assess the extent to which the theories used in the analysis are compatible.

Second, the preference for 'middle-range' theories over all-embracing grand theories is suggestive of a pluralistic strategy. It is better to use a set of target-specific theories, in which explanatory mechanisms are defined or at least purposefully left undefined, rather than to employ a theoretical perspective which either focuses on broad-sweeping topics and themes (without a clear mechanistic or analytical structure) or is too complex to be tested against empirical evidence.

Third, the specific subject of the study is defined by the concept of 'ritual', which, as is often observed, is a 'fuzzy set' or 'family-resemblance' concept (Snoek 2008; Sax 2010; Stephenson 2015: 70–3). Theories of ritual, on the other hand, generally come with definitions of the phenomenon they intend to explain, or at least with a focus on a particular aspect of the rather sweeping category of ritual. Thus McCauley and Lawson, for example, give a relatively narrow definition of 'religious ritual' in their 2002 book. They posit 'a technical sense', according to which all religious rituals involve 'agents acting upon patients' and are ultimately connected with 'actions in which CPS-agents [culturally postulated superhuman agents] play a role and which bring about some change in the religious world' (McCauley and Lawson 2002: 13). Although the precision of this definition pays dividends in the explanatory framework of cognitive science, one can object that it leaves out many activities that are usually deemed 'rituals' (for example, singing together in worship or performing secular rituals). This concern is relevant in the context of the integrative approach adopted in this study. As suggested in Chapter One, Ritual Studies, as a field focusing on a wide spectrum of actions and behaviours that scholars working from different theoretical perspectives identify as 'rituals', has the potential to shed significant new light on the study of Christian beginnings. In a work which aims at creating connections between Ritual Studies, CSR, and Biblical Studies, restricting the analysis to a single theory or definition of ritual may not be the best strategy. Theoretical pluralism, in contrast, allows more space for seeking cross-fertilization and links between the given fields in producing knowledge concerning the behavioural aspect of early Christian history. To overly narrow down the theoretical focus would also reduce the data relevant to the analysis (and data are scarce for the study of early Christianity in any case) and consequently the knowledge gained from the analysis.

On the other hand, theoretical pluralism should not be taken to extremes, to a kind of 'hyper-pluralistic' position (della Porta and Keating 2008: 33), or a post-modern epistemology which consistently resists definitions and champions a multiplicity of perspectives to the point of full relativism. In Ritual Studies, the resistance to defining ritual, and hence to developing formal theories of ritual, has most prominently been advocated by Bell, who criticizes the hegemony of theory and sees both the study of ritual and ritual practice as strategic means of exercising power (Bell 1992; see also section 1.5 above). Bell's approach can be contrasted with the strategy, adopted by many ritual theorists in the past, which attempts to define 'ritual' as a 'thing out there' and to work consistently within the boundaries of the given definition or theoretical framework. The pluralism applied in this study seeks a middle ground between these two poles—on the one hand a paradigmatic approach, starting with one clearly formulated theory or definition, on the other a hyper-pluralistic stance, which tends to be relativistic or pessimistic as to the possibility of gaining reliable knowledge about the world.

In terms of the classic philosophical debate between the nominalists (for whom scientific categories exist because we arbitrarily create them) and the realists (for whom the categories are out there to be discovered), the position taken in this study can be described as *theory-dependent realism*. According to this view, the category of ritual is helpful in achieving knowledge about human behaviour and social life, but this knowledge comes by various paths, that is, selected theories and perspectives. It remains for the analyst to decide how much of the different 'chunks' of information, arrived at via diverse pathways, are commensurable with one another and with other, independent and reliable information. The physicists Stephen Hawking and Leonard Mlodinow write about 'model-dependent realism' in a similar manner:

> It could be that the physicist's traditional expectation of a single theory of nature is untenable, and there exists no single formulation. It might be that to describe the universe, we have to employ different theories in different situations. Each theory may have its own version of reality, but according to model-dependent realism, that is acceptable so long as the theories agree in their predictions whenever they overlap, that is, whenever both can be applied.   (Hawking and Mlodinow 2010: 116–17)

We can use the approach suggested by the world's leading scientists as an analogy for the way different models and theories work in the present study. 'Ritual' as such is too fuzzy or too inclusive to be applied as an analytical category. Theoretical pluralism, as tamed by theory-dependent realism, provides a potential way to grasp some aspects of the 'ritual universe', as can be observed in the emergence of early Christian religion.

## 2.6 THREE PERSPECTIVES ON RITUAL

The foregoing review of the diverse schools and theories of ritual in CSR provide a basis for distinguishing three perspectives on ritual that will be used in the subsequent chapters. I should stress that 'perspective' should not be understood as referring to an aspect of a clearly identified entity, since 'ritual' obviously is not such a category. Each perspective on ritual opens up a realm of its own, in which 'ritual' may be understood narrowly or broadly—or it may remain undefined. Note also that the perspectives are theoretical viewpoints under which a number of middle-range theories can be organized. Although they emerge from the work done in CSR, the perspectives as such are not cognitive; they also represent classic issues in anthropology and the Study of Religion.

In the following, I discuss in more detail the three perspectives applied in this study: (1) ritual as action, (2) ritual and cooperation, and (3) ritual and religious knowledge.

### 2.6.1 Ritual as Action

This is the perspective that embraces McCauley and Lawson's definition of religious ritual. In their account, rituals are understood as actions in which agents act upon patients, which involve CPS-agents, and which 'bring about some change in the religious world' (McCauley and Lawson 2002: 13–14). But this perspective also involves other theoretical stances privileging the action dimension over the communicative or expressive aspects of ritual activities. As Laidlaw and Humphrey note, the elaboration of the latter aspects has been much more common in ritual theory than an approach focusing on ritual as action (Laidlaw and Humphrey 2008: 265). Their own theory of ritual, focusing on the non-intentional and archetypal nature of ritual actions (Humphrey and Laidlaw 1994), differs from that of Lawson and McCauley in many respects, but shares what can be called an 'action paradigm' in the study of ritual. Laidlaw and Humphrey write:

> Our own work on ritual, like that of Staal and Lawson & McCauley, departs from the widespread assumption that ritual is fundamentally a system of communication in which participants receive pre-existing meanings and messages. Instead, we argue that the attribution of meanings is a *response* to ritual, which is called for and developed to different degrees in different cultural settings and religious traditions at different times. Thus a meaning is at best a derivative feature of ritual—highly variable and indeed sometimes effectively absent. (Laidlaw and Humphrey 2008: 274; italics original)

The difference between, on the one hand, Lawson and McCauley, and, on the other, Humphrey and Laidlaw has to do with their different theoretical backgrounds, the former promoting a cognitive account of *religious* rituals (how such actions are represented in the minds of the participants), whereas the latter's theory is fundamentally about *ritualization*, that is, what distinguishes ordinary actions from ritualized actions.

Lawson and McCauley's theory also lays stress on the question of ritual efficacy: rituals are actions which 'bring about some change in the religious world'. Particularly suggestive of ritual efficacy are 'special agent rituals', which are qualified ultimately by the agency of a CPS-agent, and which therefore generate a 'superpermanent change in each ritual patient' (McCauley and Lawson 2002: 191). Ritual efficacy is intrinsically related to the question of *magic*, which has a long and complex history in the study of religion (Czachesz 2011, 2013a). One important vein in this history has been Durkheim's account of ritual as the mirror and source of the social, and as 'the direct antithesis of the utilitarian understanding of action' (Laidlaw and Humphrey 2008: 265). For Durkheim, genuine rituals give rise to and consolidate social groups, whereas the focus on the efficacy transfers rituals into the sphere of magic (cf. Durkheim 2001: 45). The question of efficacy should not, however, be detached from the analysis with such a ritual–magic dichotomy, but should be taken as an essential part of ritual theory (Sax et al. 2010).

The action perspective on ritual recognizes a number of practices that played a central role in the earliest phases of the early Christian movement. The examples analysed in this study are the ritual immersion performed by John the Baptist, Jesus' healing practices, and ritual healing in Early Christianity (Chapters Three and Four). In all these practices there are agents acting upon patients, CPS-agents are involved, and the actions are expected to bring about some change in the religious world.

### 2.6.2 Ritual and Cooperation

The action perspective shifts away from the Durkheimian tradition in its embrace of ritual efficacy and its rejection of the view which sees ritual first and foremost as a paradigm of the social. The question of how ritual facilitates social life has nevertheless not ceased to engage the attention of ritual theorists. This is also true of cognitive theorists, especially those who suggest that religion emerged in the course of evolution to support cooperation and to overcome the challenge of collective action. As we have seen, this is the starting point of behavioural ecologists, who promote the signalling approach to religion. This approach is in line with Durkheim's central tenet, that religious rituals communicate about the social and create a basis for all communal life; it diverges from the action perspective, which does not accommodate communicative aspects of ritual activities.

In the pluralistic approach applied in this study, the action and communication/cooperation perspectives are not mutually exclusive. Some ritual activities are amenable to more than one analytical perspective. For example, John's water ritual can be examined as an action upon a ritual patient generating some change in the religious world which the participants inhabit, but it can also be seen as a signal of commitment to the group that cultivated the practices and beliefs promoted by John. On the other hand, not all practices which can be reasonably subjected to ritual analysis fit easily into the action model consisting of the agent, patient, and action/instrument slots.

Chapter Five provides a critical discussion of the Durkheimian perspective in the light of recent developments in Ritual Studies and CSR. The middle-range theory applied in that chapter is Commitment (Costly) Signalling Theory, which makes some specific predictions as to the social dynamics and survival of small-scale groups in relation to the 'costliness' of the behaviours demanded of group members. Commitment Signalling does not offer a clearly formulated definition of ritual—it is more a theory of religious practices or behaviours in general—but it nevertheless provides a tool for reconsidering some of the cherished ideas in the study of the social world of early Christianity. The test case for the socio-cognitive approach to ritual and cooperation is the ritual life of the earliest Christian 'house churches', about which some evidence, even if fragmentary, can be found in the letters of Paul.

### 2.6.3 Ritual and Religious Knowledge

In symbolic anthropological theory, ritual was often understood as a kind of language, which could be decoded by means of the analytical and interpretative work done by the anthropologist. This stance was effectively criticized by Sperber in his *Rethinking Symbolism* (1974), which is often seen as an early precursor of CSR. In Sperber's account, the interpretations of symbolic anthropologists are themselves symbolic; they are acts forming part of an endless process, best understood in cognitive terms (Pyysiäinen 2001: 42–4; Boyer 2008). This view accords with the approach advocated by Laidlaw and Humphrey (cited in section 2.6.1), according to whom the attribution of meanings is a *response* to ritual (Laidlaw and Humphrey 2008: 274), not an inherent quality of ritual itself. In other words, ritual semantics and the analysis of ritual *actions* should be analytically kept apart (Lawson 2008).

This, however, does not mean that the issue of the relationship between ritual and religious knowledge has been eclipsed by the introduction of the cognitive programme. Whitehouse's Modes of Religiosity Theory centres on religious knowledge, analysing how imagistic and doctrinal rituals facilitate the *transmission* of religious traditions. His theory also connected cognitive memory to ritual theory, an approach that has been elaborated in subsequent studies (Whitehouse and Laidlaw 2004; Czachesz 2010; Uro 2011b).

In the large picture of the schools and currents in CSR, the perspective of ritual and religious knowledge is readily associated with theories of cultural evolution and embodied cognition. As depicted above, cultural evolution theorists have developed models of learning biases, some of which have direct links to ritual transmission (especially Henrich 2009). In this study, particular attention is given to embodied (extended) cognition, which sees cognition, and thus religious knowledge, as being inherently dependent on the body and its interaction with the environment. This would seem an obvious vantage point for a ritual analysis, but in fact very little research has been carried out from this perspective, either in Ritual Studies or in Cognitive Science. In Chapter Six I explore the question of how rituals convey religious knowledge, applying theories and insights from embodied and extended cognition and taking examples from early Christian baptismal practices.

The three perspectives on ritual do not cover all significant cognitive theories of ritual advanced in the history of the cognitive movement. They nevertheless organize a number of theories and approaches under larger themes, which both reflect various theoretical currents in CSR and provide links to classic issues and topics in ritual theory (see Table 2.1).

Table 2.1. Research questions, classical issues, cognitive theories, and examples from early Christianity, arranged by the three perspectives on ritual

| Perspectives | Questions | Classical issues | Theories and mechanisms | Examples from early Christianity |
|---|---|---|---|---|
| Ritual as action | – What kind of rituals are understood as powerful?<br>– How do ritual inventions function as catalysts for new movements? | – Discussions on magic, ritual healing and efficacy | – Ritual Competence Theory<br>– Cognitive theories of magic and possession | – John the Baptist<br>– Ritual healing in early Christianity |
| Ritual and cooperation | – How do rituals foster cooperation in small-scale and large-scale societies? | – Religion and ritual as a basis of social life | – Commitment Signalling | – Ritual in the Pauline assemblies |
| Ritual and religious knowledge | – How do rituals generate and accommodate religious knowledge? | – Myth and ritual<br>– Ritual symbolism and semiotics | – Memory studies<br>– Embodied and situated cognition | – Ritual knowledge transmitted in and through baptismal practices |

## 2.7 FROM COGNITIVE THEORY TO THE STUDY OF ANCIENT RITUALS

In this chapter, I have described the most important schools and currents in CSR and the different ways in which evolutionary theory has been used by cognitive scholars of religion. Although CSR is a pluralistic and manifold movement, it also shares unifying features, such as the promotion of explanatory and testable theories and a multilevel analysis, often connected to the strategy of explanatory pluralism. The original programme, sometimes referred to as the 'standard' model, has developed into a diverse set of research projects, applying various cognitive and evolutionary theories as well as experimental research. In the subsequent chapters, I will consistently refer to CSR as a broad and pluralistic approach comprising the various schools and currents introduced here.

Cognitive theories of ritual were reviewed against the background of the cognitive programme at large. This discussion helped to develop a socio-cognitive approach to ritual which seeks to integrate a social-level analysis with findings from the broadly defined CSR. For the purpose of the study of Christian beginnings, a socio-cognitive analysis of Christian beginnings is best accomplished by drawing on a theoretical pluralism which considers three perspectives on ritual: ritual as action upon a ritual patient, ritual and cooperation, and ritual and religious knowledge. We now turn to ancient texts to see how the theoretical reflections offered in this chapter can be rendered into an analysis of early Christian rituals.

# 3

# 'I Baptize You With Water'

## Ritual and the Rise of Religious Movements

In the beginning was John's baptism. This is the impression received by the reader of the New Testament, and scholarship has generally confirmed John's important role in the emergence of the Jesus movement. All four evangelists place descriptions of John the Baptist's activity at the beginning of their writings (Mark 1:2–6; Matt. 3:1–16; Luke 3:1–6; John 1:19–23), and refer to him frequently elsewhere as well (John appears in a total of fifty-three passages in the Gospels and Acts; Webb 1991: 47–91). It is even likely that 'Q', the Sayings Source used by Matthew and Luke, began with John's preaching (Q 3:7–9, 16–17; Uro 1995).[1] An overwhelming majority of New Testament scholars believe that the reports preserved in the Gospels as to the connection between the two religious figures reflect genuine historical memories (for a few dissident voices among scholars, see Enslin 1975 and Mack 1988: 54). It is widely acknowledged that Jesus was baptized by John—one of the 'almost indisputable' facts of Jesus' life, according to Sanders (Sanders 1985: 11)[2]—and that John's activity

---

[1] According to the scholarly convention, 'Q' passages are cited by their Lukan versification.

[2] Although Sander's 'indisputable fact' is widely accepted, some scholars have cast doubt on the historical reliability of the story of Jesus' baptism. Vaage (1996), for example, sees Mark's narrative of Jesus' baptism (1:9–11) as part of the evangelist's 'mythmaking' or redactional 'efforts at persuasion' (282). DeMaris (2002) argues that Jesus' visionary experience (historically very likely) was later associated with baptism as a response to the criticism that Jesus' spirit possession was uncontrolled (i.e. not induced by a ritual). Although I do not deny that the Gospel narratives involve considerable mythmaking, the massive presence of the Baptist traditions in the Gospels and Acts (and in some extra-canonical sources as well) cannot simply be

was of major importance for the subsequent ministry of Jesus. There are of course uncertainties and debated issues concerning the relationship between John and Jesus, some of which are discussed in this and the following chapter, but it is justified to state that there is a wide-ranging consensus as to the historicity of contacts between John and Jesus and their respective movements (for summaries of the discussion, see Webb 1994, 2000; Betz 2011b). The analysis of John's activity is therefore of no minor importance for understanding the emergence of the early Christian movement. There are good reasons to start our study of Christian beginnings with John.

John was best remembered for his performance of an immersion rite, the *baptisma*, a word used only in Christian sources (deriving from the verb *baptizō*, 'dip', 'immerse'; cf. also *baptō*, 'dip'; Bauer 1988, *s.v.*; Ferguson 2009: 38–59).[3] This practice produced his epithet 'Baptist' or 'Baptizer' (*baptistēs*), used by the Evangelists (except for John) and by the Jewish historian Josephus (*Ant.* 18.116;[4] cf. also the participle *ho baptizōn* 'the one immersing' in Mark 6:14, 24).

John's reputation as promulgator of a special rite that became associated with his name leads us to ask what role his ritual practice played in the formation of his movement, and consequently in its offshoot, the Jesus movement. Although scholars of early Judaism and early Christianity have written a number of detailed analyses of the meaning and function of John's rite and its religious-cultural setting (Ernst 1989: 320–46; Webb 1991: 163–214; Taylor 1997: 49–100; Rotschild 2005: 65–71), they have seldom asked questions as to how ritual inventions, such as John's immersion, function as catalysts for new movements. How do ritual innovations contribute to the consolidation of religious ideas and to the social dynamics of an emergent group or movement? These kinds of questions arise from

---

explained away in terms of the Evangelists' redactional and rhetorical interests in creating a baptism story.

[3] *Baptisma* is the usual word for the baptism of John and for Christian baptism in the New Testament. The more general word *baptismos*, is sometimes used for ritual washings in the New Testament (Mark 7:4, 8; Heb. 6:2; 9:10; Col. 2:12 v.l.), but *baptisma* is the overwhelmingly preferred expression for baptism in the early Christian literature. Josephus, on the other hand, uses the word *baptismos* to describe John's rite (*Ant.* 18.116).

[4] The abbreviations of the Latin and Greek titles of the ancient writings referred to in this book follow the style recommended in *The SBL Handbook of Style: Second Edition* (Collins et al. 2014).

recent developments in the field of Ritual Studies, which, as demonstrated in Chapter One, have not yet been brought to bear to any great extent upon the study of Christian origins. It is indeed striking how seldom perspectives from Ritual Studies have been used in the analysis of John's ministry, notwithstanding the prominent role the immersion rite played in his career. In this chapter, I seek to demonstrate how ritual theory, in particular cognitive theories of ritual, can help to answer or at least clarify questions that biblical scholars and historians have been asking about John the Baptist, and to raise questions that have not previously been asked.

## 3.1 THE NEGLECTED THEME OF RITUAL INNOVATION

What evidence we have points to the conclusion that there was something new in John's practice of immersing in the river Jordan those who came to him. John would hardly have obtained his nickname, 'the Baptizer' or 'the Immerser', unless his immersion practices were deemed somehow special by his contemporaries. What precisely was new in John's ritual is to some degree a matter of debate, but there is no doubt that John was a ritual entrepreneur of some sort.

Somewhat surprisingly, 'ritual innovation' or 'ritual invention' is not a major theme in ritual theory. It does not feature in the massive two-volume work *Theorizing Rituals*, which collects, systematizes and reviews the research carried out in the field of Ritual Studies (Kreinath et al. 2007; Kreinath et al. 2008b). Nor does it appear as an entry, or even as an item in the index, in a recent encyclopedia of religious rituals (Salamone 2004). There is a tendency to think of ritual as something traditional or essentially unchanging (Bell 1997: 223–34; Grimes 2000: 11), which has undermined the importance of this theme in ritual theory. Given the family-resemblance nature of 'ritual' itself (see sections 1.5 and 2.6 above), a grand theory of ritual innovation is perhaps not even possible. However, new rites—or behavioural patterns that may turn into full-blown rites—are invented constantly in human societies, and it is vital to try to understand the social and psychological mechanisms which operate in such processes.

One relevant concept with regard to the invention of new rites is that of 'ritualization'. Ritual theorists, however, define this in different ways. For Grimes, for example, ritualization is part of the process that may (or may not) lead to full-blown rituals (1995: 60–2); in his 2013 book, he defines ritualization as 'the act of cultivating or inventing rites' (Grimes 2014: 193). Bell sees ritualization as a way of distinguishing certain actions from other, more ordinary activities; especially affirming differences of power (1992: 88–93). Laidlaw and Humphrey argue that ritualized actions differ from ordinary actions in that they are 'non-intentional', in the sense that the identity of the action is fixed by prior stipulation. This non-intentionality makes the ritual action appear to those who perform it 'as somehow pre-existing and coming from outside themselves'. Laidlaw and Humphrey refer to this as the 'archetypal quality of ritual' (2008: esp. 277–8; see also Humphrey and Laidlaw 1994). For new rites, the challenge of course is to make them appear 'archetypal', so that participants can feel that they are replicating or achieving something pre-existing.

In her treatment of the theme 'ritual invention', Bell analyses a number of contemporary and historical rites which have arisen as the result of more or less conscious efforts at ritual invention. These include rites developed to take the place of Christian rites in the former Soviet Union, various ritual dimensions of American national identity, the rise of the modern Olympic Games in the late nineteenth century, the firewalking movement in North America, feminist and womanist rites, and therapeutic and New Age rituals (Bell 1997: 223–42). The degree to which the 'novelty' of invented rites is emphasized in these movements is variable: in some cases it seems important not to call undue attention to the fact of invention, but in other contexts both ritual specialists and participants are quite aware that they are involved in new or invented rites. Bell concludes that legitimacy and efficacy are construed differently for invented rites than for more traditional ones. For a rite which is less deeply rooted in a shared sense of tradition, there is increased pressure to show that it 'works'. In other words, efficacy is an important issue in ritual innovations, and ritual specialists/innovators have to meet the challenge that people may be disappointed (Bell 1997: 241).

Would such a tendency also be observable for John's ritual immersion? We do not have reports in our sources of people actually being disappointed with John's rite, but it is worth noting that the issue of efficacy comes up in a number of passages referring to the immersion administered by John. Luke's description of 'deficient' disciples in Ephesus in Acts (19:1-7; cf. also 18:25), for example, focuses on the inferior nature of John's baptism in relation to Christian baptism, in that immersion by John did not induce the Holy Spirit for those immersed. Josephus' account of John the Baptist (*Ant.* 18.116-19) also seems to reflect debates as to whether John's immersion was meant to wash away people's sins or merely to provide a means to purify one's body (more on this below in section 3.4). As Jesper Sørensen has argued, 'magical agency' (referring to superhuman agencies necessary for ritual efficacy) is a decisive factor in the stabilization of religious charisma (Sørensen 2005). Debates over the legitimacy of John's rite (cf. Mark 11:30-33 and parallels) can thus be seen as traces of the process in which the magical agency operating in John's ritual invention is assessed and set against the more traditional source of religious power.

Ritual innovations are seldom completely new in their historical and cultural contexts. New rituals are built on existing rituals and cultural elements—sometimes copied or modified from more distant or exotic 'primordial' contexts. This is essential in promoting the 'archetypal' quality of a new rite (cf. Laidlaw and Humphrey as referred to above). Vanessa Ochs, who has written about ritual and religious innovations in contemporary Judaism in the United States (Ochs 2007), speaks of the 'Jewish Ritual Toolbox', on which she and other ritual innovators draw in developing new forms of Jewish religious practices; the 'Toolbox' includes for example biblical passages and teachings, familiar actions, objects, and elements of Jewish *halakha* (2007: 5-7). Ritual innovators often use existing building blocks from their cultural resources to develop new rites and ritual complexes.

The number of ritual variations in the evolution of religious practices, however, is not unlimited. The range of variation is significantly constrained by the cognitive capacities of the human mind, which explain the striking regularities found in the world's religious traditions across time and space. This insight is at the heart of the cognitive approach to culture, especially of the 'standard' model, as was demonstrated in Chapter Two (see 2.2). To become truly cultural, that is shared by a sufficient number of individuals in a given population, ritual inventions must conform to selection forces largely based on human *maturationally natural* predilections (McCauley 2011). 'Maturational naturalness' is a term used by cognitive scientists of religion to refer to actions that humans learn to do effortlessly; it is distinguished from 'practised naturalness', such as the ability to read a book without consciously thinking about how to do it (McCauley 2011: 29). Cognitive scholars of ritual have focused on those natural selection forces that are important for rituals to survive and be transmitted. This is not to say that intuitive mechanisms are the only relevant factors in explaining ritual behaviour, or that conscious processes have not played a crucial role in the evolution of human cognition. Rituals should not be seen as emerging merely from the sphere of unconscious thinking. People can, for example, learn rituals which require considerable training and are thus 'cognitively costly'—ritual specialists supported by religious institutions often do so and train others to follow such practices. But a working hypothesis can be advanced that in the long run, and filtered through larger masses of 'carriers', ritual practices tend to square with the cognitive intuitions provisionally modelled by cognitive theorists of ritual.

While one should not underestimate political and institutional arrangements supporting 'weightier' forms of religiosity (cf. Whitehouse 2004a: 49–59), intuitive mechanisms are helpful for understanding the ritual innovations analysed in this chapter. This is so for at least two reasons. First, the movements triggered by the activities of John and Jesus were *popular* movements, *not* supported by ecclesiastical institutions, systematic teaching, or a dependence on literacy. Second, even in the case of religious traditions in which such guilds play a significant role—for example, the later stages of the Christian movement—religious representations are always processed by human minds. Cognitive mechanisms—many of which are beyond the individual's reflective thinking—should therefore not be isolated from the processes of cultural manipulation and the exploitation of cultural technologies, unless we want to end up in the fruitless nature vs. culture dichotomy (Bloch 2012).

## 3.2 RITUAL INNOVATIONS AS CATALYSTS FOR RELIGIOUS MOVEMENTS

To return to the initial question: how do ritual innovations function as catalysts for new movements? Sociologists of religion have suggested a variety of theories to explain the emergence and survival of religious movements and the reasons why people join them: deprivation theory, rational choice theory, theories which focus on a search for meaning, and resource mobilization, to list but a few (Furseth and Repstad 2006). The role of ritual, however, does not usually come up in such classic—or more recent—sociological explanations. Some cognitive scholars, on the other hand, have ventured to extend their theoretical work from the cognitive to the sociological level, and have attempted to determine how cognitive mechanisms underlying ritual exert an influence on the social dynamics of religious groups. McCauley and Lawson, for example, hypothesize that 'special agent rituals' (rituals in which the superhuman agent is primarily associated with the agent of the ritual) play an important role in activating members of the movement: 'no religious system can survive without at least the periodic performance of special agent rituals capable of energizing participants and motivating them to transmit their religious systems' (McCauley and Lawson 2002: 212).

Whitehouse's vivid ethnography of the Pomio Kivung provides further insights into the role of ritual inventions in the emergence of a new movement (Whitehouse 1995; see also Whitehouse 2000). During his fieldwork in the Eastern Province of New Britain, Papua New Guinea, among the adherents of a millenarian movement, Whitehouse became an eyewitness to the rise of a high-arousal splinter group; over the course of a few months, before the group exhausted itself, its leaders developed a series of increasingly intensive and emotionally laden rituals. These included a resuscitated version of the traditional Mali Baining dance, the *awan*, supplemented by a night of singing, dancing, and feasting, as well as a completely new ritual, the ring ceremony, in which the participants formed a human circle, with the leader(s) standing at the centre representing the community of the chosen ones. Inspired by a dream experienced by one of the two leaders, the rite was performed at dawn in a state of virtual nudity and was later repeated many times and in many forms over the life-span of the movement. During the climactic stage of the outburst, rituals were performed which were even more emotionally intense, culminating in a series of all-night vigils in which the participants awaited the ancestors' return and faced increasingly severe distress: stifling heat, hunger, nausea, and other forms of stress.

Whitehouse's ethnography demonstrates how high-arousal ritual innovations can provide energy for an emerging movement, motivating the members and supporting its ideology. New rituals clearly functioned as promoters or catalysts of the millenarian outburst. The main architect of the movement, Baninge, was quite aware of his role as a ritual entrepreneur, sometimes even consulting the resident anthropologist (Whitehouse) for new and imaginative ideas (Whitehouse 1995: 115). In his analysis of the two forms of religiosity among the Pomio Kivung, Whitehouse's most important observation was that the renewal involved a shift of emphasis away from the codification of the religious knowledge in language (as was largely the case in the traditional form of Kivung religiosity) 'towards the cultivation of concrete metaphors through *collective ritual performance*' (Whitehouse 1995: 124, italics original). The ring ceremony, for example, was not just an abstract conception, but 'physically experienced reality' (1995: 194). In a later work, Whitehouse uses the term 'spontaneous exegetical reflection' to describe the explicit meanings that high-arousal and low-frequency rituals tend to generate in the minds of the participants (2004a: 113–17). Such codification through cultivation of iconic processes does not support doctrinal religious systems (coherent religious ideologies), since the range of possible symbolic interpretations of the ritual episodes will always be vast.

The splinter group described by Whitehouse was fuelled by a series of increasingly imagistic rites. Sometimes a new religious movement revolves heavily around a single ritual innovation. This, apparently, is what was going on in John the Baptist's movement. Another example is a contemporary movement instigated by a female Indian guru, Mata Amritanandayami, better known as Ammachi or Amma, which provides an interesting point of comparison to the Baptist movement.[5]

## 3.3 AMMA—HOLY MOTHER

Mata Amritanandayami (born 1953), affectionately called Amma or Ammachi ('mother'), is the most famous of Indian female gurus. Her

---

[5] I thank Kimmo Ketola for the idea of comparing John the Baptist with Amma.

ashram (spiritual centre) was formally established in 1981 near Kollam, Kerala (Raj 2005). Over the past two decades the movement has grown tremendously; today she has a large following of devotees and sympathizers worldwide, representing a wide spectrum of different religious traditions. The roots of Amma's spiritual community are in the Bhakti tradition of Hinduism, which emphasizes loving devotion towards Shiva and Vishnu and their incarnations—for example Krishna (for Bhakti, see Prentiss 1999). This tradition also assigns a prominent role to the guru, who as an embodiment of God mediates between the supreme reality and human beings (Ketola 2008: 87). For her followers, Amma is *sat guru*, the true and perfect spiritual teacher, although she has never been initiated as one. At the same time she is revered as a goddess (*devi*), and her identity as divine mother is revealed in her *Devi Bhava* programmes, organized both in India and in the countries she visits (Raj 2005: 131-2; Lucia 2014: 76-106).

The most conspicuous aspect of Amma's spiritual activities is the 'divine hug' she performs with her devotees. This ritual innovation is based on the traditional *darshan*, the exchange of sight between the devotee and the deity represented by an idol, guru, or renouncer (Humphrey and Laidlaw 1994: 270; Raj 2005: 137-8). It is a central ritual act in Hindu worship, in which the devotee both sees and is seen by the deity. In striking contrast to the version of *darshan* developed by Amma, the traditional etiquette of the ritual act does not allow bodily contact with the deity, which would normally be both inauspicious and forbidden for the average devotee (Raj 2005: 137; see also Lucia 2014: 44-5). The ritual hug performed by Amma, including intense bodily contact (touching and kissing), is thus a radical and unorthodox new version of the traditional ritual act familiar to every Hindu worshipper. There is no doubt that Amma's creative ritual innovation has played an important role in the spread and popularity of the movement both in India and beyond. It is not difficult to find moving stories about the *darshan* experiences of those who have received Amma's ritual hug, reflecting people's different backgrounds and personal perspectives.[6]

---

[6] To give just one example documented by Raj: 'She leaves a permanent impression on the level that's way beyond language or thought... from her perspective, she is you. She's just trying to wake you up that you are Her [the divine]... during *darshan*, she awakes the divine in you with a smile and hug' (Raj 2005: 137). For testimonies of Amma's North American devotees, see also Lucia 2014: 161-75.

80    *Ritual and Christian Beginnings*

John the Baptist and Amma the Divine Mother come from different cultures and are two thousand years apart. Yet there are striking similarities between them. The trademark of both spiritual leaders is the performance of a new ritual. John obtained his epithet from his baptismal activity; Amma, in turn, is called a divine 'Mother' (*amma* or *ammachi* in Malayalam, Amma's native language). It is not an unwarranted assumption that the ritual entrepreneurship of both leaders is a crucial factor in the success of the respective movements. Moreover, both ritual innovations are built on religious practices that are already well-known and central in the cultures into which they were introduced. Amma relies on the traditional Hindu *darshan*, while John's immersion is a version of Jewish ritual bathing. It is widely recognized that practices of ritual bathing were widespread in Second Temple Judaism and part of widely shared cultural knowledge (Sanders 1992: 213–40; Meyers 2002; J. D. Lawrence 2006; Freyne 2011; Adler 2013). Amma's ritual hug is a *radical* new version of the traditional *darshan*, which does not normally include touching or kissing. This raises the question of the distinctive nature of John's immersion as compared to other ritual washings of his time. How radical was it in the context of Second Temple Judaism?

## 3.4 WHAT WAS NEW IN JOHN'S IMMERSION?

Perhaps the most widely cited answer to this question was given by Morton Smith, who argued that John's great innovation was 'to introduce . . . a new, inexpensive, generally available, divinely authorized rite, effective for the remission of all sins' (M. Smith 1973: 208; cited approvingly for example by Crossan 1991: 331). The only place where Jews could legally offer sacrifice was Jerusalem, and its services were expensive. John's ritual innovation was thus to provide an inexpensive means of atonement for the common peasant, who could not easily afford animal sacrifices. Webb follows this line of interpretation in arguing that one of the functions of John's baptism was a protest against the temple establishment (Webb 1991: 203–5; 1994: 197; similarly Wright 1996: 160–1). Webb emphasizes the political undertones of John's activity. With his immersion rite, John provided an alternative to the temple's sacrificial system, and his prophetic preaching was directed against the leading religious elite (Matt. 3:7–10; cf. Luke 3:7–9; see, however, Uro 1995).

Although Smith's interpretation of John's rite as a radical alternative to temple offerings has appealed to many commentators, we should be careful not to read John's ritual activity in the light of later Christian theology, which sees Christ's death as a substitute for temple sacrifices and gives pride of place to forgiveness of sins (M. Casey 2010: 46-7). As Eyal Regev points out, the Priestly Code—representing the view of the sacrificial system held by religious specialists—does not require a personal sacrifice in relation to every offence (Regev 2004: 405), and it would be anachronistic to assume that large masses of people in John's time were motivated to sacrifice by feelings of personal guilt and introspective anguish (cf. Meier 1994: 113). Ancient sacrifice should not be restricted in its interpretation by the connotations carried by the word 'sacrifice' in Christian theology (Stowers 1995: 297).[7]

Moreover, the Hebrew Bible and Second Temple literature contain several references to rites of repentance other than sacrifices (Avemarie 1999; Olyan 2004: 62–96; Hägerland 2006; see also Boda et al. 2007). Sometimes it is explicitly said that penitential prayer can replace sacrifice for those who for one reason or other cannot offer sacrifice in the Temple (1 Kgs 8:46–50 = 2 Chr. 6:36–39; see also Dan. 9:3; Hos. 14:2–3; Jonah 3:6–9). The rites of repentance mentioned in these sources include penitential prayer, confession of sins, fasting, and bodily posture (for example kneeling and extending one's hands), as well as signs of mourning (rending one's clothes, putting on sackcloth, etc.). Public (oral) confession of sins, prayer, and fasting are particularly interesting for us, since these rites of repentance also appear in the traditions attached to John the Baptist (Mark 1:5; 2:18; Luke 11:1). Penitential prayer and fasting may even have been understood in some circles as expiatory (Holmén 2001: 130–1; Hägerland 2006: 182). For example, Philo states that in the annual Day of Atonement (Lev. 16:29–31) people's penitential prayers 'bring about' God's forgiveness (*Mos.* 2.23–34; *Spec.* 1.187). The author of the Psalms of Solomon asserts that the righteous one 'atones for his (sin of) ignorance by fasting and by humbling himself' (3.8; trans. R. B. Wright in Charlesworth 1985). To what extent these and other

---

[7] For a collection of up-to-date essays on ancient Mediterranean sacrifice, see Knust and Várhelyi 2011.

practices related to atonement reflect anti-Temple or antisacrificial sentiments in Second Temple Judaism is a vexed question (Taylor 1997: 31–2 argues that they do *not* reflect rejection of the Temple cult).[8] The important point here, however, is that—although undoubtedly distinctive in its cultural setting—John's baptism can be aligned with varied practices and expressions in pre-70 CE Judaism which offer evidence for other means of atonement than the sacrificial cult in the Temple of Jerusalem (cf. also Avemarie 1999). Even if it were taken as in some regard a critique of the Temple cult, John's attitude would not have been unique in his cultural context.

To my knowledge, the most thorough analysis of John's immersion rite in relation to the ritual practices of Second Temple Judaism has been that by Joan Taylor (1997: esp. 15–100). Taylor's view is that John's immersion has to do with purification of the body, not with mediating forgiveness of sins to those who received baptism (1997: 88). This interpretation of John's baptism is in agreement with Josephus' account, in which he says that according to John the baptism should not be used 'for seeking pardon of certain sins but for purification of the body' (*Ant.* 18.117; trans. Feldman 1965). Taylor points out that in John's time purification by immersion in water was a cultural truism; everyone knew that was what an immersion was about (1997: 94). But she also recognizes that there was something 'novel or extraordinary' in John's activity, as otherwise he would not have earned his title of 'Immerser' (1997: 94). Taylor's answer to the question asked in the heading of this section is that John's novelty was not so much in his immersion practice as in his teaching that 'previous immersions and ablutions were ineffective for Jews without the practice of true righteousness' (1997: 99–100). She notes that (according to Mark) John proclaimed a 'baptism of repentance' (*baptisma metanoias*; Mark 1:4), and argues that the genitive case in Greek renders the Aramaic prefix *dī* or *d*, which can indicate either purpose or result. Taylor prefers the latter, and interprets Mark's words *baptisma metanoiās eis aphesin hamartiōn* to mean 'an immersion *resulting from* repentance for the remission of sins' (1997: 197).

---

[8] This relates to the larger, much-debated issue of cult criticism and supersessionism in ancient Judaism and early Christianity. For a balanced treatment of the question, see Klawans 2006. See also Ego et al. 1999 and Hendel 2012.

Taylor's contention, that immersion in water would have been largely associated among John's contemporaries with bodily purification, is reasonable. Ritual bathing practices were an important part of everyday life in Jewish society at large (Meyers 2002: 220; Freyne 2011: 231; Adler 2013: 247–8), and it would be strange if the shared cultural knowledge of bodily purification had not influenced people's understanding of John's immersion.[9] This does not mean, however, that we should attempt to reconcile Josephus' and Mark's accounts of the purpose of John's baptism (cf. also Rotschild 2005: 65). Taylor's reading of Mark 1:4 is forced; the phrase *eis aphesin hamartiōn* ('for the remission of sins') more naturally refers to the whole genitive construction *baptisma metanoiās* ('baptism of repentance')[10] than to 'repentance' alone. As pointed out by Whitehouse (see section 3.2), emotional and powerful rituals evoke a variety of interpretations, and there is no reason to assume that John or his followers (including Jesus) were able to create doctrinal unity with regard to immersion.

Most importantly, it is difficult to see how Taylor's interpretation would explain why John's immersion was regarded as something noteworthy by his contemporaries (cf. Taylor 1997: 63). If the thrust of John's message was that previous purifications were ineffective without moral reform, what makes the *immersion* practised by him so outstanding? In what way was it different from ordinary purification in a *miqveh* or in the sea, according to biblical Law? Why was an immersion performed by John necessary in the first place?

Some scholars argue that John's immersion was a rite of initiation into the Baptist movement, administered only once for each individual (Webb 1991: 197–202, 216 n. 139; cf. also Yarbro Collins 1989: 32; Ferguson 2009: 87). According to this account, John's rite differed significantly from other forms of Jewish ritual bathing in that the latter were normally repeated many times over a lifetime to regain purity after various events, such as menstruation or emission of

---

[9] It is also possible to add a cognitive argument in support of the view that John's immersion was largely associated with purification. Pascal Boyer and Pierre Liénard have advanced an account of ritual behaviour which assumes an evolved Hazard-Precaution System, a system specialized in the detection of and response to potential threats (Boyer and Liénard 2006; Liénard and Boyer 2006). This would explain why ritual behaviours are often associated with the theme of pollution and cleansing.

[10] The genitive is best understood as the *genetivus qualitativus* or descriptive genitive, which describes the head noun in a loose manner ('baptism that is related to repentance'); see von Dobbeler 1988: 172–3; Blass et al. 1979: § 165; Wallace 1996: 80.

semen.¹¹ Webb connects his view of John's immersion as a rite of initiation into 'True Israel' with his argument that John instigated a sectarian movement within Second Temple Judaism. Some scholars reject the latter view, maintaining that since John did not establish a 'closed community', his rite could not function as an initiation into any such community (Becker 1972: 39–40; cf. also Lupieri 1993). Webb rightly refutes the argument that 'initiation' needs to be into a fully segregated group; he contends that in the Judaism of John's time 'sectarian movements flourished which distinguished themselves in some way from ethnic Israel as a whole, yet the individuals remained as functioning members of society' (1991: 199).¹² It seems indeed obvious that John's activity gave rise to a socially distinctive group consisting of his followers and sympathizers, although adherents probably did not cut their ties to the rest of society.

This conclusion, however, does not logically entail the further conclusion that John's immersion functioned as a once-in-a-lifetime initiation into membership in John's movement. It may have been so, but we can imagine other functions as well. John's immersion could have been similar to Amma's hugging ritual, which is not an initiation or rite of passage, typically experienced only once by any given individual. It is in fact quite common for devotees to participate multiple times in Amma's ritual embrace to receive a divine blessing (Lucia 2014: 11). This is a possible scenario for John's adherents as well. Again, we should be careful not to see John's rite in terms of Christian baptism and baptismal theology (Taylor 1997: 70). Moreover, early Christian baptismal practices should not be understood as quite so uniform as is often assumed (see for example 1 Cor. 15:29 and Heb. 6:2; DeMaris 2008: 14–36).

It thus remains uncertain whether John's immersion functioned as a once-and-for-all initiation into his group. How, then, to describe the originality of his ritual practice? The most obvious difference

---

¹¹ Later rabbinic sources have references to proselyte baptism, i.e. purification immersion as part of the process of conversion to Judaism (e.g. '*Eduyyoth* 5.2 and *b. Yebamot* 47a–b). There is no evidence, however, for this practice being followed in the time of John. For an overview of the discussion, see Ferguson 2009: 76–82.

¹² Calling John's movement a 'sect' does not mean that we assume a 'heterodox' Baptist movement, out of line with 'mainstream' Judaism (cf. Taylor 1997: 29–32, who argues against such an outdated view). For applications of sociological models of sectarianism to early Judaism, see Chalcraft 2007.

between John's baptism and other types of Jewish ritual bathing has to do with the form of the ritual, rather than its function. Other Jewish ritual washings were self-administered, while in John's immersion there is an agent of the ritual (John or his disciple) *and* a ritual patient (someone who came to him to be baptized). The most likely procedure is that John (or his assistant) stood in the water with the ritual patients and submerged them (Taylor 1997: 50). This structure of John's ritual practice is often recognized by scholars, but its relevance for an analysis of John's ritual activity is seldom noted. In what follows, my purpose is to demonstrate how an analysis of ritual structure can contribute to an understanding of the ritual dynamic in John's movement.

## 3.5 IMMERSION AS A SPECIAL AGENT RITUAL

It was Thomas Lawson and Robert McCauley's Theory of Ritual Competence (or Ritual Form Theory) that inaugurated the movement in Religious Studies which later came to be referred to as the Cognitive Science of Religion (Lawson and McCauley 1990; see also McCauley and Lawson 2002). As explained earlier (sections 1.6 and 2.4), their competence approach was inspired by Noam Chomsky's idea of a 'universal grammar', an innate competence of the human mind which enables children to learn a language quickly (for the linguistic background to their theory, see Lawson and McCauley 1990: 61–8). The Chomskyan hypothesis of a 'language module' is often contested in studies of the evolution of human cognition (for example, Donald 2001; Jablonka and Lamb 2005: 212–9, 298–206; Gärdenfors 2006: 141–65), and it is wise not to build our case too axiomatically on specific linguistic claims about language competence (see, however, Biró 2013 for a development of the linguistic aspect of Lawson and McCauley's theory). For our purposes, what is important is that the theory of ritual form opens up a perspective in which rituals can be analysed as *actions*, irrespective of the functions or verbal interpretations attached to them by participants, observers, or religious specialists. This is what I have called the 'action perspective' on ritual (cf. also Laidlaw and Humphrey 2008), as distinguished from other dimensions of ritual analysed in this book, such as the perspectives of signalling or transmission.

The central postulates of Ritual Competence Theory were introduced in section 1.6. To summarize briefly: Lawson and McCauley's theory is based on the observation that the action representation system of ritual follows the general pattern of ordinary *actions* (vs. something just happening). The basic categories of action are agent, action/instrument, and patient. The difference from ordinary actions is that in *religious* rituals, 'culturally postulated superhuman agents' (CPS- agents) are associated with one of these categories, producing different kinds of ritual structures or profiles. More specifically, two ritual profiles are suggested: (1) special agent rituals, in which CPS-agents are associated with the agent of a ritual and (2) special instrument/patient rituals, in which either the instrument or the patient of a ritual has the most direct links to CPS-agents.

It is clear that John's immersion can be described as a special agent ritual. In a structural account of the ritual, a CPS-agent is primarily associated with the agent of the ritual, that is, with John, a God-sent prophet (Q 7:26), or with someone who has received a baptism from him. A more difficult question is how to describe various forms of self-administered ritual bathing in Judaism in terms of Lawson and McCauley's theory. Probably the best way is to understand them as special instrument (action) rituals, in which the means of purification must meet certain conditions stipulated in the *halakha*, such as the requirements of a valid *miqveh* in the Mishnah and other authoritative texts (forty *seahs* of valid water, etc., see e.g. *Miqwa'ot* 7.1), while the action itself follows the orders given by God in the *Torah*. In this description, the instrument/action slot in the structure of ritual bathing is primarily associated with a CPS-agent (see Figure 1.1 in section 1.6).

An important part of Lawson and McCauley's theory involves the predictions they formulate as to how a ritual's profile determines participants' intuitive judgements about the ritual's properties. Lawson and McCauley hypothesize, for example, that special agent rituals are generally understood as ones that cannot be repeated ('when gods do things, they are done once and for all'), can be reversed (for example by defrocking priests), and involve sensory pageantry (see Lawson and McCauley 1990: 121–36; McCauley and Lawson 2002: 26–35, 179–212).

Not all of these predictions are supported by the evidence discussed in this book. Amma's ritual hugging, for instance, can be structurally described as a special agent ritual, in which a CPS agent is primarily connected with the agent of the ritual. As noted above, however, the ritual is repeatable. It is an emotionally powerful ritual and is not frequently performed upon a particular ritual patient, but its performance does not leave a 'super-permanent' effect on the patient (cf. McCauley and Lawson 2002: 32). The question of whether John's immersion was a once-and-for-all ritual is connected to the question whether it was construed as an initiation into John's group, which, as we have seen, remains uncertain. It is indeed arguable that the fact that some special agent rituals are unrepeatable is explained by their function as rites of passage, rather than by their structure as special agent rituals (Pyysiäinen 2001: 93; see also Boyer 2002: 299–300). The references to CPS agents in such life-cycle rituals may be more a consequence of gods being summoned at one-time turning points than a reason why they are performed only once upon a single person (Pyysiäinen 2001: 93).

Our evidence underlines the need to modify Lawson and McCauley's predictions; it does not entail their outright rejection. A hypothesis can be formulated that special agent rituals are intuitively sensed as more powerful than rituals with other structural profiles. For this reason they often trigger emotional arousal and play a significant role in motivating and energizing members of a movement (cf. McCauley and Lawson 2002: 212). Special agent rituals are normally less frequently performed on one ritual patient because frequent performance would bring about either sensory overload or habitation (McCauley and Lawson 2002: 184–92). A causal mechanism that would explain such representations of religious rituals in the human mind, however, remains to be further investigated (Malley and Barrett 2003; for an analysis of mechanisms in cognitive theories of ritual, see Uro 2011c).

## 3.6 WHY CONSIDER RITUAL INTUITIONS?

The application of such tentative hypotheses to historical materials is challenging. Do we have enough evidence in our sources to test and validate the theory? Can cognitive theories be used deductively to add to the data concerning historical movements, such as the Baptist movement?[13] Although a full discussion of these methodological issues would need more space than is available here, I offer three considerations to support the application of Lawson and McCauley's theory to an analysis of John's immersion rite.

First, McCauley and Lawson's claim that special agent rituals can play a significant role in motivating and energizing ritual participants helps us to conceptualize ways in which ritual innovations can influence the rise of religious movements. Introducing an emotionally strong special agent ritual may be a way to recruit and mobilize new members. Although McCauley and Lawson's assertion that 'no religious ritual system can survive without at least the periodic performance of special agent rituals' (McCauley and Lawson 2002: 212) remains uncertain (at least in view of the evidence from mainstream Judaism; see Biró 2013), it is possible to suggest that the introduction of special agent rituals is *one* way to revitalize a ritual system and to instigate a religious reform.

Second, the cognitive theory is useful in evaluating interpretations of John's immersion by biblical scholars. For example, Taylor's view that the 'speciality' of John's rite relates only to the ethical prerequisites set by John for his baptism overlooks the ritual structure of John's innovation. According to the hypothesis advanced in this chapter, John's special agent ritual would have intuitively been felt to be more powerful than a self-administered ritual purification. This is confirmed by the historical record: people came to John to be baptized *by him*, and his immersion rite gained unprecedented success among his contemporaries. People certainly believed they were receiving *more* by letting John press them down under the water than by immersing themselves in a pool or a river. What verbal interpretations John or his ritual patients attached to this ritual action is irrelevant to an analysis of ritual structure, and the question is best treated as a separate issue.

Third, to develop the second point a little further: a cognitive analysis of John's rite helps us to see why symbolic and cultural analyses, without recognition of intuitive psychological constraints, do not lead to a sufficient account of the role of the ritual in the emergence of John's movement. Assessing various culturally plausible interpretations is important and indeed indispensable in many ways.

---

[13] Cf. Meeks' criticism of a 'deductive use of sociological and anthropological theory' in Early Christian studies (Meeks 2005: 161). See also the discussion in 1.5.

Such analyses focus on the few extant references and interpretations that have been preserved in our sources (in the Gospels and Josephus), as well as on the wider cultural background (such as ritual bathing in early Judaism). What is important is to realize that such public narrative manifestations have only limited value for explaining people's actual behaviour. Three reasons can be given to support this claim: first, people are not always willing or able to explain why they participate in a ritual (Humphrey and Laidlaw 1994: 100). Second, preserved reports may not be representative of the majority of the movement; they may be randomly preserved, derive mostly from the educated elite, etc. The last is almost certainly true of those few explicit interpretations that have been preserved for John's immersion. Third, even if they were representative, they do not necessarily reveal the cognitive processes which trigger the behaviour in the first place, and which, as noted above, play an important role in directing the course of events in the long run. As Bloch argues, explicit statements are always second-order interpretations, only remotely connected to the inner states that lead to action (Bloch 2012: 199).

## 3.7 IMMERSION AND TEACHING

Explicit statements are related to the teaching John gave in the context of his baptismal gatherings. All of our sources (i.e. the Gospels and Josephus) are unanimous that John was a teacher (*didaskalos* or rabbi; Luke 3:12; John 3:26) of religious and moral knowledge, not just a practitioner of a magical rite. As we have argued (section 2.6), one important dimension of ritual is that it supports the spread and the transmission of religious knowledge. Ritual can endorse religious knowledge in a number of different ways. Rituals may, among other things, generate religious traditions (for example by evoking exegetical interpretations or aetiological myths); they may consolidate religious concepts and doctrines; and they may serve to accommodate auxiliary forms of communication, such as sermons, images, and recitations of religious texts (more on this in Chapter Six).

New Testament scholars have different views as to how much of the teaching of John preserved in the gospel tradition goes back to historically reliable information (von Dobbeler 1988; Ernst 1989: 290–319; Webb 1991: 261–306; Lupieri 1993; Uro 1995; Taylor 1997: 101–54;

Rotschild 2005). One problem in evaluating the historical accuracy of these traditions is the fact that, except for the very general statement in Josephus' account, all teachings attributed to John are filtered through the tradition process in early Christian communities and are therefore suspect of being modified or created to serve the ideological interests of the Christian movement. Cognitive theories do not give us a shortcut for deciding which traditions are historically reliable, but they may enrich the historian's understanding of the tradition process and the mechanisms that operate in its transmission (Czachesz 2013b). In what follows, I elaborate upon three cognitive perspectives on the relationship between ritual and the transmission of religious knowledge: (1) Whitehouse's idea of 'spontaneous exegetical reflection'; (2) Czachesz' analysis of rituals' effect on long-term memories; and (3) the significance of 'credibility-enhancing displays' in transmission.

The main focus of Whitehouse's theory of the modes of religiosity is on transmission. Whitehouse proposes that religious traditions tend to evolve either around high-arousal, infrequent ('imagistic') rituals or around often-repeated ('doctrinal') ones (see section 1.6). The imagistic and doctrinal modes are based on different memory systems: on episodic or semantic memory respectively. An important aspect of Whitehouse's theory is his suggestion that imagistic rituals evoke 'spontaneous exegetical reflection', but do *not* support the transmission of systematic doctrines or religious narratives. Rarely performed high arousal rituals do trigger enduring memories (ultimately in the semantic memory) and sustain transmission, but spontaneous exegetical reflection leads to *diversity of religious representations*, not to doctrinal orthodoxies (Whitehouse 2004a: 72). Whitehouse's idea that high arousal rituals often produce idiosyncratic religious knowledge provides further support to our view that we should not limit our analysis of John's immersion to the preserved explicit interpretations, let alone decide which interpretation is the 'correct' one.

One problem with Whitehouse's distinction between doctrinal and imagistic rituals and the corresponding modes of religion is that his term 'imagistic' lumps together a variety of different types of emotional rituals. A nuanced analysis of different ways in which emotional stimulation in rituals can affect long-term explicit memory has been offered by István Czachesz (2010). Czachesz discusses four different types of emotional stimulation: thematically arousing stimuli, salient visual and sensory stimuli, the effect of stress on the formation of memories (which may also narrow down the amount of details remembered), and self-relatedness. The last point signifies that a participant sees himself or herself as an agent in the ritual or attributes personal significance to the actions involved.

The factor of self-relatedness is particularly relevant to an analysis of John's immersion. Czachesz refers to a number of psychological studies which demonstrate that items related to the self are better remembered than items not so related (Symons and Johnson 1997; Cloutier and Macrae 2008). John's immersion fosters self-relatedness and hence the memorability of the rite in several ways. The participants have made a personal decision to undergo John's immersion and are not simply following the general rules and conventions of their society (Cloutier and Macrae 2008; Czachesz 2010: 334). The ritual structure (special agent ritual) reinforces the idea that the ritual patient is receiving special attention from a counterintuitive being. Moreover, the patient is him-/herself an agent in the action of confession, which makes the experience personal and memorable.

The third perspective on conceptualizing the relationship between ritual and the transmission of religious knowledge has been suggested by Joseph Henrich (2009). His approach draws on theories of cultural evolution (Richerson and Boyd 2005; see section 2.2), and is related to the signalling perspective discussed in the next section of this chapter. The core idea of Henrich's theory is that cultural/religious traditions spread as 'belief–ritual packages'. Cultural learners do not adopt ideas, beliefs, values, etc. separately from these packages, but have evolved a bias to attend to 'credibility enhancing displays' alongside the verbal expressions of their learning models. Since 'actions speak louder than words', costly displays play a crucial role in the transmission of belief systems; successful beliefs are often associated with costly behaviour by those who promote the beliefs to others.

In view of this theory, it is interesting to observe that the traditions attributed to John contain several references to John's special diet, attire, and lifestyle (Mark 1:6; Matt. 3:4; Mark 2:18; Matt. 9:14; Q 7:33–34). Although the significance of John's fasting practices, his garment of camel's hair and leather belt, and especially his diet (locusts and wild honey) may be explained in various ways (Vielhauer 1965; S. L. Davies 1983; Ernst 1989: 284–9; Kelhoffer 2005), it seems obvious that they functioned as 'credibility-enhancing displays', promoting his status as a prophet and providing people with a means to evaluate the truth value of his message.

In sum, John's immersion may be seen as a high-arousal ritual, creating long-term—though not necessarily uniform—memories for the participants. In particular self-relatedness was an important memory-enhancing feature in John's baptism. His powerful ritual performance and austere lifestyle supported the spread and the transmission of his message. These conclusions do not mean that the traditions concerning John in the New Testament and Josephus are historically particularly reliable, but they explain in part why so many traditions about him survived and his ritual innovation became so persistent.

## 3.8 IMMERSION AS A SIGNAL OF COMMITMENT

The signalling perspective is one of the three perspectives on ritual introduced in sections 1.6 and 2.6; it takes ritual as a form of communication. The signalling perspective, however, should not be confused with the view according to which rituals are construed in the symbolist approach in traditional anthropology. In signalling theories, unlike in the symbolist approach, communication is not understood as encoded information (Sperber 1974; Uro 2011d: 501–2). 'Signalling' is understood in a rather straightforward sense, for example, as indicating one's commitment to the aims and moral values of a group. Rather than analysing the 'ritual grammar' (structure) of a religious ritual, the signalling perspective focuses on the capacity of ritual to enhance cooperation in social groups. This is suggestive of the classical Durkheimian view of ritual; rather than building on a sociological tradition, however, the Signalling Theory of Ritual draws on evolutionary biology and theories of biocultural evolution, and is part of a broader interdisciplinary discussion concerning the roots of human prosociality and the adaptive nature of religion (for a more detailed discussion, see section 5.2).

Two versions of Signalling Theory have been formulated. Commitment (Costly) Signalling postulates that religious rituals function as hard-to-fake signals of commitment which increase group cohesion and solidarity and deter free-riders (Irons 2001; Sosis 2003, 2004, 2006; Sosis and Alcorta 2003; Bulbulia and Sosis 2011; Heimola

2012). A further version of Signalling Theory, Charismatic Signalling, has been advanced by Joseph Bulbulia (Bulbulia 2009b; Bulbulia et al. 2013). Whereas Commitment Signalling assumes relatively small-scale interaction in which costly signals can increase solidarity and social cohesion, Charismatic Signalling addresses the problem of cooperation on large interactive scales. Signalling theories provide a further tool for analysing the social dynamics of the Baptist movement, focusing on the way in which John's rite functioned as a signal of cooperation in social interaction.

Our sources contain some scattered information about the organization of John's movement. We know that John had disciples who shared his lifestyle, followed his teachings, and probably also assisted him in his baptismal work.[14] Many scholars have suggested that Jesus was one of these disciples, and even that some of Jesus' own associates were originally John's (Meier 1994: 116–30; Rotschild 2005: 52–6). In contrast to the Gospels, Josephus does not specifically mention that John had 'disciples' or give information about his special lifestyle. He presents John as the leader of a popular movement and as a moral teacher, who summoned people 'to gather together by means of baptism' (*baptismō synienai*; *Ant.* 18.117). It is somewhat unclear how the dative *baptismō* should be interpreted. I follow Webb's interpretation of the dative as instrumental, underlining the role of baptism in the gathering of people in John's movement (Webb 1991: 199–200). However, translations as 'for baptism' or 'in baptism' are also possible (cf. Ferguson 2009: 84 n. 7). Whichever translation we choose, Josephus' account seems to suggest that John's baptizing activity created a community of some kind. Interestingly, Josephus refers to 'others' (*allōn*), who also gathered around John and were excited about his words (*Ant.* 18.118). Josephus' reference may be taken as an indication that John's movement consisted of an inner circle along with a larger group of sympathizers, something that is also confirmed by the general picture given in the New Testament: John drew large crowds of people, at least some of whom received his baptism, but also had a more intimate group of followers, 'disciples' or 'students' (Taylor 1997: 102).

John's immersion can be analysed as a hard-to-fake signal of commitment for those who received his baptism. Matthew and

---

[14] See Mark 2:18; 6:29; Matt. 9:14; 11:2; 14:12; Luke 5:33; 7:18; 11:1; John 1:22, 32, 35, 37; 3:25, 27; Acts 19:1–7.

Mark report that John's baptism was accompanied by an act of confession of sins: '... they were baptized by him in the river Jordan, confessing their sins' (Mark 1:5, cf. Matt. 3:6). This brief description is open to various interpretations.

The act of confessing (*exomologoumenoi*) can be understood in various ways. In principle, it may refer to public or private confession of sins. The latter would mean that it took place in the hearing of John alone, which I regard as implausible given the public setting of the immersion itself. Moreover, public 'confession' can be interpreted as referring to a confession of specific sins or merely of a general sinfulness. There are some examples of public confession of specific sins in the Greco-Roman world, although most of the comparative materials indicate general confessions (see evidence in Yarbro Collins 2007: 142–5; Pettazzoni 1954: 55–67; Kudlien 1978). Drawing on examples from Qumran which seem to imply communal recitations of penitential prayers and a sense of collective sinfulness (e.g. 1 QS 1:22–2:1; 4Q393; see also Russell 2006) Yarbro Collins concludes that the confession of sins in connection with John's immersion was communal and general (Yarbro Collins 2007: 144). A comparison to liturgical forms in Qumran may, however, be misleading since the time-span of John's movement would hardly have allowed the development of elaborate collective ceremonies. I find it plausible that confession in the context of John's baptism was individual and also personal rather than strictly formulaic, although we have little means to determine the precise forms it took.

The whole ritual process of John's immersion, including the confession of sins, thus seems to possess three traits; it was public (i.e. it took place in front of other participants), individual (both the immersion and the confession were conducted separately for each ritual patient), and in some way personal. It is therefore arguable that it involved emotional and social costs which worked as costly signals to enhance social cohesion and solidarity in John's community, along with other symbolic markers, such as specific practices of fasting and prayer. A central tenet of the Commitment Signalling Theory is that there is a positive correlation between the costliness of (ritual) practices and the level of devotion and commitment in a religious group (Sosis 2006: 78; see also Iannaccone 1994). Is there any means to assess *how* costly the practice of immersion demanded by John was in the particular historical situation in which it was introduced? Can we draw any inferences as to the level of social cohesion and solidarity in John's movement?

Interesting parallels to the public confession of sins among the followers of John are found in descriptions of similar ritual practices in early Christian communities. Rikard Roitto has analysed the practices of confession, intercession, and forgiveness in 1 John 1:9 and 5:16 from a perspective of Commitment Signalling (Roitto 2012). As in the case of the confession accompanying John's immersion, the passages in the First Epistle of John seem to suggest a *public* confession of sins in front of other participants ('brothers and sisters' in 1 John). What is different in the practices reflected in 1 John is that the role played by the other group members in the ritual process is much more central than in the confession promoted by John the Baptist. In the ritual reflected in 1 John 5:16a, as reconstructed by Roitto, a fellow congregant functions as a mediator of forgiveness by praying to God on behalf of a transgressing brother or sister and by mediating forgiveness to the transgressor ('if someone sees his brother sinning a sin not unto death, *he* shall ask and give him life'; trans. Roitto, my italics).[15] Such a practice was probably costly for a sinning member since he or she was receiving forgiveness from a fellow member, not from God or a human whose status was clearly higher than that of the transgressor. As Roitto notes, in antiquity submissive confession of wrongdoing was an appropriate strategy for inferiors as a way to appease their superiors (Roitto 2012: 245; see Konstan 2010; Griswold and Konstan 2012). Between equals, however, it was a costly behaviour; this is why the ritual of forgiveness described in 1 John was experienced as a loss of status within the group. Although confessing sins to equals and receiving forgiveness from them was a costly behaviour, the risk of being exploited is experienced as smaller by committed members than by the less committed. The practice of confession in 1 John can thus be interpreted as an effective costly signal that repelled

---

[15] Many interpreters find it problematic that the subject of the phrase *dōsei autō zōēn* ('shall give him life') is the same as that of the previous verb *aitēsei* ('he shall ask'), that is, a fellow congregant, and therefore interpret the third person form as referring to God (cf. e.g. RSV: '... and God will give him life'). From a syntactic point of view, however, it is much more plausible to regard the subjects of the verbs as the same. Cf. also John 20:23, which asserts that Jesus' followers have the authority to forgive sins. Roitto 2012: 239–40.

less committed group members but attracted committed ones (Roitto 2012: 148–9).

Compared to the practice of confession reflected in the passages of 1 John (cf. also Jas. 5:16; *Did.* 4:14; 14:1), the ritual confession that accompanied John's immersion was not an act between equal members; the whole ritual process was administered by a figure who, as a man of God (or the representative of such a man), was clearly above those who were passing through the ritual. The practice of confession in John's movement was apparently in line with general penitential practices in early Judaism, in which repentance was always in relation to God (Roitto 2012: 245; referring to Morgan 2012). We may then speculate that participating in John's ritual would not have involved as much loss of face as the practice of confession in the community of 1 John, and that consequently the level of costly signalling does not indicate such strong cohesion and group identity in the Baptist movement as in the Christian community to which 1 John was addressed.

As already suggested above, the boundaries of John's movement were not clearly defined; the movement embraced both intimate followers and a larger group of sympathizers, whose ties to the inner circle were more or less loose. Not all of those who came to John and participated in his gatherings became active members, that is, such as were engaged in his baptismal mission and shared his lifestyle. For both groups, however, John's immersion was a powerful signal to which they all responded positively. Charismatic Signalling provides a way to model how John's immersion worked in a larger movement.

Commitment Signalling is at its best in explaining relatively small-scale interactions, in which costly signals can increase solidarity and social cohesion. Charismatic Signalling, on the other hand, accounts for cooperation in a large-scale and anonymous population, where it is more difficult to recognize cooperators and defectors. It is reasonable to assume that most of those who came to John and received his baptism did not stay with him but returned to their home villages and continued their everyday lives; they were thus unable to monitor the behaviour of the other sympathizers. For such followers of John, the immersion rite did not function as a 'costly signal' in terms of Commitment Signalling Theory, but rather as a 'charismatic signal'. According to Bulbulia, cooperative signals in larger-scale religious cultures occur by means of 'synchronous cues', that is, signals that 'predictably coordinate social interaction by design' (Bulbulia 2009b: 531). In other words, such signals are so robust that they are able to coordinate a religious culture in anonymous, larger-scale populations. The model predicts that in large-scale religious cultures individuals will be able to anticipate the responses of unknown others around these cues. Bulbulia summarizes:

> Charismatic culture 'affords' synchronous outcomes by a potentially wide variety of means, affecting partners through music, symbolic arrays, architectural arrangements, the management of landscape, body entrainment, the production of altered states of consciousness.

(Bulbulia 2009b: 545)

Charismatic Signalling is an attempt to answer much larger questions than we are dealing with in this chapter, but the basic idea is helpful in conceptualizing how signalling works in the rise of larger-scale religious movements. John's immersion rite was sufficiently robust to coordinate people's thinking and behaviour so that a popular movement could arise. To be sure, this coordination was rudimentary, involving perhaps no more than that people *came* to John and believed that he was a true prophet. But we can see a cooperative signal here similar to the one which was operating later with full effect in the presence of Christian saints, relics, and other sources of miraculous power. John's immersion can be viewed in similar terms. It is a good candidate for a ritual functioning as a robust synchronous cue: it was emotionally strong, it involved the whole body and it centred on the individual ritual patient. In the light of the story of Jesus' baptism in the Gospels, which is described as a visionary and auditory experience (esp. Mark 1:9–11; cf. Matt. 3:13–17; Luke 3:31–2; cf. also stories about the temptations of Jesus in the wilderness; Mark 1:12–13; Q 4:1–13), we may even speculate that the ritual triggered an altered state of consciousness among John's followers.[16] However, we cannot know how common such experiences were in John's movement, and it is equally possible that the ACS/spirit possession phenomena in the Jesus movement (see 4.4 and 5.6) influenced Mark's story of Jesus' baptism.

---

[16] For Jesus' baptism as an ASC/spirit possession experience, see S. L. Davies 1995: 52–65; DeMaris 2002; Craffert 2008: 213–44.

## 3.9 FROM JOHN THE BAPTIST TO THE JESUS MOVEMENT

The scholarship on Christian origins has often emphasized the difference between John the Baptist and Jesus. John was a strict ascetic, 'eating no bread and drinking no wine'; Jesus in contrast was 'a glutton and a drunkard, a friend of tax collectors and sinners' (Q 7:33–34). John was a preacher of the coming wrath, whereas Jesus placed more emphasis on the offer of salvation. John's message was concerned with imminent futuristic eschatology, while Jesus proclaimed that the future kingdom was already present in some way. A number of scholars even see a conflict between John and Jesus, not just a contrast (Linnemann 1973; Ebertz 1987: 69–71; cf. also Hollenbach 1982: 214). Without entering into a discussion of these interpretations, it is important to point out that there are many elements of continuity in the relationship between John and Jesus and their movements (see Allison 2003; cf. also Rotschild 2005). Our ritual analysis highlights this continuity. The most obvious point, of course, is John's baptism, a ritual innovation which was adopted by the early followers of Jesus and which was eventually turned into an initiation rite of the early Christian church. Jesus did not become known as a baptizer (cf. however John 3:26 and 4:1), but we can recognize the same ritual structure in his healing practice as in John's immersion.

There are also other elements of continuity which emerge from the above analysis. Practices of confessing and forgiving sins were continued in early Christian communities (1 John 1:9; 5:16; Jas. 5:16; *Did.* 4:14; 14:1). There is some evidence for the view that Jesus also forgave sins when he healed people (Mark 2:10; Luke 7:47; Hägerland 2012). Moreover, both movements were organized in the form of an inner circle of close associates, 'disciples', together with a larger group of sympathizers and supporters. Cohesion and solidarity within the inner circle was maintained by costly signalling. In the Jesus movement costly signalling was high, including renunciation of family and kinship ties and acceptance of an itinerant lifestyle (Uro 2012). Finally, both religious leaders gained a reputation with their powerful ritual performances; John with his rite of immersion, Jesus by practising ritual healing.

In the next chapter, we move on to an analysis of Jesus' healing activity from the perspective of ritual theory.

# 4

# 'Are Any Among You Sick?'

## Ritual, Possession, and Healing

In the previous chapter, I argued that John's ritual innovation is a good point to start an analysis of Christian beginnings and that there is a great deal of continuity in the historical trajectory from the Baptist movement to the Jesus movement. Although we have only little detailed information about the ways in which John and the early Christians performed their water rites, it is important to recognize that according to the information preserved in our sources the ritual profile of the baptisms in the respective movements was the same. In terms of Lawson and McCauley, both John's baptism and the baptism performed by early Christians were special agent rituals. In the case of John's baptism, John (or his follower) can be understood as an agent who is more closely associated with God than with the instrument or the patient of the ritual. Descriptions of early Christian baptismal practices, in turn, assume ritual agents who baptize 'in the name of Jesus Christ' (Acts 2:38; 10:48) or 'into the name of the Lord Jesus' (Acts 8:16; 19:5; cf. also 1 Cor. 1:13; 'in the name of Father and of the Son and of the Holy Spirit' in Matt 28:19). In the preceding analysis, a modified version of Lawson and McCauley's theory was used to show how the ritual innovation contributed to the rise of the movements instigated by John. The account of John's movement was supplemented with other perspectives from cognitive theories of ritual.

### 4.1 FROM BAPTISM TO HEALING

There is, however, a historical conundrum in the ritual trajectory from John's movement to early Christian communities. Jesus did not baptize; or, if John 3:22, 27 and 4:1 preserve reliable historical information, his baptismal activity did not become a distinctive part of his public ministry. Unlike John, Jesus was not remembered as a baptizer but as a preacher of the kingdom and as a healer. Scholars who have focused on the historical development from John's prophetic activity to the Jesus movement have sometimes argued that healing replaced baptism in Jesus' ministry after the ways of the two movements parted. Paul Hollenbach (1982), for example, has suggested that Jesus ceased baptizing when he realized that he was able to heal and exorcize demons; Hollenbach interprets this new orientation as a conversion of Jesus. John Dominic Crossan, on the other hand, sees a striking parallelism between John's ritual action and Jesus' healing, claiming that while John the Baptist cured with 'a magical rite', Jesus did the same with 'a magical touch' (Crossan 1991: 324). This is a provocative statement, and raises the issue of whether John's baptism and Jesus' curative actions are comparable from a ritual point of view.

Ritual healing is a specific type of ritual action, the function of which is to restore or enhance the health of the patient. According to the traditional classification, healing rituals have been seen as a subcategory of so-called 'crisis rituals' or 'rites of affliction', which are performed when an unfavourable change has affected the group or when the group faces a threat or a calamity of some kind (Kärkkäinen Terian 2004: 101; see also Bell 1997: 115–20). Healing rites usually conform closely to the action structure discussed above: they include agents, actions, and—quite literally—patients, often also instruments. It is not quite clear, however, how Jesus' curative actions described in the Gospels should be understood as rituals, in view of the characteristics ritual theorists usually ascribe to 'ritual'. According to one often cited definition, ritual is constituted by 'patterned and ordered sequences of words and acts', characterized by 'formality (conventionality), stereotype (rigidity), condensation (fusion) and redundancy (repetition)' (Tambiah 1979: 119). The healing activity of Jesus in the Gospels reveals too much lability to accord with definitions that focus on formality and rigidity. Moreover, if we understand ritual as somehow compared or contrasted to the intentionality of normal or everyday human action, arguing for example that rituals are lacking in 'direct functionality' or are 'goal-demoted' (Liénard and Lawson 2008: 158, 162–3), healing rituals are not always the best examples of such actions, since it may be difficult to draw the line between direct and indirect functionality in some therapeutic treatments (for example, in exorcisms).

It is also often argued that ritualized actions 'cannot fail because they reach no goal beyond themselves' (Kreinath 2008: 451; discussing Staal 1989). Ritual healers—more than performers of other types of rituals—have to face failures with regard to the outcomes of their rituals.[1] I return to this issue later in this chapter. At this point, it suffices to repeat the point made earlier in this study, that one definition of ritual is not always the most productive point of departure for a ritual analysis. The theme of 'healing ritual' overlaps with a number of phenomena which have been studied intensively by anthropologists and scholars of Comparative Religion, and more recently by cognitive scientists: shamanism, spirit possession, and altered states of consciousness (ASC). Studies of these phenomena, often subsumed under the field of medical anthropology, have inspired New Testament scholars in their research on the healing activities of Jesus and the early Christians. There are important convergences between these areas of study and Ritual Studies, and my argument in this chapter is that it is helpful for analytical purposes to include healings by Jesus and the early Christians in the ritual analysis of Christian beginnings.

I first survey some recent attempts to understand and explain Jesus' healing activity from a social-scientific perspective, which has been a dominant approach to the topic in New Testament Studies over the last three decades or so. I then return to ritual theories: I ask what and how ritual theory can contribute to the study of Jesus' exorcisms and healings, and of therapeutic actions in the Jesus movement in general. I also look at recent cognitive explanations for spirit possession, and consider their applicability and relevance to the study of early Christianity. The final part of the chapter offers some examples of

---

[1] According to Pyysiäinen (2011b: 157–8), there is a difference between rites of passage and crisis rituals in this regard. In the first type of ritual, failure is absolutely impossible, if the ritual is correctly performed. The participants can believe this because the outcome of the ritual cannot be empirically verified. The case of crisis rituals is different, since people have more means to judge whether the ritual has produced the desired outcome (recovery, rain, avoidance of calamity, and so forth). However, lack of the desired outcome does not necessarily mean a failure in the ritual but rather a failure of the participants to understand the working of the will of counterintuitive agents. Pyysiäinen's insights would also explain why 'ritual failure' is often a matter of political contestation (Schieffelin 2007).

further developments in the process whereby healing and exorcistic practices were ritualized in the life of early Christian communities.

## 4.2 JESUS AS A SPIRIT-POSSESSED HEALER

Although there is a general trend in recent Jesus scholarship to accept the fact that Jesus was well known in his time as a healer and exorcist (Sanders 1985; Crossan 1991; Twelftree 1993; Evans 1999; Eve 2009; Theissen 2010; Vermes 2012; for a sceptical view, see Mack 1988), there is much less consensus on how significant a role healings played in the public ministry of Jesus or how many historically reliable details we can reconstruct from the stories in the Gospels. Scholarly views concerning the stories of healings or miracles in general vary from attempts to integrate the healings into Jesus' overall eschatology or theology (Eve 2009: 118–44) to full-blown reconstructions of Jesus as a 'shamanic' figure (Craffert 2008). While the present chapter is not primarily a contribution to the thorny and often theology-laden quest for the historical Jesus, I hope that the points I make will strengthen the view that healing and exorcistic practices were present in the Christian movement from its earliest beginnings.

There is an interesting trajectory in Jesus research, which rather than starting from Jesus' sapiential or eschatological *teaching* has focused on the magico-religious aspects of his activity. This trajectory starts with Morton Smith (1978), and continues by way of Stevan Davies (1995) to more recent social-scientific analyses of Jesus' exorcisms and healings, such as those by Craffert (see also Hollenbach 1982, 1993; Crossan 1991; Rousseau 1993; Kollmann 1996; Strecker 2002; Klutz 2004; Eve 2009).

Although approaches and points of view vary, most historical analyses of Jesus' healing activity falling within this 'magico-religious trajectory' strand of Jesus research agree on at least the following points:

- Jesus acted as a spirit-possessed healer. Jesus' baptism by John is often seen as a crucial moment, in which Jesus was possessed by the Spirit; or at least the story is seen as important evidence for the central role of possession in Jesus' ministry.

- Since Smith, who built his case mainly on comparative materials from the magical papyri—an approach that has been largely rejected by subsequent scholars—it has often been argued that cross-cultural anthropological studies and ethnographies on phenomena of spirit possession and altered states of consciousness (ASC) can shed light on the activity of Jesus, his methods of healing, his social role, the aetiology of illness in Jesus' time, and more generally on the question of what type of religious personage Jesus was.

- A great deal of other materials in the Gospels and elsewhere in the New Testament (Jesus' preaching of the Kingdom, stories about controversies, so-called nature miracles, transfiguration, resurrection stories, Paul's slight interest in Jesus' teaching, ecstatic practices in early Christian communities, and so forth) are explained in terms of the fact that spirit possession and the ASC were an integral part of the movement from its earliest beginnings.

There are, however, considerable differences in scholars' views as to what kind of magico-religious practitioner Jesus actually was. For example, applying Winkelman's five-fold classification of magico-religious practitioners (shaman, shaman/healer, healer, medium, priest; Winkelman 1992), Davies concludes that Jesus fits best into the category of 'medium': one who practises healing and divination, provides protection from spirits and malevolent magic, and practices ASC possession (S. L. Davies 1995: 100). Craffert, on the other hand, argues passionately for the view that the cultural processes and dynamics related to Jesus' social personage are best explained by what he calls a 'shamanic complex' (see also Ashton 2000: 62–72 and Klutz 2004). The approaches and theoretical models used to explain the phenomena of spirit possession and the ASC in the stories of the Gospels also vary greatly. Some have been inspired by the sociological analysis of spirit possession by I. M. Lewis (1971), who distinguishes between peripheral and central possession cults. Peripheral possession, according to Lewis, often functions as self-promotion and as a protest on the part of the humiliated and weak; and therefore manifests itself as a kind of 'ritual rebellion' (1971: 127).

Several New Testament scholars have provided political interpretations of Jesus' exorcisms along these lines, the Gerasene demoniac (Mark 5: 1–17) being the most common point of reference, and have attempted to show that the colonial situation in Roman Palestine was generating cases of spirit possession as expressions of passive resistance against oppression (Hollenbach 1981, 1993; Horsley 1987; Crossan 1991; cf. also Theissen 1983: 256). It is not possible to discuss Lewis' sociological theory in full length here (see Cohen 2007: 91–4). Suffice it to note that the specific colonial explanation offered by New Testament scholars runs into difficulties, since (1) there is no theme of opposition against Rome in Mark; (2) the word 'legion' can be well understood in a figurative sense, not as a reference to a Roman military unit (cf. Matt. 26:53); and (3) it is not at all clear that Roman colonialism in first-century Palestine was so thorough-going as to provide the most important single explanation for the appearance of demoniacs in the world of Jesus or Mark (see Davies 1995: 78-81; Kazen 2002: 334–35; Klutz 2004: 82; Twelftree 2007b: 105–11; Yarbro Collins 2007: 269–72). It is furthermore doubtful that Jesus' exorcisms and healings as such would have been interpreted by Romans or by the Jewish ruling elite as a subversive protest against exploitation (Eve 2009: 136). This is not to argue that Jesus' exorcistic activity did not more generally involve elements of rebellion against social constraints (see Klutz 2004: 144; referring to Bell 1997: 117) or that the socio-economic situation in first-century Galilee did not have an impact on people's health.

Many scholars have tackled the issue of whether the analyst should give etic (outsider's) or emic (insider's) accounts of Jesus' healing practices. At some point, generalizing theories about spirit possession and shamanic practices fell into disfavour in anthropology, and this way of thinking has resulted in a growing number of ethnographic studies in which possession is examined on its own terms in the societies where it is found (Boddy 1994; Znamenski 2007; DuBois 2009). Many New Testament scholars using social-scientific approaches have adopted this view, and have sought to offer culturally sensitive readings of the Gospel stories (for a strong defence of the emic approach to healing in the New Testament, see Pilch 2000).

Good examples of such research are Christian Strecker's performative approach to Jesus' exorcisms (2002; relying on Kapferer 1983) and Craffert's 'anthropological historiography' or 'cultural bundubashing' (a metaphor derived from a South-African term for off-road driving) (Craffert 2008). The latter approach programmatically rejects any attempt to identify an authentic kernel to the Gospel stories for the reconstruction of the historical figure of Jesus; it is also critical of efforts at distinguishing diachronic layers in the history of Gospel traditions. This position is related to the critique of the tendency to view many (or most) of Jesus' healings, as well as the so-called natural miracles, as 'literary constructions'. Making a sharp distinction between the Western 'monophasic' culture (not open to ASC experiences) and non-Western 'polyphasic' cultures (which accept the reality of ASC experiences), many New Testament scholars with a social-scientific orientation have argued that not only healings but also such stories as Jesus' transfiguration or his walking on the sea are reports of *real* ASC experiences, not theological constructions by later faith communities (in addition to Craffert 2008, see Pilch 1993, 1998; Malina 1999).

I fully agree that we should recognize the cultural reality of the healing stories, and that our theoretical work should be based on and tested against valid historical and ethnographic research. What I question, however, is the sharp dichotomy suggested by Craffert and others between the Western and non-Western world with regard to such phenomena as possession, ASC, and shamanism. The anthropologists, to be sure, have often pointed out the radical 'otherness' of these phenomena (Boddy 1994; see also Cohen and Barrett 2008a: 250–1), but it is also striking how widely held beliefs in possession of various kinds are today in many Western cultures. One need only read Michael W. Cuneo's study on *American Exorcism* (2001) to be convinced that what Craffert calls 'polyphasic consciousness' is experienced by a surprising number of ordinary, respectable North American people. Even though beliefs and practices related to exorcism seem to have become popular only after the publication of William Peter Blatty's book *The Exorcist* (1971), and its release as a Hollywood film two years later, it is still necessary to explain why exorcistic rituals spread so easily in different segments of a modern, medically advanced, and certainly 'Western' society.[2] Exorcistic practices are not restricted to the USA. The Catholic Church in my own country (Finland), for example, has a designated exorcist; the job is assigned to a priest whose task it is to investigate potential cases of diabolic possession, and—if the case turns out to be genuine—to expel

---

[2] True, the symptoms of possession must be socially learned (cf. Theissen 1983: 250; referring to Berger and Luckmann 1967: 175–6). From the cognitive point of view, however, it is striking how easily beliefs in possessing spirits spread in favourable contexts.

the demon.³ Similar more or less official exorcists have been appointed in most other Catholic Churches, and charismatic or evangelical 'deliverances' are practised in the USA as well as all around the world (Cuneo 2001: 309–23).

Moreover, the vivid and intense descriptions of possession and exorcism by anthropologists show that the anthropologists do not come from a 'different planet' but can empathize and identify with their research subjects. Sometimes anthropologists themselves learn to practise sorcery in a way that is effective in the field, and they even find it helpful in their personal situation (Stoller and Olkes 1987; Stoller 2004). And even if we were not willing to personally foster or practise exorcism, our mindset has no difficulty in dealing with possession beliefs in popular fantasy literature, video games, and sci-fi stories.⁴ Quite the contrary, many of us are often fascinated by them. Finally, as I will argue later, possession includes aspects of magic that psychologists have demonstrated to be part of the everyday behaviour and beliefs of modern secular people (Vyse 1997; cf. Czachesz 2011).

There is another point I want to make with regard to the emphasis placed by Craffert and other scholars on the 'reality' of ASC experiences reflected in many New Testament stories, and their reluctance to engage in stratification of the sources or in source-critical work. I admit that it is extremely difficult to decide which aspects of the healing stories most reliably reflect the actual healing practices of the historical Jesus, and that the legends and embellishments created around the figure of Jesus are valuable sources for the cultural world within which Christianity emerged. Perhaps we should also be prepared to see more continuity than scholars usually assume between

---

³ See the interview in *Helsingin Sanomat* (the largest subscription newspaper in Finland), 20 June 2010.

⁴ A good example is the science-fiction franchise *Stargate*, initially created by Roland Emmerich and Dean Devlin. *Stargate* envisages three kinds of parasite races, the Goa'uld, the Tok'ra, and the Jaffa. The Goa'uld are hostile parasites, integrated within a host, most of the time human. The Tok'ra take only willing human hosts, providing long life and perfect health, and share the body equally. The human host of a Tok'ra speaks in a normal voice, while the symbiote speaks with the flanged, bass-augmented 'Goa'uld voice'. The Jaffa are modified humans genetically engineered by the Goa'uld in antiquity to serve as soldiers and as incubators for their young. See https://en.wikipedia.org/wiki/Stargate (visited 8 October 2013). Similar beliefs can easily be found in other sci-fi movies and television series. I thank my son Ilkka Uro for drawing my attention to the possession beliefs in sci-fi lore.

the historical person of Jesus and later wonder stories and legends about him. As Craffert writes, 'until proven otherwise, all documents from antiquity claiming to be about Jesus of Nazareth should be reconsidered as some form of residue of his life as social personage' (2008: 94–95). Although Craffert may push his case too far, this perspective may open up some intriguing insights. For one thing, what else are later Christological beliefs and doctrines about Jesus' divinity than theological constructions and developments of possession which, as suggested earlier, might well have been present in the Jesus movement from its earliest beginnings? So we may see some sort of continuity from Jesus as a spirit-possessed healer and preacher to later Christological doctrines, the same point that was made already by Morton Smith and Stevan Davies.

On the other hand, if we suggest that the synoptic stories, Johannine speeches, Paul's statements about Jesus, later Christologies, the birth stories of the Gospels, and even the Infancy Gospels, derive from the same polyphasic system (in contrast to our monophysic culture), and at the same time deny the relevance of historical stratification and source criticism, we end up with a very abstract generalization of Jesus as a typical representative of his culture and lose sight of chronological, specific, and historical developments (see also van Aarde 2008). The best option, it seems to me, is to take 'anthropological history' (Craffert's term) and historical criticism not as epistemological alternatives but as complementary approaches (van Aarde, relying on Elliott 1993), just as ethnography and anthropological theory are often interrelated. Of course, insights from social-scientific and comparative approaches to religion may sometimes lead to a re-evaluation of some traditional historical-critical hypotheses. Moreover, some social-scientific and cognitive perspectives can be informative in tracing historical developments and trajectories.

To conclude: descriptions of Jesus as a magico-religious practitioner are not helpful if they are used merely for assigning various controversial labels to Jesus, such as 'magician' or 'shaman'. Cross-cultural and social-scientific analyses should not lead us to abandon solid source-critical and tradition-critical work, nor should we embrace extreme cultural relativism or adopt a one-sided picture of Jesus which ignores other important aspects of his activity. Although much evidence supports his being 'the most successful exorcist and healer of his time', there was certainly 'more than that to his ministry',

108 *Ritual and Christian Beginnings*

as the point is aptly made by Maurice Casey (2010: 278-9). But what I have called the 'Smith—Davies—Craffert trajectory' has been valuable in bringing to the fore the often over-looked reason for the cultural success of both Jesus and his movement. As already pointed out in relation to John the Baptist, adherents of a religious movement usually acquire their religious knowledge in the form of 'belief–practice packages', not as beliefs alone (Henrich 2009). Cultural learners tend to pay attention to 'credibility-enhancing displays' in determining how much to commit to a particular mental representation, such as Jesus' teaching of the kingdom of God. The teaching alone would hardly have made Jesus' success possible, but his effective healing functioned as a perfect credibility-enhancing display.

## 4.3 HEALING AND RITUAL THEORY

Why take a ritual approach to Jesus' healing activity? Would it not be more natural just to speak of therapeutic actions, not rituals? The stories in the Gospels about Jesus healing the sick and the possessed, after all, do not display the degree of formality and rigidity usually associated with many other types of ritual behaviour, described above.

Anthropologists have tackled a similar problem in attempting to conceptualize shamanic practices as rituals. For the sake of clarity, they have described shamanic séances as 'performance-centred' rituals in distinction from 'liturgy-centred' rituals (Humphrey and Laidlaw 1994: 8-12; relying on J. M. Atkinson 1989).[5] In the former type of ritual one finds much more improvisation and selection from a wide range of possible scenarios; the latter type is closer to the traditional definitions of ritual discussed at the beginning of this chapter.

Jane Atkinson writes of Wana shamanic performance (*mabolong*): 'As a performance-centred ritual, a *mabolong* cannot be described or analysed as a preordained progression of delineated steps to which

---

[5] Humphrey and Laidlaw (1994: 8-10) argue that performance-centred rituals are 'weakly ritualized', but compare their different conclusion in Laidlaw and Humphrey 2008. In the latter, they argue that 'performance-centred rites may differ from the liturgical not in being less ritualized but in ritualization applying at a more inclusive and higher-order level, to larger and more encompassing actions' (2008: 280-1).

ritual practitioners and congregants collectively conform. It is rather a repertoire of ritual actions available to performers acting independently in the ritual arena' (Atkinson 1989: 15).[6] Jesus, as described in the Gospels, can be seen as acting in a 'shamanic' manner, drawing on various ritual techniques which probably partly conformed to the expectations of the audience and readers but which could also include innovations. I put 'shamanic' in quotation marks here because my argument is not that Jesus is described as having used many of the typical shamanic techniques recorded in various cultures (sophisticated methods of entering into a shamanic trance, for example), but rather that in their discussion of shamanic practices, anthropologists are confronted with a problem similar to our own. There is a long tradition among anthropologists and shamanic scholars of discussing shamanic or folk healings in ritual terms, and it is natural to utilize their insights in the study of Christian beginnings.

Jesus' healing repertoire can be approached from two different perspectives. We can either emphasize the *similarity* between Jesus' healing activity and those of other ritual healers across time and space, or focus on the *distinctive* nature of his healing against his cultural background. In a wider cross-cultural perspective, Jesus' healing activity as described in the Synoptic Gospels seems to fall relatively neatly into certain categories of healing techniques that anthropologists have identified in various cultures of the world. Susan Sered and Linda Barnes, for example, list seven such categories or clusters (Sered and Barnes 2007):

1. Manipulation of sacred or symbolic objects.
2. Prayer and meditation.
3. Removing the object, experience, emotion, force, spirit, or person that is understood to be causing the illness. This cluster includes concession, exorcism, and purification of various sorts.
4. Inserting something into the person in need of healing.
5. Touching the person in need of healing (laying of hands of different kinds).
6. Induction of trance and other altered states of consciousness (in the healer or the sick person or both).

---

[6] For further ethnographic examples, see Laderman and Roseman 1996.

7. Use of performative elements, such as music, visual stimuli, taste, and kinaesthesia.
8. Practices that encourage the patient or other participants to see or construe their affliction in a new or 'healthier' way.

The healing techniques that appear most frequently in the Gospel stories are removal of the malignant spirit or spirits from the patient by commanding (exorcism; number 3) or touching the sick person (number 5). There are signs of other techniques as well. In addition to the fact that the ASC is apparent in most of the demoniacs Jesus is reported to have healed, scholars have pointed to a number of passages which seem to imply that Jesus himself was thought to have been possessed by the Spirit, an ancestor or Beelzebul (number 6). Especially closely related to healing are Mark 3:21, in which Jesus is said to be 'out of his senses', *exestē*, and 3:22, where his opponents claim that Jesus is possessed by Beelzebul; but the idea that Jesus is possessed by a spiritual entity is relatively common in the Gospels.[7] The scholars representing the 'Smith–Davies–Craffert trajectory' have greatly elaborated this aspect of the Jesus tradition. One narrative, the healing of the man who is deaf and mute (Mark 7:31–37), may indicate that Jesus was in some sort of meditative trance while healing (Mark 7:34, where Jesus looks up to heaven and 'sighs' or 'groans', *estenaxen*).[8] Looking up to heaven and sighing may also indicate prayer as Jesus' healing technique (number 2; see Meier 1994: 713); this is probably also implied in Mark 9:29 (Casey 2010: 251). On the other hand, it is clear that the references to prayer are relatively marginal in the tradition of Jesus' healings. No elaborate prayers or incantations are attributed to Jesus.

Although the stories of Jesus' healings and exorcisms do not present elements that can be characterized as manipulations of sacred or symbolic objects (number 1), there are symbolic gestures (stretching of hands), contagious magic (Jesus touching the sick person or the afflicted body part or the sick person touching Jesus' garments), even sympathetic magic (Mark 7:33, which probably assumes that Jesus touched the deaf man's tongue with his own tongue; Theissen 2010: 60–1); the use of medication (saliva, clay made out of mud and

---

[7] See Mark 3:22; 6:14–15; 8:28–30; Luke 4:1; 5:17; John 7:20; 8:48–52; 10:20–21.
[8] Or alternatively, sighing can signify a demonstration of spiritual power. Thus Yarbro Collins (2007: 371), referring to *PGM* XIII.942–46.

saliva, oil; number 4); and 'antagonistic magic' (Theissen 2010: 49) in exorcisms.[9] It is also possible to argue that the specific Aramaic phrases *ephphatha* and *talitha koum* were preserved by Mark because they could have special effects in a Greek or Latin linguistic environment.

We can hardly compare Jesus' exorcisms and healings to the dramatic Sri Lankan 'celebrations of demons' analysed by Kapferer (1983). Nevertheless, the public and demonstrative character of Jesus' exorcistic actions in the Gospels and their play with the transformation of identities and with the cosmic drama, as reflected in the sayings tradition (most conspicuously in Q 11:20), make them amenable to a performative approach (number 7 in Sered and Barnes' list), as has been demonstrated by Strecker (2002). The theatre-like nature of healing rituals (and many others) is certainly part of the explanation of their efficacy.

Scholars have often noted that many of the more elaborate healing techniques or challenges in healings attributed to Jesus occur in the Gospel of Mark (especially Mark 7:31–37 and 8:22–26, omitted by Matthew and Luke) and that the other evangelists seem to have, to some degree, suppressed such features (Meier 1994: 709–10). It is not easy to determine to what degree such features as praying and fasting, (ecstatic?) sighing or groaning, the use of saliva, physician-like questions and coping with failure are informative about Jesus' healing practices and/or early Christian practices more generally. A full discussion is beyond the limit of this chapter; but I find it difficult to argue that all these details can be attributed to Mark's theological or narrative interests, although miracles and healings do undoubtedly play a major role in Mark's presentation in general (Eve 2009: 92–117). Many features in Mark's stories, for example the Son of David Christology in Mark 10:46 (probably referring to King Solomon, who had the reputation of a great exorcist and healer), specific names, topographies, Aramaic formulas, and other details (Meier 1994: 646–772), give cause to believe that such stories circulated among the members of the early Jesus movement, who arguably continued his therapeutic work (see Mark 6:13 and Q 10:9; Theissen 1979, 2004; Uro 1987; Kollmann 1996). It is more probable that stories of miraculous healings *interacted* with magical practices among early

---

[9] Commanding or rebuking a demon was not an unknown exorcistic technique in Jesus' world; see *Apocalypse of Abraham*, 14.5–8 and 4Q560; Penney and Wise 1994; Sorensen 2002: 58–74.

Christian groups than that they were transmitted without any evidence of or encouragement for performing miracles by members of the movement (Czachesz 2013a). It is also easier to hypothesize that some of these elements were removed from the tradition for Christological reasons than that they were added at a later point (cf. Klutz 2004: 205–6). It is also worth noting that the theme of ritual failure is not restricted to Mark (see Q 11:24–26), and it would be unrealistic to suggest that Jesus and his disciples did not have to deal with failure. Traces of more elaborated healing techniques, however, should not lead us to ignore the fact that the most distinctive techniques preserved in the tradition are exorcism by commanding and touching the sick. Spirit possession is also a striking element, although no specific trance inductions are described (cf. the discussion of spirit possession later in this chapter in section 4.4).

In addition to the cross-cultural comparison which in very general terms aligns Jesus with other folk healers and shamans, it is legitimate to focus on the distinctive nature or profile of Jesus' curative work in his particular cultural context. This question should be kept separate from the theological issue of Jesus' 'uniqueness'.[10] As argued in the previous chapter, people produce religious innovations, and sometimes these innovations are successful enough to meet with a response among contemporaries and to be imitated by others. If Casey is right in his claim that 'Jesus was the most successful healer and exorcist of his time'—I am inclined to regard this as a valid statement—there must have been features in his healing/preaching activity that contributed to this success.

A number of scholars have taken notice of the differences between Jesus' therapeutic actions and those of other contemporary healers and exorcists (in different ways, Rousseau 1993; Twelftree 1993; Strecker 2002; Theissen 2010). Twelftree (2007a, 2007b: 48–9) lists some of the distinctive features of Jesus as exorcist: there is no evidence that he used artefacts or a library of incantations; he expressed no interest in the control of unwanted demons or protection from them, or in exorcizing buildings or places; and, while he acknowledged his power-authority, according to the *reports* about his

---

[10] This question seems to be at stake in Mack's (1988: 210–11) criticism of Theissen's early work on miracles in the early Christian tradition (Theissen 1983 [orig. 1974]).

healings, he did not mention his source of power.[11] As for the last, Twelftree does admit that the sayings tradition includes a reference to the power-authority used by Jesus, that is, the finger or spirit of God (Q 11:20). Twelftree concludes that Jesus 'deliberately draws attention to himself and his own resources in his ability to expel demons', and is best described as a 'charismatic magician' (2007a: 48).

Due to the near or total absence of ritual gestures, special magical objects, prayers, charms, odours and so forth in the Jesus tradition, Theissen argues that the ritual elements in Jesus' healings are minimal and that they should be taken as rituals *in statu nascendi*, rituals under development (cf. the full-blown healing ritual described in James 5:13–18) (Theissen 2010: 60). Theissen also notes that Jesus' selection of ritual elements out of a much larger repertoire conveys a message: it highlights the personal relationship between healer and sick person. By reducing external ritual elements, Jesus 'underlines immediate personal contact by laying hands and by gestures comparable to a kiss' (cf. Mark 7:33; Theissen 2010: 63). A further distinctive aspect of Jesus' healing activity, according to Theissen, is the emphasis on active faith, which is lacking in contemporary miracle stories (2010: 53–7). Healing at a distance, which appears in a number of stories, also underlines the faith element (Mark 7:25–30/Matt. 15:21–28; Matt. 8:5–13/Luke 7:1–10; cf. John 4:46–54; Luke 17:11–19).

Although we cannot achieve any certainty about the details of Jesus' healing activity, the descriptions by Twelftree and Theissen are plausible historical conjectures.[12] Jesus must have been able to create a special combination of healing techniques somehow distinct from other healers, which, together with his own personal charisma, contributed to his reputation as a successful healer and exorcist. Jesus' minimal use of external elements and his strong focus on his own ability to expel demons is in line with John the Baptist's emphasis on his own ritual power; in technical terms, John's introduction of a special agent ritual. Had Jesus used, for example, elaborated prayers,

---

[11] Twelftree also mentions that prayer was not part of Jesus' technique, but (as argued earlier in this section) it is possible to find some evidence of Jesus having used prayer in his healing.
[12] In his earlier study, Theissen was somewhat more sceptical about the historical details of healing stories than in his 2010 article. Cf. Theissen 1983: 282: 'To attempt to reconstruct a vivid picture of the historical Jesus from the miracle stories would be as nonsensical as to attempt to reconstruct the Pauline teaching of justification from Acts 13.38f. or the Baptist's preaching of repentance from Mk 6.17ff.'

incantations or magical objects in his healing activity, the ritual structure would have moved toward special instrument or special patient rituals. In other words, a CPS-agent would have been associated with the instrument (for example, a magical object or an incantation) or with the patient of a ritual, as happens in intercession with God. Since according to Lawson and McCauley's Ritual Competence Theory—more accurately, according to the modified version suggested in Chapter Three (3.5)—special agent rituals are usually understood to be more powerful than special instrument or patient rituals, the theory would give a partial explanation for Jesus' success as a healer and for the fact that his style of healing remained relatively consistent in the Gospel tradition.

A ritual approach to Jesus' healings is a complex issue. As William Sax (2010) has noted, our definition of ritual is inherently connected with the issue of the apparent nonrationality and ineffectiveness of ritual healing. We tend to call Jesus' healings 'rituals' or 'symbolic healings' (cf. Theissen) because, according to our biomedical understanding, healing an epileptic with an exorcism or someone with malaria by laying a hand on her is not actually effective. But by assuming that Jesus worked as a successful ritual healer we concede that ritual healings sometimes work, by means of the placebo effect or hypnosis, by focusing on 'illness' instead of 'disease', by using the functional effects of the ASC, by catharsis, 'group therapy' and so forth.[13] Granted 'the conceptual category of "ritual" is a specific modern Western tool of self-reflection and intellectual *modus operandi*' (Stausberg 2008: 98), there is nevertheless no good alternative to the term in the academic tradition of the study of ritual. As I. M. Lewis puts it, 'how else can we understand "other cultures" except comparatively in terms of our concepts, constructs, and language?' (quoted from Boddy 1994: 408). Moreover, as I have argued earlier in this chapter, etic (scientific) explanations of ritual, spirit possession, and magic are also informative with regard to similar magical concepts and behaviour in our *own* culture.[14]

---

[13] Cf., for example, McClenon's (2002) ritual healing theory, which argues that suggestibility and hypnotizability gave humans an adaptive edge in evolution and explains why ritual healings are so widespread in the world's cultures and why religion is so frequently associated with health and healing. For placebo research and ritual efficacy, see Brody 2010.

[14] Many healing activities in conventional Western medicine may helpfully be analysed as rituals (Brody 2010: 153).

## 4.4 COGNITIVE EXPLANATIONS FOR SPIRIT POSSESSION

Despite the resistance against universalizing theories among many anthropologists, the frequency with which shamanic-type behaviours have occurred in human history, from ancient rock art to present-day neoshamanism (DuBois 2009), is nevertheless striking. Michael Winkelman, for example, has explored in a number of studies the physiological nature, the evolutionary background, and ecological settings of shamanism, the ASC, and magico-religious practices (Winkelman 1986, 1992, 2000, 2002; see also McClenon 2002). Winkelman and others argue that shamanism and shamanic trance have functioned as an adaptive feature, facilitating human responses to stimuli such as pain, illness, and threat. These behaviours have a neural basis, which can be scientifically explored; in Winkelman's words, 'Shamanic traditions have arisen throughout the world because of the interaction between the inner structures of the human brain-mind with the ecological and social conditions of hunter-gatherer societies' (2000: 77). Winkelman outlines a course of cultural-evolutionary development: from hunter-gatherer societies, with shamans, to more complex societies, generating various types of magico-religious practitioners such as mediums, priests, sorcerers, and witches. The shift, however, is gradual, and many residues of shamanic practices survive in more complex societies. In very broad terms, Jesus can be understood as a magico-religious practitioner whose ministry involves some residues of shamanic practices.[15]

Although it may be questioned whether 'shamanism' is a coherent sets of beliefs and practices, or whether, as Eliade argued, it represents humankind's *ur-religion* (Eliade 1964),[16] many features associated with the 'shamanic complex' and spirit possession can reasonably be subjected to cognitive analysis (Pearson 2002; Pyysiäinen 2009: 57–94; see also DuBois 2009: 132).

A pioneering ethnographic study of spirit possession, drawing on insights and theories from the Cognitive Science of Religion, was undertaken by Emma Cohen (2007). Cohen's ethnographic research

---

[15] For an application of Winkelman's insights to Pauline studies, see Shantz 2009.
[16] For a recent harsh criticism of Eliade, see Sidky 2010. See also Znamenski 2007, who provides a cultural explanation for the popularity of the shamanism idiom in Western intellectual culture.

was conducted over a period of eighteen months (2002–04) with a group of Afro-Brazilian religionists in the northern Brazilian city of Belém. The possession movement involves small, house-based communities (*terreiros*). The house cult within which Cohen conducted her research consisted of some five initiated members and a larger core group of about twenty members, the house being the venue for daily ceremonies of possession and healing. Although in some cases the members of the cult regard the spirits temporarily possessing people's bodies as unwelcome intruders, the spirits are not generally regarded as evil. Rather, people warmly welcome them after weeks or months of preparation and waiting. Cohen's study is the first attempt to chart the ways in which possession concepts are cognitively represented in the human mind, and the causal structures that characterize these concepts. The results were later tested and developed in an experimental research project together with the cognitive psychologist Justin Barrett (see Cohen and Barrett 2008a, 2008b).

In a follow-up article (2008), Cohen suggests that, in the world's cultures, concepts of spirit possession fall broadly into two categories: one entailing the transformation or replacement of identity, *executive possession*, the other envisaging the possessing spirits as the cause of illness and misfortune, *pathogenic possession*. According to Cohen, these cross-culturally recurrent features of divergent conceptual structures may be explained at least in part with reference to distinct processes of human cognition: one dealing with representations of person–identity, the other with notions of contamination.

Let us take a parallel look at the two mechanisms:

Executive possession

- Causing a change of identity (temporarily or for longer period)
- Total loss of control of body and mind during séance
- Based on parallel cognitive systems engaged in perception of bodies and persons (intuitive dualism; see e.g. Bloom 2004)

Pathogenic possession

- Spirit seen as contaminating substance or essence
- No displacement or transformation of person-identity
- Spirits agentized only secondarily
- Based on universal beliefs about contamination (e.g. Nemeroff and Rozin 2000)

Can these cognitive processes shed light on the stories of Jesus' exorcisms and early Christian healing practices? The cases of demonic possession described in the Synoptic Gospels do not fall quite neatly into the two categories suggested by Cohen. We do find several examples of 'executive possession' in the Gospels. According to Cohen, this form of possession is signalled for example by the replacement of proper names, alterations of voice and vocabulary, temporary or more permanent loss of control of the body: all characteristics occurring in a number of the possession stories.[17] However, in many other stories the change of identity is not emphasized, nor is it made explicitly clear whether the condition of the patient is to be understood in terms of executive or pathogenic possession. Sometimes it is obvious that an illness is caused by an executive type of demonic possession (for example the Matthean version of the epileptic boy, Matt. 17:14–20); in other cases it is equally clear that possession does not give rise to a total change of identity (see, for example, Luke 13:11, where Jesus heals a woman who had suffered from a 'spirit of infirmity' for eighteen years; cf. also Luke 4:39). The two cognitive mechanisms suggested by Cohen apparently do not translate into two different aetiologies in the world of the Synoptic authors. However, if we take Cohen's typology as a model which emphasizes interaction and interface between the cognitive mechanisms involved in possession concepts, we can explain certain peculiar features in the Jesus tradition and in Second Temple Judaism.

Although some scholars want to preserve a clear distinction between demonic possession and disease in the cultural environment of Jesus, many have also observed that both in aetiologies and in healing practices the categories are often blurred (Kazen 2002: 300–39; see also Klutz 1999, 2004). Exorcistic and therapeutic language often co-occur in Second Temple Jewish sources, and diseases and contaminating conditions, such as scale disease and corpse impurity, are not infrequently associated with the activities of demons (Kazen 2002; Klutz 2004: 121–51; Wassen 2008). Since demonological aetiologies were relatively common, it is not surprising to find pathogenic possession in the healing stories of the Gospels. Demons are

---

[17] For example in Mark 1:24; 3:12; 5:5 the demons 'cry out' and in 5:9 the demon calls himself Legion. For loss of control, see Mark 5:3–5; 9:8; note also the raging sons of Sceva in Acts 19:11–20.

often called 'unclean spirits' (*ta pneumata ta akatharta*).[18] But while beliefs in malicious spirits and demonic affliction do occur for example in the Enochic literature, in the Qumran and in Josephus (Alexander 1999; Sorensen 2002: 47–74; Wassen 2008; Eve 2009: 26–39), it is not easy to find passages where demonic affliction is understood in terms of executive possession comparable to that found in some of the Gospel stories—suggesting a total change of identity, the demon speaking through its host, and so on. It seems that the idea of pathogenic possession was more prevalent in Second Temple Judaism, although mental disabilities could be seen as evidence of demonic possession.[19] Cecilia Wassen, for example, has argued that the exclusion of blemished people from the Qumran movement was based on the fear of demonic influence: various ailments and disabilities were thought to be due to demonic affliction, and persons afflicted by demons were believed to have a polluting quality (Wassen 2008).

We may, then, argue that the emphasis in the Synoptic Gospels on what Cohen calls executive possession is to some degree characteristic of the Jesus tradition and perhaps of Christian beginnings more generally. While further research is needed on the phenomenon of possession in early Christianity, we should not overlook the fact that possession (both negative and positive), often construed as being taken over by a spirit, appears in several strands of the early Christian tradition. In the Gospels, Jesus is described as a spirit-possessed healer who successfully confronts evil spirits which have captured or harmed their human victims. In the Pauline epistles we have less evidence of negative possession—although Paul references 'signs and wonders' in Rom. 15:18–19 and 2 Cor. 12:12. However, Paul's discussions of *charismata* or *pneumatika*, especially concerning glossolalia and prophecy (1 Cor. 12–14), show that at least in the Corinthian assembly positive spirit possession was greatly esteemed (see also section 5.6). Paul's own attitude toward such religious experiences seems to have been somewhat ambiguous. He boasted about his visionary journey to heaven (2 Cor. 12:1–5; Shantz 2009: 87–109) and about his competence in tongue-speaking (1 Cor. 14:18–19). His overall emphasis, however, may have been less on ecstatic religious

---

[18] Especially in Mark: 1:23; 26, 27; 3:11, 30; 5:2, 8, 13; 6:7; 7:25; 9:25; see also Luke 4:36; 6:18; 8:29; 9:42; Matt. 10:1; Wahlen 2004.
[19] This may be implied in CD XV-17/4Q266 8i, in which the 'stupid and deranged' are excluded from the Qumran community (Wassen 2008).

experience and more on doctrinal (Whitehouse) or 'volitional' religiosity (investing in the study of textual traditions and of symbolic/theological concepts), which does not foster an instant and autonomous takeover by a divine being or spirit (Czachesz 2012a: 81).[20]

In addition to the Gospels and the Pauline letters, certain other early Christian texts contain representations of religious experiences, often labelled under the category of 'prophecy' (Aune 1983; Nissinen 2013),[21] which can be analysed in terms of spirit possession; most notably in Revelation, in the *Odes of Solomon*, and in later reports of such 'heretic' movements as Montanism (for the last, see Marjanen 2008). While there is no way of deciding whether a particular early Christian text reflects a 'real' experience of executive possession or merely a literary fiction, we can use these texts as evidence for the mindsets and expectations of the writers and their audiences (cf. Czachesz 2013a). It would be probably generalizing too much to argue that the whole of primitive Christianity was a possession cult (or an 'exorcistic movement', cf. Theissen 1983: 250), but it certainly hosted groups that can be called such.

In sum, Cohen's proposal of the two cognitive mechanisms operating in spirit possession is helpful in conceptualizing some of the questions concerning Jesus' healings and the healthcare system of his culture which have occupied New Testament and early Christian scholars. While it is obvious that these mechanisms often interact or oscillate in people's representations of spirit possession, we can also recognize a somewhat more prevalent role of executive possession in the early Jesus movement than can be gleaned from its cultural background. The emphasis on both negative and positive possession

---

[20] Drawing on recent neuroimaging research, Czachesz 2012a (see also 2013c) has advanced a typology of two styles of religious experience, 'volitional' and 'resonant'. The first style is induced by focusing on attention (e.g. by reading religious texts or practising meditation) and is characterized by increased activation of the prefrontal cortex. The second style of religious experience is primarily triggered by means of some routinized activity (e.g. rhythmic body movements) or external stimuli (such as music) and is characterized by decreased activation in the prefrontal cortex. Religious communities usually give prominence to one of these styles. Although Czachesz does not focus on spirit possession, I suggest that Cohen's 'executive possession' is best understood as an expression of resonant religious experience. Czachesz argues that Paul's central aim in 1 Cor. is 'to shift the operation of the community away from the resonant style and toward the volitional style of religiosity' (2012a: 84).

[21] Nissinen (2013) makes a strong case for 'prophecy' as a cultural construct. Even so, however, there are phenomena falling under this construct (such as 'executive possession') that can be cross-culturally studied and cognitively explained.

continues in later versions of the Christian movement. The positive form of possession often comes up, but the abundance of incantations, amulets, and magical texts surviving from the world of early Judaism and Christianity shows that at the time of Jesus and the earliest Christians, the threat of being contaminated or occupied by hostile spirits was a real concern for a large part of the population (Aune 1980; Naveh and Shaked 1985; Betz 1992; Meyer and Smith 1994; Alexander 2003; Eshel 2003; Bohak 2008).[22] A movement that offered effective therapeutic and protective rituals with regard to such threats, as well as ritual techniques to induce an experience of tutelary spirits, would certainly find a market and satisfy a need.

## 4.5 RITES OF HEALING AND EXORCISM IN EARLY CHURCHES

Stories of exorcisms and healings similar to those performed by Jesus in the Gospels continued to be told about apostles and other Christian heroes, as evidenced by the Acts of the Apostles, the *Apocryphal Acts*, and later lives of the saints, such as the *Life of Antony* by Athanasius of Alexandria (*ca.* 357). Some second-century Christian authors lay considerable emphasis on Christian exorcistic practices, which they regard as proof of the truth and superiority of the Christian religion. Justin Martyr, for example, devotes much attention to demon possession and evil spirits in his writings, boldly stating:

> numberless demoniacs throughout the whole world, and in your city—many of our Christian people exorcizing them in the name of Jesus Christ, who was crucified under Pontius Pilatus, have healed and do heal, rendering helpless and driving the possessing demons out of them,

---

[22] It may be noted that much of the Jewish and Christian 'magical' material was produced two or more centuries later than the time of Jesus or the Gospels; as Klutz has pointed out, however, 'an equally impressive volume of it survives from earlier times—in some instances as early as the third millennium BCE' (from ancient Egypt, Assyria, and Phoenicia; Klutz 2004: 70–1). There is no reason to assume that the practices reflected in these materials became common only centuries after the beginning of the Christian movement. For an argument that miraculous healing enjoyed little prominence in early Christianity until the fourth century, see Ferngren 2009: 64–85.

though they could not be cured by all the older exorcists, and those who used incantations and drugs. (*2 Apol.* 6.6; trans. Barnard 1997: 78)

Similarly Irenaeus, writing toward the end of the second century, appeals to the reality of miracles, exorcisms, and healings which have taken place and continue to do so in his own time (for example *Haer.* 2.32.4; see also 1.23.4 and 1.13.3; see Barrett-Lennard 1994: 151–65). Irenaeus also tells us that his theological rivals and opponents perform exorcisms, although he claims that all they can do is to transfer demons from one person to another (*Haer.* 2.31.2). In another context he writes that the Simonian mystic priests 'make use of exorcisms and incantations, love-potions too and philters and the so-called familiars (*paredri*) and dream-senders' (*Haer.* 1.23.4) and that Menander, the successor of Simon, was 'most skilful in magic' (1.23.5; trans. Unger 1992). The frequency with which Christian and Jewish symbols and formulas appear in the magical texts collected in the *Greek Magical Papyri* (*PGM*) also supports the conclusion that exorcisms, along with protective and curative rituals, were a significant factor in the spread and the growth of the Christian movement (MacMullen 1984: 27, 108–9; see also Brown 1971; Kollmann 1996: 377–8).[23] It can even be argued that fourth- and fifth-century monastic communities were the most likely venues for the scribal production of magical papyri (Brakke 2006: 227).

In addition to the use of miraculous stories as proof of the superiority of Christian religion, and evidence of the use of ritual power centred on specific spells, incantations, manuals, etc., early Christian sources also provide examples of more institutionalized and communal ritualized practices related to healing and demon expulsion. In James 5:13–18, a unique late first-century description of (or prescription for) a healing ritual has survived, in which the elders of the community (*ekklesia*) are singled out as the central agents of the ritual (cf. also Polycarp, *Phil.* 6.1, where a similar role of caring for the sick is assigned to the *presbyteroi*).

> Are any among you sick? They should call for the elders of the church and have them pray over them, anointing them with oil in the name of the Lord. The prayer of faith will save the sick, and the Lord will raise them up; and anyone who has committed sins will be forgiven.

---

[23] Twelftree (2007a) criticizes MacMullen's view but much of the evidence he himself discusses supports the contrary.

Therefore confess your sins to one another, and pray for one another, so that you may be healed. The prayer of the righteous is powerful and effective. (Jas. 5:14-16)

Although there is no reason to downplay the role of the group in the 'performance-centred' or charismatic healings discussed in the previous sections, it is evident that the ecclesiastical authorities and communal praying are at the very heart of the ritual described in James. The instruments of healing—'praying over' the patient (probably including the action of placing hands on the patient; Albl 2002: 136) and anointing in the name of the Lord—are both methods that were widely used in early Christianity for therapeutic and exorcistic purposes (Mark 6:13 and 16:18; Barrett-Lennard 1994: 240-4; Sorensen 2002: 184-85, 214; see also the discussion on the *Apostolic Tradition* below). The ritual described by James, however, contains no direct reference to exorcism, and the ritual should probably not be understood as an exorcistic rite (*pace* Dibelius and Greeven 1976: 252). Illness and sin are connected in the passage, although the author avoids expressing a direct causal relationship between sin and illness or giving a demonic aetiology for illness (Albl 2002: 134-5). The association between sin and illness in James recalls the relationship we find between them in some of the stories about Jesus' healings (Hägerland 2012). Forgiveness of sins is explicitly mentioned in Mark 2:1-12; cf. Matt. 9:1-8 and Luke 5:17-26 (where a causal relationship is also avoided) and the association may be implicit in many other stories because of the blurred boundaries between sin, impurity, and illness in Second Temple Judaism. It may be possible to see here a longer ritual trajectory, from John's baptismal activity to the forgiveness rituals in early Christian communities.

A particularly striking link exists between the communal confession in Jas. 5:16, the practices prescribed in 1 John (1:9; 5:16), and the *Didache* (4:14; 14:1). These passages speak of the ritualized confession of sins in a community context, although it remains somewhat unclear whether they all refer to confessions of particular sins (as in 1 John 5:16) or to general confessions. It is nevertheless interesting that, unlike the healing ritual stipulated in Jas. 5:14-15, the 'confession of sins' in Jas. 5:16 and First John is not connected with the ritual agency of individuals with a particular status in the community ('elders'); the whole community, or any brother who 'sees' someone transgressing (1 John 5:16), can function as a mediator of forgiveness

(Roitto 2012). This may be explained by the tradition in early Christianity, whereby healing was firmly associated with a specific charismatic gift (cf. 1 Cor. 12:9, 28, 30), or, as here, with an honorific status.[24] In James, the structure of the healing ritual is still that of a special agent ritual, but the increasing emphasis on authentic praying (Hartin 1999: 121–4) adds a dimension of a 'special patient ritual' to the ritual complex.

## 4.6 LITURGICAL EXORCISMS

In many early Christian circles, exorcistic practices became firmly institutionalized and integrated into the Christian initiation process (Dölger 1909; Kelly 1985; Leeper 1990). Signs of this development can be recognized in the *Excerpts of Theodotus*, preserved to us by Clement of Alexandria. Theodotus was a Christian teacher active in Alexandria around the middle of the second century and a student of Valentinus, the founder of a movement which was denounced as heretical in the early Church (Dunderberg 2008). Although it is difficult to reconstruct an accurate picture of the baptismal practices and doctrines envisioned by the author, it seems clear enough that baptism was believed to break the bonds of Fate and translate the baptized person from death into life (*Exc.* 74–78). The baptismal process nevertheless involves the risk of demonic contamination, revealing several indications of the pathogenic view of spirit possession discussed above. The water must be exorcized, so that it will be able to ward off evil and confer sanctification (*Exc.* 82), but even then it is possible for unclean spirits to enter the baptismal waters and gain the 'seal' together with the candidate. In that case no future cure is possible (*Exc.* 83). The candidate should therefore take strict precautions and practice prebaptismal 'fastings, supplications, prayers, raising of hands, kneeling' so that the soul 'is being saved from the world and from the mouth of lions' (*Exc.* 84; trans. R. P. Casey 1934: 91).

A set of more elaborate exorcistic rituals in the context of the baptismal process is documented in the *Apostolic Tradition,* a church order which is often ascribed to Hippolytus and dated to the early

---

[24] The charismatic gift of healing was also recognized in the third century, as demonstrated, for example, by *Trad. ap.* 5 (see Barrett-Lennard 1994: 252–6).

third century, but which may in fact be an aggregation of material from different sources and periods from the mid-second to the mid-fourth century (Bradshaw et al. 2002: 1–17). The *Apostolic Tradition* prescribes daily exorcisms of the baptismal candidates (those elected from among the catechumens) with a laying of hands over them during the unspecified period of the final baptismal preparation,[25] which culminates in the exorcism performed by the bishop (*Trad. ap.* 20.3). Another prebaptismal exorcism carried out by the bishop is ordered to be performed on Saturday, before the Sunday of baptism, including kneeling and laying of hands and followed by breathing on the candidates and sealing their foreheads, ears, and nostrils (*Trad. ap.* 20.8). In the actual baptismal ceremony, celebrated after an all-night vigil from Saturday evening till cockcrow Sunday morning, several antidemonic and exorcistic rituals are acted out.

The most distinctive and most universal antidemonic element in the Christian liturgical tradition is the act of renunciation (Kelly 1985: 94–105), in which each baptismal candidate says 'I renounce you, Satan, with all your service and all your works' (*Trad. ap.* 21.9 Sahidic, trans. from Bradshaw et al. 2002). In the *Apostolic Tradition*, the renunciation is followed by anointing with 'the oil of exorcism' (21.10). As in the *Excerpts of Theodotus*, there is a strong concern for contamination and cleansing throughout the process of initiation. The baptismal candidates are instructed to wash themselves on the day before the baptism (20.5). Menstruating women should be put aside and receive baptism some other day (20.6). On the morning of the baptism day, the water must be 'prayed over' (21.1). The oil used in the exorcistic anointing is 'exorcised' (21.7) in the baptismal liturgy and a severe warning is given against taking 'any foreign substance' (*allotrion*, which may have demonic connotations) down into the baptismal water (21.5). Much emphasis is placed on the purity and power of the ritual instruments.

It would be unrealistic to suggest that the compilation of liturgical traditions and instructions in the *Apostolic Tradition*, deriving from a lengthy period of time, faithfully mirrors the actual practices of a particular church or churches in the third or fourth century. Still there is sufficient evidence that exorcistic rituals were practised in the context of Christian initiation and the catechumenate from the third or at the latest fourth century onwards (for detailed discussion of the evidence,

---

[25] *Trad. ap.* 17 assumes a three-year general catechumenate.

see Dölger 1909 and Kelly 1985). The *Apostolic Tradition* gives us some glimpses of such antidemonic rites, whether in the form of theological prescriptions or reflections of some actual practices, or, most likely, a combination of the two (see also Barrett-Lennard 1994: 233–75).

The stories of Jesus' exorcisms and the evidence for exorcistic rituals in early Christian liturgical documents reflect conceptions of spirit possession similar to those documented by anthropologists in many different cultures around the world. In terms of the two cognitive mechanisms operating in representations of spirit possession (Cohen), the liturgical documents do not reveal evidence of executive possession (total replacement of the host's identity by the possessing spirit), but rather show a concern for contamination and cleansing, indicating that pathogenic possession is more prominent in the arena of early Christian liturgy. From the perspective of ritual analysis, the 'performance-centred' healing which is so abundant in the stories of Jesus' and the apostles' curative activity does not occur in the rituals prescribed in James and the liturgical sources, which fit more neatly into conventional definitions of ritual.

Moreover, the strong concern for contamination in the liturgical documents, and the almost neurotic repetition of purificatory and apotropaic rites—a feature not present in the Jesus tradition—reflect actions which can aptly be explained by an approach to ritual theory that focuses on the compulsiveness of ritual behaviour. The fear of contamination, present in many ritual practices, has made some researchers ask whether there is a common cognitive mechanism behind obsessive neuroses and collective ritualized behaviour (Freud 1963; Dulaney and Fiske 1994; Fiske and Haslam 1997). Drawing on this research tradition, Pascal Boyer and Pierre Liénard have developed a theory of 'ritualized behaviour' which uses evidence from evolutionary psychology, neuropsychology, and neuroimaging, and seeks to explain the motivational ground of human ritual behaviour (Boyer and Liénard 2006; Liénard and Boyer 2006). Boyer and Liénard propose a cognitive explanation in terms of an evolved Hazard-Precaution System, a mechanism specialized in detecting and responding to potential threats. While Boyer and Liénard's theory is not very informative as to the analysis of historical details and social dynamics, the panhuman inclination toward ritualized behaviour in response to potential threats may indeed explain why the kind of rituals prescribed in the liturgical documents gained hold in early Christianity.

## 4.7 RITUAL ACTION—RITUAL COMMUNICATION

Our discussion of ritual healing and exorcisms from Jesus to the *Apostolic Tradition* has not exhausted the range of topics and texts that would require attention in a full treatment of this theme. The examples analysed in this chapter nevertheless reveal the importance of healing for the rise and formation of the Christian movement— although there is no reason to suggest that the emphasis on exorcistic practices and miraculous healings was similar in all early Christian groups; for example, the *Gospel of Thomas* makes no explicit reference to Jesus' healings (cf. however *Gos. Thom.* 14), and the Gospel of John does not contain any mention of Jesus expelling demons.

The stories and the textual evidence analysed in this chapter cannot be lumped together under a single definition or theory of 'ritual'. This should not be taken as an argument against the usefulness of a ritual perspective on early Christian healing, but rather as a sign of the very nature of the pluralistic approach applied in this study. Jesus' healings were amenable to analysis as 'performance-centred rituals', following the model employed by anthropologists in the study of shamanic and folk medical practices in various cultures. This approach is in line with the theory-dependent realism elaborated upon in Chapter Two (2.6).

New Testament scholars with a social-scientific orientation have been eager to apply insights from medical anthropology to Jesus' curative actions and early Christian healthcare, but the bias toward cultural relativism has sometimes led them to overly polarized conclusions and has prevented them from recognizing the diversity of people's experiences of sickness and spirit possession. Here the cognitive approach to ritual healing can offer complementary perspectives on, and to some degree correctives to, the previous discussion. In particular, the interaction and variation among representations of both executive and pathogenic possessions in early Christian materials show that beliefs in spirit possession are produced by different cognitive mechanisms, which may also be seen as generating different types of magico-religious practices. The spirit possession movement instigated by Jesus continued in some strands of early Christianity, but many sources are dominated by representations of pathogenic possession, indicating that demonic or spiritual forces were not often understood in terms of a takeover or transformation of person-identity. Liturgical sources show a preoccupation with pathogenic possession, while other accounts, such as the rite of healing in Jas. 5:13-18, give no sign of possession beliefs.

Although several theories of ritual have been discussed and applied, the predominant perspective in the preceding two chapters—and in this chapter in particular—has been that inspired by the pioneering cognitive theory of Lawson and McCauley. Rituals are analysed as *actions*, in which CPS-agents play a role and which are performed to bring about some change in the world—for example, the recovery of the ritual patient. Such a perspective, however, does not capture all the activities and dimensions that have been the chief focus of the field of Ritual Studies. People do not merely perform ritual actions on ritual patients or objects; they also sing, dance, and move together, as well as send signals to each other, with behaviours that can be analysed in ritual terms. This dimension of ritual will be the topic of the following chapter.

# 5

## 'When You Come Together'

### Ritual and Cooperation

The question of ritual's facilitation of social life has a long history in both social anthropology and ritual theory. The point from which ritual theorists often begin their discussion is Émile Durkheim's *Elementary Forms of Religious Life* (2001 [orig. 1912]), especially his description of religious rites as an activity in which 'the social group periodically reaffirms itself' (2001: 287). Durkheim's understanding of ritual was based on his critical distinction between profane time, which is 'monotonous, lazy, and dull' ('uniforme, languissante et terne'[1]), and sacred time, which he characterizes as 'collective effervescence' (2001: 162-4). Although the profane everyday life includes rites—in particular actions that are described as a 'negative cult' (prohibitions, taboos, etc.)—it is the sacred time that is primarily dedicated to ritual. For Durkheim, the most fundamental ritual actions were exemplified in the collective ceremonies of the Australian aborigines, who from time to time come together around their sacred emblems to reaffirm themselves as a unified group. Durkheim famously argued that by worshipping their religious representations people are unconsciously worshipping themselves as a moral community or 'church'. To put it bluntly, Durkheim's somewhat circular argument is that 'the sacred is the social, the religious is the sacred, and thus the religious is the social' (Pyysiäinen 2001: 55; see also Pals 1996: 115). Rites that are not defined by the social fall under the category of magic. The magician does not have a church, only clients (Durkheim 2001: 43). In terms of Durkheim's distinction, the healing

---

[1] Durkheim 1912: 308.

of the epileptic boy (Matt. 9:37–43) would show Jesus as practising magic, while Paul, who gives instructions as to how the Corinthians should 'come together' for a common meal,[2] each having 'a hymn, a lesson, a revelation, a tongue, or an interpretation' (1 Cor. 14:26), would be advocating proper religious rituals.

That, of course, is not my argument in this book. Magic is best understood as an aspect of many religious rituals, related to but not identical with the concept of ritual efficacy (Czachesz 2013a: 165–66; Gudme 2013: 154–7; see also Grimes 1995: 48–9); not as the opposite of religion. But Durkheim's approach to ritual is suggestive of a different approach from the one dominating in two previous chapters. Not all rituals—more accurately, not all practices largely considered as rituals by ritual theorists—are similarly amenable to the analysis of the ritual action grammar postulated by Lawson and McCauley, involving agents, patients, and actions/instruments. This is true of many collective rituals which are not best described as actions in which 'someone does something for someone by means of something' (Pyysiäinen 2004b: 140, summarizing Lawson and McCauley's action representation system) and/or which invite other analytical perspectives than Ritual Competence Theory.[3] McCauley and Lawson do not regard singing, praying, dancing, and kneeling (which are typically performed together in the context of religious activities) as religious rituals in the technical sense they propose (McCauley and Lawson 2002: 13). This should not be taken as a flaw in their theory—theories need to be kept simple enough to generate meaningful explanations; but the socio-cognitive and pluralistic approach applied in this study requires us to consider the Durkheimian perspective as well. It has after all been one of the most influential traditions in the academic study of ritual. As

---

[2] I assume that Paul's discussion of the whole *ekklēsia* 'coming together' (1 Cor. 14:23, 26; cf. 11:17, 18, 20, 33, and 34) relates to the same gathering that began with the meal in chapter 1 Cor. 11. According to the recent consensus, the description in 1 Cor. 11–14 fits the standard pattern of the Graeco-Roman dinner party, in which the meal proper (*deipnon*) was followed by learned conversation or entertainments (*symposium*). Osiek and Balch 1997: 203; D. E. Smith 2003: 188–214; E. Adams 2013: 26–7. See also Lampe 1994.

[3] While some ritual activities do not fit very well into Lawson and McCauley's action representation system, there are many rituals that can be analysed and explained from a number of theoretical perspectives, including that of Lawson and McCauley. Cf., for example, John's immersion (Chapter Three), in relation to which all three perspectives on ritual chosen for this book were considered.

we will see, Durkheim's legacy is still to be recognized in recent approaches which emphasize the crucial role played by rituals in generating social cohesion and solidarity, and indeed 'the possibility of the social world' (Bellah 2005: 194).

## 5.1 RITUAL AND COMMITMENT

To summarize the entire Durkheimian tradition in anthropology and Comparative Religion would go beyond the limits of this study (for an insightful survey, see Bellah 2005; note also Bell 1997: 23–60 and Throop and Laughlin 2002). I focus on just one important theme, which has links to Durkheim's understanding of ritual: the capacity of ritual to express commitment and generate cooperation.

One of the most illustrious examples of the Durkheimian tradition in recent years is Roy Rappaport's monumental and posthumously published treatment of ritual, *Ritual and Religion in the Making of Humanity* (1999). Rappaport starts with a highly condensed definition of ritual as 'the performance of more or less invariant sequences of formal acts and utterances not entirely encoded by the performers' (1999: 34), which he then unfolds and elaborates in the subsequent parts of his book. Rappaport stresses that his definition is neither substantial nor functional, but describes the universal form of ritual behaviours, including non-religious rituals and even stylized displays among non-human animals. The following key passage illustrates Rappaport's basic view:

> It would be well to reiterate I am raising no objections to symbolic, structural, or any other forms of analysis of ritual contexts. I am only insisting that to view ritual as no more than an alternative symbolic medium for expressing or accomplishing what might just as well—or perhaps better—be expressed or accomplished in other ways is, obviously, to ignore that which is distinctive of ritual itself. It seems apparent... that ritual is not simply an alternative way to express any manner of thing, but that certain meanings and effects can best, or even *only*, be expressed or achieved in ritual. Inasmuch as the substance of rituals is infinitely various, this must mean that these meanings follow from ritual's universal form. This form, moreover, cannot lie hidden in symbolic depths where all rituals differ from all others and each awaits its particular culture-specific exegesis. It must lie at or near ritual's

## Ritual and Cooperation 131

'surfaces', in, that is to say, relations among the *perceptual* features by which ritual is recognized as such and by which it has been defined here. (Rappaport 1999: 30–1, italics original; cf. Rappaport 1979: 174)

In complete agreement with Durkheim, Rappaport sees ritual as *the* basic ingredient in the formation of human social life. Ritual 'is not simply a symbolic representation of social contract, but tacit social contract itself'. It is '*the* basic social act' (1999: 138, italics original). Although Rappaport does not focus on the symbolic meanings of ritual or on the content of religious knowledge associated with it (such as myth), he contends that ritual is a form of communication. By taking part in ritual activities, people send messages both to each other and to themselves.

In ritual transmission, Rappaport distinguishes between two kinds of messages, which he calls 'self-referential' and 'canonical' respectively. Self-referential messages are related to the transmission of information concerning the participants' 'own current, psychic, and social states', whereas canonical messages 'do not *in themselves* represent or express the current states of those uttering and performing them' (1999: 52–3, italics original). Self-referential messages are transmitted in all rituals, human and non-human, but canonical messages are typical only of human ritual activities. The latter are *not* encoded by the participants, since they are already encoded for them in a 'liturgy' or 'liturgical order'. Rappaport does not offer a single or easily cited definition of the latter terms, but they seem to refer to the contexts of rituals and ritual sequences which are the source of the messages coming *outside* the participants' inner 'psychic and social states' (in contrast to self-referential messages). Canonical messages and liturgical orders may thus be seen as including the embedded and extended religious knowledge analysed in the next chapter, although the terminology used in this book and Rappaport's theoretical world coincide only partially.[4]

Rappaport combines a great amount of work done in anthropology and information theory, part of which is relevant for the sociocognitive approach promoted in this book. For the theme discussed in this chapter, two basic insights emerge from Rappaport's discussion of ritual. First, all rituals (including non-human ones) involve communication. The most basic form of messages sent by the participants

---

[4] See section 6.3, note 7.

is self-referential. In terms of Peirce's theory of signs (Rappaport 1999: 462–3; Sosis and Bulbulia 2011), self-referential messages are indexical (according to Rappaport, indexical signs refer to the object by being actually affected by that object), not symbolic (arbitrary) or iconic (based on likeness). Note, however, that much of Rappaport's analysis describes how indexical, iconic, and symbolic signs interact in ritual performance.

The second insight important for us in this chapter is the assertion that ritual is intrinsically about acceptance. According to Rappaport, the first of 'ritual's fundamental offices' is the act of acceptance: 'by performing a liturgical order the participants accept, and indicate to themselves that they accept whatever is encoded in the canon of that order' (1999: 119). The acceptance indicated by liturgical performance is more profound than a belief or conviction expressed by words. Rappaport's emphasis on acceptance comes close to what signalling theorists, focusing on ritual's capacity to support cooperation, have more recently called honest signalling. In expressing acceptance (Rappaport's term) by ritual public performance, the participants are also indicating commitment (the term used in Signalling Theory).[5]

Rappaport's appreciation of ritual as humanity's basic social act, and as the keystone of morality, cosmology, and religion, may be criticized as presenting a 'foundational academic narrative', rather than a testable theory (Grimes 2014: 300).[6] It is worth noting, however, that the insights mentioned in the preceding paragraph, as well as Rappaport's general contention as to ritual's fundamental role in the rise of human social life, are consistent with many recent studies on the evolution of human social cognition. Terrence Deacon, for example, in his book *The Symbolic Species: The Co-Evolution of Language and the Brain* (1997) offers an intriguing co-evolutionary theory concerning the emergence of symbolic language. Ritual occupies a central place in his account, which seeks to depict how ritual repetition helped ancient

---

[5] Rappaport stresses the distinction between belief and acceptance. Developing Rappaport's insights, Sosis notes that while performing a ritual can be a *hard-to-fake* signal of the belief in the moral values and doctrines of the group, it does not function as an *impossible-to-fake* (indexical) signal of belief (Sosis 2006: 71–2).

[6] According to Grimes (2014: 190), Rappaport's treatment of ritual is 'the most provocative' among the recent theoretical works on ritual, but also 'the least testable'. Robert Segal describes Rappaport's approach in *Ritual and Religion* as 'almost metaphysical' (Segal 2009: 68). He also points out that '[f]or Rappaport, ritual means religious ritual, and religion means ritual' (2009: 67).

hominids to establish a 'symbolic relationship from its component indexical relationships', in other words, to surmount the symbolic threshold (see esp. 1997: 401–10). 'In ritual frenzy, one can be induced to see everyday activities and objects in a very different light' (1997: 403). According to Deacon, the roots of symbolic communication lie in the peace-making, marriage, and puberty rituals of early humans.[7] Other theorists have pointed out the significance of keeping in time as well as of dance and music in improving the possibilities of cooperation and in strengthening social relations (McNeill 1995). These were certainly important aspects of early human rituals. Furthermore, the developmental psychologist Michael Tomasello—although not writing in relation to religion or ritual—has put forward the hypothesis that the decisive capacity that differentiates humans from the other big apes is our capacity for collaborative action and shared interaction (Tomasello 2014). All these and other theories as to the pivotal role of both ritual and cooperation in the evolution of human thinking and sociality lead us to ask in more specific terms, what role is played by ritual in cooperative communication (see also Sosis and Alcorta 2003; Alcorta and Sosis 2005).

## 5.2 COMMITMENT SIGNALLING

The most detailed answer to this question has been provided by theorists who apply a signalling approach to religious rituals. Certain recent developments in the area of Signalling Theory, such as the emergence of Charismatic Signalling, have already been discussed in Chapter Three (3.7); here, however, my focus is on the more original version of the theory, usually called Costly Signalling or Commitment Signalling.[8] The point of departure of the signalling approach—in

---

[7] A different evolutionary scenario has been suggested by Joseph Henrich (2009: 247), who hypothesizes that the emergence of symbolic language dramatically increased opportunities for Machiavellian manipulators. Hence the need for commitment signalling and costly ritual signals.

[8] The theory was originally referred to as Costly Signalling, but more recently signalling theorists have preferred Honest Signalling (Bulbulia and Sosis 2011) or Commitment Signalling (Bulbulia et al. 2013: 391 n. 2: '... signals do not need to be costly to evolve'). In this volume, I use the term Commitment Signalling, although I also refer to Costly Signalling, which is still widely known and used.

whatever version—is the conjecture that 'religions evolve, at least in part, to support cooperation' (Bulbulia and Sosis 2011: 363). In this respect, Signalling Theory can be seen against the background of the evolutionary considerations described above. In the (broadly defined) field of the Cognitive Science of Religion, Signalling Theory and especially Commitment Signalling can be seen as the most important example of the Durkheimian approach to ritual and religion. However, it has often been contrasted with other cognitive approaches, which argue that religion is a by-product of certain more general cognitive capacities; not an adaptation helping to solve problems of survival, such as challenges in cooperation (Boyer 2002; Sosis and Ruffle 2004; see also Pyysiäinen and Hauser 2010). Moreover, as already noted in Chapter Two (2.2), signalling theorists largely draw on behavioural ecology, a subfield of the evolutionary study of human culture and behaviour; this has resulted in some significant methodological and theoretical differences as compared to the by-product approach. Behavioural ecology applies evolutionary theory to the study of behavioural adaptation and design in an ecological setting. Behavioural ecologists are much less interested in the underlying psychological mechanisms that produce adaptive responses to ecological conditions—in contrast to the approach employed, for example, by evolutionary psychologists (Sosis and Bulbulia 2011).

Since the beginning of the twenty-first century a large number of studies have been published arguing for and testing the hypothesis that religious rituals can operate as honest, hard-to-fake signals that enhance cooperation in religious groups (Irons 2001; Sosis 2003, 2004, 2006; Sosis and Alcorta 2003; Atran and Norenzayan 2004; Bulbulia 2004, 2013; Alcorta and Sosis 2005; Ruffle and Sosis 2007; Bulbulia and Sosis 2011; Heimola 2012). The discussion of Commitment Signalling as a theory of religion covers many aspects, but its major propositions can be conveniently listed as follows (see also Uro 2011d):

- The primary adaptive benefit of religion is its ability to facilitate cooperation.
- Religious rituals are a form of communication (cf. non-human rituals).
- Religious rituals signal commitment to the members of the group.
- A reliable signal for cooperation is one that is too costly to fake.

- Religious rituals promote group cohesion by requiring members to engage in behaviour that is too costly to fake.
- Costly rituals are an efficient mechanism for overcoming the problem of free-riders.

These propositions require a few comments and clarifications. The debate over the adaptive benefit of religion in the evolution of the human species has gained relatively a great amount of attention among cognitive and evolutionary scholars of religion. The issue is complicated and involves many questions, such as what exactly is the trait (religion) that is claimed to be adaptive or a by-product, in what context it is assumed to produce benefits for its carrier, and what is meant by 'adaptation' (Sosis 2009; Sosis and Bulbulia 2011). The confusions and misunderstandings with regard to the issue may derive in part at least from the different disciplinary backgrounds of the researchers. As Sosis and Bulbulia point out, in asking whether a trait is adaptive, many evolutionary psychologists and cognitive scientists are in fact asking whether there exists a universal psychological mechanism that has produced a particular behavioural pattern (Sosis and Bulbulia 2011: 348). Behavioural ecologists, in contrast, are not interested in creating hypotheses about such underlying mechanisms, but instead ask whether a particular behavioural pattern results in fitness gains in a specific environment, relative to other available strategies. The explanations proffered by the 'adaptationist' and 'by-product' schools seem to be operating, to some degree at least, on different evolutionary levels, and are thus not necessarily contradictory or mutually exclusive. Moreover, certain intermediate positions have been suggested, arguing, for example, that 'religion originally evolved from pre-existing cognitive functions', but that 'it may then have been subject to selection, creating an adaptively designed system for solving the problem of cooperation' (Pyysiäinen and Hauser 2010).

## 5.3 COMMITMENT SIGNALLING AS A MIDDLE-RANGE THEORY

How important is evolutionary theory in applying Costly Signalling to historical materials? It is in principle possible to separate Costly Signalling from its evolutionary underpinnings, and to take it simply as a neo-functionalist social theory. One can analyse societies or groups to test whether they work as the theory predicts, without taking sides in the debate over the adaptive nature of religion.[9] In terms of biological evolution that would roughly mean that Costly Signalling provides 'proximate', not ultimate explanations for ritual behaviour.[10] It is important to realize, however, that it is precisely the evolutionary framework that has helped theorists to develop the functionalist approach into a testable theory, designed to avoid the causal tautology plaguing classical functionalism. As often noted, the problem with functionalism is that any explanation based on it may easily turn circular. In other words, if every social phenomenon must serve some positive function to survive, and if nothing without such a function does survive, how can we argue against a functionalist explanation (Pyysiäinen 2001: 67; see also Penner 1971)?

The methodological and theoretical resources derived from behavioural ecology and other evolutionary sciences have supported more scientific formulations of the theory. Commitment (Costly) Signalling has indeed been tested in a number of studies, against both historical and contemporary data. The results have been encouraging. An analysis of nineteenth-century collectivist communes, for example, has demonstrated that religious communes were four times more likely to outlast their secular counterparts, and that the most successful communes had the strictest entrance rules (Sosis 2000; see also Sosis and Bressler 2003). A study conducted in contemporary Israeli kibbutzim using an economic game gave support to the hypothesis that the frequency of ritual participation was positively correlated

---

[9] Pyysiäinen, oral communication. For an insightful discussion and an application of evolutionary approaches to cooperation to historical materials (Finnish early nineteenth-century revival movements), see Heimola 2012.

[10] A distinction between proximate and ultimate causation has been highly influential in biology and evolutionary studies since the publication of Ernst Mayr's classic article (1961). A proximate cause is an immediate, mechanical influence on a trait: say, the influence of a day's length on a bird's brain. Ultimate causes relate to natural selection; they explain in evolutionary terms why an organism has one trait rather than another. More recently, however, this dichotomy has been relativized and more nuanced theories of causation have been advanced in biology. See, for example, Laland et al. 2011 (I am grateful to Vojtěch Kaše for pointing out this article to me). More complex theories have been developed, for example, by niche constructionists, who argue that the environmental alterations caused by an organism are as important to evolution as natural selection. The signalling approach concurs well with niche construction theory; see Bulbulia and Sosis 2011.

with levels of generosity (Sosis and Ruffle 2003, 2004). Similar results have been achieved in studies outside Israel, for example in Brazil (Soler 2008), New Zealand (Bulbulia and Mahoney 2008), and Mauritius (Xygalatas et al. 2013). Importantly, most of the data used for testing Commitment Signalling have been derived from small-scale religious or secular groups.

Commitment Signalling theorists have not always been quite specific as to whether the theory should be understood as a theory of religion or as a tool for analysing specifically ritual behaviour. This ambivalence may be due in part to the fact that behavioural ecologists are interested in religious beliefs only to the extent that they affect behavioural patterns (Sosis and Bulbulia 2011: 348). This approach has led to some conundrums in the application of the theory, also noted by signalling theorists themselves. The empirical studies mentioned above, for example, have produced puzzling results, which cannot be explained without taking religious beliefs into account: why, for example, do religious communes with costly rituals outlast secular ones which impose similarly costly demands on their members? On the other hand, Sosis has also sought to integrate beliefs in supernatural agents into the theory, as 'proximate mechanisms that facilitate the efficient functioning of religious signals' (Sosis 2006).

For our purposes, Commitment Signalling is best used as a middle-range theory of ritual or religious practices (cf. section 2.5 above); not as a general theory of religion, that would explain, for example, why religious phenomena are pancultural or why religions incorporate so many similarities across time and place (for a critique from this point of view, see Murray and Moore 2009). It may not even work as a general model of ritualized behaviour, since many costly displays are not ritualized; furthermore, even if such ritualization did occur with sufficient frequency, the theory does not explain *why* such behaviours are ritualized (Boyer and Liénard 2006: 640). Neither is it a very good tool for defining 'ritual', in contrast to some other theories of ritual used in this book. Moreover, the word 'costly', central for the original formulations of the theory, may be open to misunderstandings, since many rituals do not involve extravagant sacrifice or investment. One can, however, safely argue that religious rituals offer rich opportunities for costly signalling. Moreover, religious behaviours often entail at least minimal costs, such as time, energy and material costs, as well as physical and psychological ones (cf. Sosis and Alcorta 2003: 264).

The question raised by signalling theorists is why election has favoured such seemingly counterproductive behaviour. Taking a cue from biological signalling theory, in particular from the so-called Handicap Principle advanced by Amotz Zahavi (Zahavi and Zahavi 1997), they suggest that costly rituals are adaptive because they can function as reliable signals for cooperation. The Handicap Principle suggests that evolution has sometimes favoured signalling which is strikingly costly for animals (e.g. the energetic jumping, 'stotting', of Thomson's gazelles in the presence of predators). A costly trait signals that the organism is fit enough to thrive despite having to bear the cost; in other words, the trait is an honest, hard-to-fake signal. In the case of human behaviour, signalling theorists argue that the adaptive benefit of human costly rituals is that they promote cooperation by engaging practitioners in behaviour that is 'too-costly-to-fake'—just as a gazelle's stotting is a hard-to-fake signal of the strength of that particular individual. To operate as an honest signal and to overcome the problem of free-riders, religious practices must be difficult to fake.

This insight can be compared to Rappaport's idea of indexical ritual signals. As we saw above, Rappaport argued that by engaging in ritual behaviour people send self-referential, that is indexical messages—a form of communication that human rituals share with non-human ritual behaviour. For Rappaport, an indexical ritual sign means above all that 'the sign brings the state of affairs into being ... and having brought it into being cannot help but indicate it' (Rappaport 1999: 108). Combined with the canonical order—Rappaport's term for the meaning of ritual transcending the physical and social states of the performers—indexical messages bring about 'the first of ritual's fundamental offices', the acceptance of the moral values (or the like) encoded in the ritual. It remains somewhat unclear how Rappaport defines 'indexical' in relation to self-referential messages,[11] but for our purposes here it is useful to distinguish between 'impossible-to-fake' indices and 'hard-to-fake' signals of commitment (Sosis 2006: 71–2). From the perspective of cooperation, successful ritual signalling is often of the latter kind, difficult but not impossible to fake. This is particularly true of emotions as costly signals, an issue to which I return in a moment.

---

[11] In his 1979: 181, Rappaport seems to suggest that he is not using 'indexical' in the strict sense of Peirce's communication theory.

## Ritual and Cooperation

One final comment is in order. Adopting a commitment signal perspective on ritual does not mean that the potential cooperat benefits of ritual should be seen as the only factor contributing to t evolution of religious rituals and behaviours. While cooperative sig nalling has received much attention in recent years, evolutionary scientists have focused on other benefits as well, such as reproductive control (Boster et al. 1998), health and stress (Sosis and Handwerker 2011), and the manipulative use of signals (Cronk 1994). It should also not go unnoticed that Rappaport's classic analysis of the ecological significance of Maring *kaiko* ceremonies was an important pioneering work for evolutionary and ecological studies (Rappaport 1984; for further studies applying evolutionary approaches to religion, see Sosis and Alcorta 2003).

Commitment Signalling is an established theory, developed by evolutionary anthropologists to analyse and predict how religious practices motivate cooperation. It is not designed to work as a comprehensive theory of religion, or even as a general model of ritualization which would explain why cooperative signals often take ritualized forms. It is best considered as a middle-range theory which sheds light on the social dynamics of small-scale communities, including early Christian groups.

### 5.4 PAULINE CHRISTIANITY AS A TEST CASE

In the light of the general design of the theory, Commitment Signalling would seem a potentially useful tool for analysing the social dynamics of the earliest Christian groups: those small assemblies that gathered in private houses or other meeting places available to them in a few Graeco-Roman cities during the first decades of the Christian movement.[12] The closest (almost first-hand) information

---

[12] Edward Adams (2013) has provided some important evidence against the usual consensus that the early Christians met in houses (villas) offered by wealthy members of the movement. For the meeting places of the Pauline groups there are indeed other plausible options, such as workshop dwellings and rented dining rooms. Moreover, 1 Cor. 11:22 ('Do you not have homes to eat and drink in?') and 34 might be taken to suggest other venues than a private house as the meeting place of the Corinthian Christians (the rhetorical questions would have been less persuasive if some of the Corinthians were in fact eating in their own homes). This does not mean that private

... gatherings comes from the undisputed letters ... been the subject of intensive study by scholars ... social life and formation of early Christians ... Meeks 1983; Ascough 1998; Still and Horrell 2009). ... correspondence, in particular, may be seen as pro-... important glimpses of Christian gatherings in the city ... (Horrell 1996; Horrell and Adams 2004; Cameron and ... 11).

... may thus pose the question of the nature of cooperative ...ding in the Pauline groups, insofar as it can be inferred from ... letters of Paul. What was the level of costly signalling in the ...ssemblies that he addressed? How did ritual practices performed among Pauline Christians facilitate cooperative behaviour and group solidarity—if indeed they did? Any attempt to answer these questions, however, faces severe challenges.

One obvious problem is the paucity of the data from which we can draw inferences concerning the social and ritual life of Pauline groups. The handful of authentic letters addressed to the small and diverse social formations that we are accustomed to calling Pauline 'communities' or 'churches' hardly resemble the ethnographies drawn on by ritual scholars, or the kind of historical data used by Sosis and Bressler in their analysis of nineteenth-century utopian communes (Sosis and Bressler 2003). The latter researchers drew up a questionnaire aimed at collecting behavioural data on the known utopian communities of the period from a relatively large set of mostly secondary sources (thirty-seven books). The survey covered a wide range of topics, including consumption, material possessions, membership, dress, communal activities, rituals and taboos, marriage, sexual relations, family, social control, finances, and so on. Sufficient data for drawing relevant conclusions were found for eighty-three of the 200 communes in the original dataset.

Researchers applying evolutionary theories to cultural phenomena typically use quantitative methods to statistically evaluate the hypotheses they posit (Mesoudi 2011). Such an analysis would be quite difficult for New Testament specialists who wish to collect data about Paul's assemblies. While quantitative analysis is a potentially

homes were not among the places where early Christians met more generally. For alternative meeting places, see also Horrell 2004.

helpful method for the study of early Christianity,[13] the scanty, sporadic, and definitely one-sided evidence for the ritual life reflected in Paul's letters does not offer sufficient data for *testing* Commitment Signalling against it. This, however, does not mean that Commitment Signalling Theory is useless for an analysis of Pauline Christianity, or that no relevant connection can be established between it and the historical material in question. Theories can be helpful in a number of ways. We may, for example, ask whether Commitment Signalling can enrich the social-scientific interpretation of Pauline rituals, and whether the mechanisms of social dynamics suggested by signalling theorists might shed some light on the issues tackled by New Testament scholars.

The focus on Pauline 'communities' also encounters a challenge related to our modern imagination of the social formations reflected in Paul's letters. Stanley Stowers (2011b) has put this problem sharply in his provocative analysis of Paul and the Corinthians. Stowers argues that our scholarly assumptions with regard to Pauline Christianity have been dominated by 'academic Christian theological modernism', which takes religion as a matter of right and wrong beliefs and assumes that 'people consciously adopt beliefs and are conscious of their beliefs/ positions as beliefs/positions'. In the modernist theological imagination, 'community' implies 'the idea of the highly integrated social group based on a common ethos, practices and beliefs'. Stowers hence asserts that '[t]he concept of community and communities has been enormously constraining for scholarship on ancient Christianity. Community is a highly ideal and ideological concept' (2011b: 108).

More specifically, Stowers offers the following summary concerning the social formations in Corinth:

> In my view two things are very clear from the evidence of the Corinthian letters: first, Paul very much wanted the people to whom he wrote to be a community, and held a theory saying that God had miraculously made them into a community 'in Christ'; second, the Corinthians never did sociologically form a community and only partly and differentially

---

[13] See, for example, The Database of Religious History (DRH), a project of Cultural Evolution of Religion Research Consortium (CERC) at the University of British Columbia, directed by Edward Slingerland. This 'big history' project collects data from six priority areas (the Indus Valley; Latium; Egypt; the Mayan Lowlands of Mesoamerica; and Hawai'i) and includes materials from early Christianity. See <http://www.religiondatabase.arts.ubc.ca/> (accessed 11 June 2015).

shared Paul's interests and formation. In my estimation, it is very unlikely that 'the Corinthians' ever had any more social organization than households that may have had previous ties with other households, and after Paul, a roughly shared knowledge that Paul wanted them to be an *ekklēsia* in Christ and that he kept telling them that God had transformed them into one. (Stowers 2011b: 109)

Stowers' considerations should make us cautious about assuming a priori too much social cohesion and organization in the groups of people Paul is addressing in his letters. The social formations in Corinth somehow connected with Paul's activity should not be understood as similar to the utopian communes studied by Sosis, or to what the term 'religious community' generally implies in modern usage. This is an important reminder, since the words commonly used by scholars to designate Paul's addressees—'church', 'congregation', 'community'—are all theologically and ideologically loaded, easily contributing to anachronistic interpretations ('assembly' may be somewhat less loaded; hence my preference for it). For the purposes of the present analysis, however, the crucial question is whether Paul's letters, despite their highly idealistic and rhetorical language, allow us to draw conclusions as to cooperative signalling in Corinth or in the Pauline assemblies in general. As Stowers writes, 'community or even groupness more broadly is something to be demonstrated, not assumed' (2011b: 110). Our tacit assumptions concerning the Pauline 'communities' should, therefore, be translated into research questions.[14]

## 5.5 COOPERATIVE SIGNALLING IN THE PAULINE ASSEMBLIES

To begin from a broader perspective, commitment or costly signalling is ubiquitous in many New Testament texts and related documents. In the Synoptic Gospels and the *Gospel of Thomas*, for example,

---

[14] There are also obvious problems in using the designation 'Pauline' to describe the groups of which we have some knowledge through the letters of Paul; see Horrell 2008. I deploy the term 'Pauline' here in a loose sense, referring to the evidence of social life gleaned from the letters, without assuming that there were no significant differences between the groups or that Paul had similar control over all the groups to whom he writes.

abandoning one's family and property for the sake of Jesus is a frequent theme (Uro 2012). Breaking with one's natural family ties and home, and accepting the itinerant lifestyle of Jesus and his followers, would certainly look like honest signals of commitment.[15] Ideas of persecution and martyrdom also abound in early Christian writings, in fact constituting one of the basic elements of Christian mythmaking (Mack 2001). Similarly, the metaphor of sacrifice, readily resonating with costly signalling, continued to be central in early Christian discourse, even when the sacrificial cult was no longer practised (Eberhart 2011). Demands for asceticism increase in early Christian sources toward the second century CE (Uro 1998).

Nor is it difficult to find references to commitment signalling in the letters of Paul. To take one letter, Philippians, as an example, we read about Paul's imprisonment for Christ (1:13); his and the congregation's constant prayers (1:3; 2:19); giving up one's self-interest for the welfare of others (2:4); Christ's *kenosis* (2: 5–11); sacrificing one's life (2:17); unselfishly serving the gospel (2:22); risking one's life (2:30); Paul being circumcised, blameless under the law (3:5–6), losing everything for the Lord's sake (3:8); pressing on toward the goal like an athlete (3:14); suffering want for the sake of the gospel (4:11–14); and the Philippians giving material help to Paul (4:15–20). The letters to the Corinthians, especially Second Corinthians, reveal a similar emphasis on the performing of costly displays by Paul and his addressees, for the sake of Christ and the gospel.[16]

However, if we try to estimate the level of commitment signalling in the Pauline assemblies in terms of *concrete practices* demanded of the people Paul is addressing, the information available suggests greater caution in drawing conclusions as to costly practices than the general commitment-signalling ethos implied in the Pauline letters. To be sure, the social cohesion of the assemblies is of great concern to Paul.[17] As has been elaborated by commentators, Paul employs the ancient rhetoric of concord and 'body politics' to foster unity among his addressees (for Paul's rhetoric in First Corinthians, see M. M. Mitchell 1991 and D. B. Martin 1995). On a translocal level,

---

[15] E.g. Mark 10:29–30; Q 9:58–60; 10:4–7; 14:26; see also *Gos. Thom.* 16; 55; 79; 86; 99; 101; 105.

[16] See 1 Cor. 4:12; 7:5; 9:15–23; 10:24, 33; 13:1; 16:1–2; 2 Cor. 1:4–11; 4:2–18; 5:15; 6:4–10; 8–9; 11:16–33; 12:10; 13:4.

[17] See e.g. 1 Cor. 1:10, 12:13–27; 2 Cor. 13:11; Phil. 2:2; Rom. 12:16.

Paul works hard to organize a collection for the 'poor' in Jerusalem as a sign of inter-group solidarity,[18] although we do not know how successful he eventually was in achieving this aim (Wedderburn 2002). The general impression we gain from reading Paul, however, is that he did not attempt to increase internal cohesion and solidarity by means of excessive and costly demands. On many issues he is modest rather than strict; compare, for example, Paul's interpretation of Jesus' teaching on divorce (1 Cor. 7: 11–16; cf. Q16:18), his somewhat liberal attitude toward eating idol meat (1 Cor. 10:25, but compare 1 Cor. 8:10) and his discussion of sexual abstinence (1 Cor. 7:1–7). Significantly, Paul is very determined that the non-Jewish members of his assemblies not receive circumcision or other symbolic markers of Jewish ethnicity (Gal. 5:1–12).[19] It is difficult to see Paul's teaching as being laden with particularly costly demands. As has been observed by a number of scholars, Paul's attitude toward Christians' participation in the economic and social life of the society at large is more lenient than that found in some other early Christian writings, most notably in Revelation (for example, Räisänen 2001: 141–89; for the issue of idol meat, see Acts 15:20, 28–29; *Did.* 6.3).

This general overview of commitment signalling in Paul is somewhat at odds with many analyses by scholars who have used socialscientific approaches to study the ritual life of Pauline Christians. Wayne Meeks' groundbreaking chapter on ritual in *The First Urban Christians* is typical in that regard (1983: 140–63). Meeks divides the material into three categories: 'minor', 'major', and 'unknown and controverted' rituals. Major rituals constitute, not surprisingly, baptism and 'the Lord's Supper'. Minor rituals include the variegated and fluid ritualized actions for which Paul's letters give some clues, such as 'coming together'(regular meetings), music and hymns, blessings, reading of scriptures, prayer, glossolalia, and the 'holy kiss'. Finally, under the last rubric, Meeks briefly discusses practices related to death and marriage as well as calendrical rites, on which we have very little evidence for Pauline Christians. Notably, he mentions the

---

[18] See Gal. 2:10; 1 Cor. 16:1–4; 2 Cor. 8–9; Rom. 15:22–29.
[19] Circumcision seems to have been a universal practice for male proselytes in Second Temple Judaism. Its obvious costliness explains why converts were more often women and why there developed a group of adherents to Jewish communities, 'Godfearers', who adopted Jewish observances without taking the full step of circumcision and complete conversion. See Grabbe 2000: 295–6.

vicarious 'baptism for the dead' practised by some Corinthians (1 Cor. 15:29) as being 'mystifying to us' (1983: 162).[20]

Meeks' 'moderate functionalist' and eclectic approach (1983: 6–7) emphasizes that the major and minor ritual complexes in the Pauline assemblies foster social cohesion and togetherness. The Lord's Supper, in particular, is a 'ritual of solidarity'. According to Meeks, Paul uses the symbolism of the Supper ritual 'to enhance the internal coherence, unity, and equality of the Christian group' as well as 'to protect its boundaries vis-à-vis other kinds of cultic association' (1983: 160). It is not difficult to find similar interpretations in subsequent analyses of Pauline rituals. Margaret MacDonald, for example, describing the institutionalization of the Pauline churches, notes that the rituals of the Pauline Christians are 'at the heart of the process of community-building' and 'stimulate group solidarity' (MacDonald 1988: 61–71, esp. 65). Ekkehard and Wolfgang Stegemann similarly contend that the Pauline rituals 'reinforce in a prominent way the specific, somehow divinely ordained, cohesion of the Christ-confessing group, which is defined metaphorically in the image of one "body" of many believers in Christ' (Stegemann and Stegemann 1999: 283; for a survey of literature on ritual after Meeks, see L. J. Lawrence 2009).[21]

Moreover, Meeks' analysis relies heavily on Victor Turner's ideas of *communitas* and liminality. According to Turner's influential theory of ritual process, societies oscillate between well-defined and ordered social strata (structure) on the one hand and ambiguous and egalitarian social movements on the other (V. Turner 1969). Turner extended Van Gennep's structural analysis of rites of passage (van Gennep 1960), according to which the transition from one social identity to another requires a liminal stage (from Lat.

---

[20] Meeks' analysis of the diverse practices in the Pauline assemblies has been charged with lacking 'conceptual specificity'. Bruce Malina (1985), for example, asks why all aspects of Christian practice that foster solidarity in a variety of contexts are not also classified as rituals. Moreover, Meeks' distinction between 'major', 'minor', and 'unknown/ controverted' rituals has been criticized as obscuring rather than illuminating the analysis (DeMaris 2008: 59–60). Although this criticism is relevant to a general analysis of Pauline rituals, the Commitment Signalling perspective does not have much to offer with respect to such questions as how 'ritual' should be defined in the letters of Paul, or what categories they should be divided into.

[21] Cf. also Turley 2013, which similarly describes Pauline ritual life in rather idealized terms. Turley's analysis nevertheless, relying heuristically on Rappaport, rightly emphasizes both the expressive and generative nature of ritual.

*limen*, threshold), creating an egalitarian spirit of *communitas*. Turner suggests that the oscillation between structure and anti-structure can produce a state of what he calls 'permanent liminality'. This form of liminality can be observed in groups which seek to maintain conditions for the realization of *communitas* indefinitely. Turner obviously thinks that the rituals practised in such a group somehow support the social processes of permanent liminality (or vice versa), although he does not explain how exactly this takes place.

Meeks follows Turner in arguing that the many elements of early Christian/Pauline baptism (nudity, symbolic death, rebirth as a child, abolition of distinctions of role and status) are all typical of the transitional or liminal phase of initiation. Permanent liminality is at least ideally present, since '[the community] sees itself, as a whole, distinct from the world', although it also suffers from 'some tension between the mode of socialization, which opposes normal structures of the macrosociety, and the old structures' (Meeks 1983: 157). In his analysis of Pauline Christianity, Meeks points out that 'the dialectic between "structure and anti-structure" that Turner describes appears again and again in the tensions addressed by the Pauline letters' (for example in the 'status inconsistency' experienced by Pauline Christians; see Meeks 1983: 51–73, 89). Turner's processual approach and terminology have been influential in subsequent analyses of Pauline rituals (see, for example, Wedderburn 1987; Taussig 2009), most prominently in the study by Christian Strecker (1999), for whom Turner's concept of the liminal phase provides a key not only to Pauline ritual practice but to the entire thought world of Paul that he calls 'transformation theology' (Transformationstheologie).

Commitment Signalling offers a means for the critical evaluation of scholarly interpretations and explanations of Pauline rituals, without shifting our focus from the question of how ritual facilitates social life and enhances cooperation. It is true that many former approaches to Pauline rituals based on functionalist theories and Turner's idea of *communitas* are 'susceptible to imprecise and anachronistic redescriptions' (Turley 2013: 12). The idea of community, involving social cohesion, solidarity, togetherness and so on, is simply assumed, without truly testing it in the light of the available evidence (cf. Stowers' criticism cited in section 5.4). Moreover, it is not clear how Turner's tripartite structure applies to Pauline rituals (for example to baptism; see DeMaris 2008: 19–20) or how the assumed liminality experienced in rituals is connected to social processes.[22] On the other hand, generations of social scientists and ritual theorists have suggested, with Durkheim, that collective rituals promote cooperation and play an essential role in the formation of the society or community. Earlier functionalist explanations were perhaps not very good, or in fact explanations at all in the proper sense of the word; but more recent work, based on articulated theories and/or evolutionary theory, gives cause not to reject the general logic of functionalism, at least as one perspective on ritual behaviour. The 'effervescence' generated by ritual performance is still a relevant topic for researchers applying controlled scientific measures (Bulbulia and Reddish 2013).

How much 'groupness', then, do we find in the Pauline evidence if we examine it from the perspective of Commitment Signalling? We may ask whether the generally low level of costly signalling observed above leads to a view similar to that suggested by Stowers on the Corinthians: that the latter never sociologically formed a 'community', beyond the loose network of households that held 'a roughly shared knowledge that Paul wanted them to be an *ekklēsia* in Christ' (Stowers 2011b: 109; see the full quotation towards the end of section 5.4). There is an offshoot of the signalling approach that can cast further light on the question: the discussion of emotional rituals as honest signals.

## 5.6 HIGH-AROUSAL RITUALS IN CORINTH

Meeks' description of the communal meal held by Paul's addressees as a 'ritual of solidarity' has prevailed in subsequent scholarship, and has gained further support from our deepened understanding of the banquet as a central social institution in the Graeco-Roman world (Klinghardt 1996; D. E. Smith 2003; Taussig 2009). While meals in the Pauline assemblies were real meals, providing nourishment for the participants (cf. 1 Cor. 11:22), they were also significantly—or even primarily—about social bonding, about drawing boundaries and constructing identities. In that regard, early Christian meals were in

---

[22] In his later career, Turner himself turned from the analysis of social processes toward exploring ritual as performance and social drama. See e.g. V. Turner 1988.

general no different from the dining practices in other associations and clubs in the Graeco-Roman world (Harland 2009).

It is not easy, however, to determine in more concrete terms how the meal itself promoted cooperation and social cohesion, at least beyond what happened in other social contexts in Paul's society. It is obvious that for Paul himself partaking of 'one bread' and of the 'table of the Lord' (1 Cor. 10:17, 21) was a key symbol of unity, the *ekklēsia* being one social body in Christ. We can conjecture as to practices of sharing food at meals; it is possible, for example, that well-to-do members shared their food with poorer ones (Alikin 2010: 104) or that each member brought his or her own food-basket, albeit not necessarily of equal size and quality (Lampe 1994). Whatever dining protocol the Corinthians followed, Paul's critical comments on their practice show that, against his best intentions, eating caused disunity and division rather than fostering harmony (1 Cor. 11:27-33; cf. also Gal. 2:11-14). While there is no reason to contest 'the power of the banquet to create bonds' in general (D. E. Smith 2003: 200), it is difficult to see how exactly these eating practices worked as honest signals, promoting trust and social cohesion in Corinth. Paul's discussion in First Corinthians gives an impression of clashes and tensions between different understandings of the Lord's Supper, rather than of a celebration of unity and mutual love.

If we look for cooperative cues in the Corinthian assembly, the best candidates are the other activities described by Paul in 1 Cor. 11-14 aside from the meal proper (*deipnon*), namely music and spiritual gifts, such as prophecy and speaking in tongues. It is now commonly assumed that such ritual activities took place in the *symposium* part of the dinner party, dedicated in antiquity to entertainment, conversation, and religious actions (see D. E. Smith 2003 and note 1 above). Paul's discussion of the assembly's activities clearly indicates that everyone was free to take part in them. The members are described as bringing contributions to the group's common affairs: 'When you come together, each one has a hymn, a lesson, a revelation, a tongue, or an interpretation' (1 Cor. 14:26). We can thus assume that the *symposium* part of the gathering was a time especially suitable for cooperative signalling. In this respect, it is noteworthy that Stowers, who argues—not, as we have seen, without grounds—for a rather low level of 'groupness' among the Corinthians, does not place much emphasis on these emotional rituals. In the same volume that contains Stowers' essay, Jonathan Z. Smith downplays the usual interpretation of tongue-speaking among the Corinthians as ecstatic and non-linguistic utterance, suggesting that Paul misunderstood the Corinthians' 'xenoglossia'—their ceremonial communication with ancestral spirits in their native languages—and confused it with the Delphic model of ecstatic speech (J. Z. Smith 2011: 31; cf. Acts 2:4). Smith's reading would, however, mean that Paul's description of glossolalia was misleading in almost all respects. According to Paul, speaking in tongues is unintelligible without an interpreter (1 Cor 14:2–19); it sounds like the speech of a madman (14:23); moreover, Paul boasts that he himself is a greater tongue-speaker than any of the Corinthians (14:17).

Of the two forms of spiritual activity discussed by Paul in 1 Cor. 12–14, glossolalia and prophecy, the nature of the latter phenomenon has been subject to debate. While a few scholars have been eager to make a clear distinction between Christian (Corinthian) prophecy and that involving altered states of consciousness, comparable to the Graeco-Roman mantic oracles (for example, Grudem 1982), others have taken Paul's references to prophecy as evidence of religious ecstasy in Corinth. Shantz, for example, argues that 'privileging of dissociation trance seems to have been an active part of prophetic activity within the major cultures of the Mediterranean', and contends that the Pauline data fit well into that context (Shantz 2009, esp. 189). She sees Corinthian prophecy as a form of spirit possession, and draws on Michael Winkelman's cross-cultural category of mediumship (Winkelman 2000). Applying a different approach to religious experience, Czachesz concludes that prophecy, glossolalia, and other spiritual activities in Corinth are witness to what he calls 'resonant religious experience', typically represented by music, synchrony, dance, and other emotionally contagious activities (Czachesz 2012a). Paul's comments on the Corinthian situation, in contrast, display a different style of religious experience, described as 'volitional'; it is characterized by an emphasis on learning, symbolic interpretation, transmission of religious texts, etc.,[23] and is generated by a different pattern of neural activity from the 'resonant' experience (see also section 4.4, note 19).

---

[23] Similarly, Stowers (2011b: 141) argues that Paul didn't much like the rituals practised by a number of Corinthians because they did not 'fit Paul's intellectual mode'. For a different reading of Paul's attitude toward ecstatic religiosity, see Shantz 2009: 194–7.

However we see Paul's own position on ecstasy, the evidence in First Corinthians is suggestive of high-arousal ritual activities in the Corinthian assembly. Paul's instructions that prophets should not speak simultaneously in the meeting, and that 'the spirits of the prophets are under the control of the prophets' (1 Cor. 14:29–33) indicates that the prophets lacked conscious control while they were prophesying. The implied participation in prophecy as a collective ritual is best understood as being induced by what the psychologists call 'emotion sharing' or 'emotional contagion' (Czachesz 2012a: 82; Harmon-Jones and Winkielman 2007: 250–56). The fact that some Corinthian women prophesied with their heads uncovered (1 Cor. 11:2–15) is also informative for our understanding of Corinthian prophecy. Although it is difficult to say what exactly is Paul's concern and argument in the section—for example, whether he is referring to women prophesying unveiled or with their hair loose—it seems clear that the Corinthian practice was somehow inappropriate for Paul, and that he tried to use his intellectual power to redirect their behaviour.[24] Such behaviour could thus be emotionally stimulating and also costly, insofar as it also has to do with the issue of women's honour. Read together with Paul's warning about disorder in the assembly, Paul's discussion in 11:2–15 seems to speak for the view that prophecy involved both emotional arousal and synchrony.

Glossolalia is usually taken as the most striking evidence of imagistic practices in Corinth. Paul's several references to it in 1 Cor. 12–14 indicate that it was a central and highly valued practice among the Corinthians. Shantz sees it as the 'predominant form of spirit possession' in Corinth (2009: 157). It is indeed likely that the Corinthians saw in glossolalia the main manifestation of the *pneuma* Paul had taught they were to receive in baptism and share 'in Christ'.

There has been a considerable body of anthropological research on modern tongue speaking. The findings show that many of the basic features of glossolalia are cross-culturally similar (the sounds of tongue speaking, for example, do not necessarily reflect the speaker's language) and that the phenomenon can be reasonably compared with other traditional forms of non-linguistic speech uttered by religious specialists or members of secret associations in traditional societies (for a survey of this research, see F. D. Goodman 2005). It is

---

[24] For the sexual connotations of unveiling in antiquity, see D. B. Martin 1995: 233–9.

difficult, however, to find comparative examples for glossolalia in the Graeco-Roman culture of Paul (Forbes 1995), lending support to the view that, at least in the form described in First Corinthians, it is a Christian ritual innovation. The references to tongue speaking in the Acts of the Apostles, although misconceived by Luke as xenoglossia in Acts 2:4 (cf. 10:46; 19:6), may be based on recollection of the role it once played in some other early Christian groups as well (cf. Esler 1994: 37–51).

There has been considerable discussion concerning the role of emotions and high-arousal rituals as honest signals, facilitating group cohesion and cooperation. Many signalling theorists have argued that emotions can function as honest signals and thus enhance cooperation. One can lie with words, but producing tears is harder. The explanation behind such an assumption is that emotions are generated by the limbic structures of the brain, which are out of conscious control and are thus difficult to 'fake' (Sosis 2006; Levenson 2003). Bulbulia lists five properties of emotions that support their role as reliable signals: emotions index felt reality, integrate perception to motivation, are clearly recognizable, speak truly, and can be used to manipulate audiences (Bulbulia 2013: 77–78; see also Alcorta and Sosis 2005; Emmons and McNamara 2006). It can of course be argued that emotional contagion may make emotions less reliable as signs of a deeper commitment, but then again this psychological mechanism seems to speak in favour of a general human inclination to respond to a performance of emotional rituals with synchrony. Emotional states, however, wear off relatively quickly, and may thus be less stable as indications of commitment than some more steady symbolic markers (food taboos, tattoos, cognitively costly practices).

As shown by the above-mentioned examples from the anthropological literature, the idea that synchronous activity or collective effervescence produce emotions that weaken the psychological boundaries between the self and the group is not new. More recent empirical research has sought to provide support for this suggestion, using quantitative measures and also searching for a causal link between synchrony and cooperation. Note, for example:

- Cooperative effects have been found among pairs of individuals who mimic each other (van Baaren et al. 2003).
- Synchrony promotes generalized prosociality (Reddish et al. 2014; van Baaren et al. 2004).

152    *Ritual and Christian Beginnings*

- An investigation of the physiological effects of a highly arousing Spanish firewalking ritual demonstrates that the ritual evokes synchronized arousal over time between active participants and bystanders (Konvalinka et al. 2011; for a comprehensive account of a Greek firewalking ritual, see Xygalatas 2013).
- Extreme rituals increase cooperation (Xygalatas et al. 2013).
- The role of music, singing, dance, and rhythmic movement in evoking congruent emotions and generating cooperation is well documented (Anshel and Kipper 1988; McNeill 1995; Alcorta and Sosis 2005; Weimer 2015).
- Some studies suggest that synchronous actions need not entail 'muscular bonding' (cf. McNeill 1995), or even positive emotions, to foster cooperation (Wiltermuth and Heath 2009).

The analysis of the Pauline evidence, especially that in 1 Cor. 11–14, together with the research on synchrony and emotions, seem to support the view that prophecy and glossolalia, along with other emotional rituals in the Pauline assemblies, functioned as cooperative signals. Prophecy and glossolalia may be seen as rituals that evoked synchronized arousal, as described in Paul's comments on the Corinthian practice. The empirical research cited above allows the conjecture that such synchrony led those involved in the behaviour to cooperate with the other group members (it may even have increased prosocial actions toward outsiders; Reddish et al. 2014). While prophecy and glossolalia can hardly be characterized as extreme rituals in comparison to such practices as firewalking, they are nevertheless arousing and emotionally salient. Glossolalia, possibly an early Christian ritual innovation, is a particularly striking example of a ritual that evokes synchronized arousal. Music, prayer, and healing, as well as other spiritual gifts, provide further evidence in the same direction: cooperative signalling did take place in Corinth after all.

## 5.7 IDEALISTIC RHETORIC VS. SOCIAL REALITY

Theories focusing on the cooperative benefits of ritual provide a different analytical perspective on early Christian rituals from the 'action paradigm' discussed in previous chapters. Commitment Signalling in particular offers a way to evaluate earlier analyses, which often assumed quite anachronistically that the Pauline assemblies functioned as 'churches' or cohesive 'communities'. The analysis presented in this chapter concurs with Stowers' contention: that social cohesion or 'groupness' should not be taken as a point of departure, but rather as a research question, to be tested critically in the light of the evidence available to us. It is crucial to draw an analytical distinction between Paul's idealistic rhetoric and the social reality of the assemblies he addressed. Commitment Signalling is helpful because it focuses on people's actual behaviour in a specific ecological context. Paul's many comments on the behaviour of the Corinthians, when analysed from the perspective of signalling, offer some interesting insights.

The above analysis, however, does not suggest quite as low a level of social formation in Corinth as does that of Stowers. The recent empirical research on synchrony and emotional rituals reveals that emotions can function as honest signals, generating prosocial behaviour. Even minimal synchronic bodily movements can produce measurable effects on cooperation. The role of arousing rituals and synchrony should not thus be underestimated in the account of ritual life in Corinth, and in the earliest Christian groups more generally. How far should we move from the almost zero position of Stowers toward more cohesive social formations? Czachesz (2012a) argues that the 'resonant religiosity' in Corinth, manifested in glossolalia and other synchronic rituals, entailed a social dynamic without clear leadership, power structures, or consistent belief systems. That is undoubtedly true. But it is also important to remember that the Corinthian assembly did survive, as demonstrated, for example, by First Clement—even if not on its own but as part of the emerging network of early Christian groups. Commitment Signalling cannot account for the whole story, but may provide a partial explanation for the social dynamic and survival of early Christian groups.

# 6

## 'Baptizing... and Teaching'

### Ritual and Religious Knowledge

How do rituals generate religious knowledge? How do rituals enhance religious beliefs and cognition? How do rituals function as instruments of teaching and transmission? My purpose in this chapter is to find answers to these questions, taking examples from early Christian baptismal practices.

Although ritual can be reasonably analysed as actions designed to produce effects or as signals fostering cooperation within a group, early Christianity also provides abundant examples of interactions between ritual practices and the transmission of religious knowledge. People invest meanings in rituals, which may generate verbal interpretations and traditions, while ritual itself often functions as an instrument of teaching and transmission. It is extremely difficult to imagine any culture of shared beliefs without its knowledge being sustained by ritual practices. The role of ritual in the transmission and consolidation of religious knowledge, the third perspective on ritual examined in this study, resonates with many classic and more recent themes in ritual theory, such as myth and ritual theory (Segal 1998), ritual symbolism and semiotics (V. Turner 1967; Kreinath 2008), and the relationship between ritual and belief (Harvey 2005; Pyysiäinen 2011b). The theme of ritual and religious knowledge also partly overlaps with the signalling perspective discussed in Chapter Five, since cooperative cues in religious communities include beliefs as well (Sosis 2006). The *coordinative* and *transmissive* components of human sociality are interrelated, but they can also be kept apart and analysed as different dimensions of ritual behaviour, as in this study. Human cultural life consists of these two components: people aim at coordinating their actions, which in turn requires a common cognitive ground facilitated by collectively known and hence transmitted cultural knowledge (Tomasello 2014). It is obvious that rituals serve an important function in this facilitation. For the biblical scholar, the latter aspect of ritual is relevant since transmission has been a key issue in the study of biblical texts and the cultural world of the Bible (Uro 2011b).

## 6.1 WHAT IS 'RELIGIOUS KNOWLEDGE'?

Before we can go into a more detailed discussion on the transmissive aspect of ritual in early Christianity, we need to define what 'religious knowledge' means in the present context. A simple answer to this question is that religious knowledge encompasses all aspects of knowledge, that is information stored in memory, that relate to counterintuitive agents (or the 'sacred', if that concept is preferred), for example myths, beliefs, and knowledge about religious institutions, norms, practices, etc. It is thus a very broad concept. However, some further elaboration is in order.

The issue of religious knowledge inevitably invokes the notoriously difficult question, what do we mean by 'religious' or 'religion'? The tentative description of religious knowledge offered above assumes the general approach applied in the Cognitive Science of Religion (CSR), where the analysis of counterintuitiveness plays an important role. To be sure, cognitive scholars generally understand religion as a family resemblance category and an academic construct, and no ready definition of the category is offered to start with (J. L. Barrett 2007; but compare Franek 2014). It is indeed unclear how to differentiate scientifically between religious and other cultural representations (McCauley and Cohen 2010). The qualifier 'religious' is used here because most of the early Christian themes discussed in this chapter fall under the traditional domain of Religious Studies, where the term 'religious knowledge' is widely used. The general expression *ritual knowledge*, however, is employed in this chapter as well.

Moreover, a broad definition of religious knowledge does not allow us to distinguish between different types of religious knowledge, for example between firm belief or faith, which evokes worship and deep commitment, and mental representations about supernatural concepts (ghosts, fictional characters, fairy tales, etc.), which evoke neither. In CSR, this is often called the 'Mickey Mouse problem' (Atran 2002: 13; cf. also J. L. Barrett 2008a; Gervais et al. 2011). I admit that the distinction between mental representations and belief-commitment is crucial to explaining certain important aspects of religious behaviour, for example, why some counterintuitive concepts evoke deep devotion, while others do not. Such questions, however, are not the focus of this chapter.

For the present analysis, more important than the distinction between belief and mental representation is the one between intuitive and reflective knowledge/thinking. The focus on the intuitive (or automatic) mental mechanisms producing or contributing to religious thinking has been a central interest in CSR, and perhaps also the most familiar aspect of the cognitive approach in general (see section 2.2 above). It should be noted that intuitive knowledge can refer either to innate processes that develop very early in childhood (such as panhuman expectations about ontological categories) or to the intuitive patterns of behaviour acquired later through practice and routinization (Pyysiäinen 2004a). Robert McCauley has used the expressions 'maturational naturalness' and 'practiced naturalness' to describe these different patterns of cognitive activity (McCauley 2011). McCauley and many other cognitive scholars of religion have emphasized the key role played by maturationally natural predilections or innate ('hard-wired') processes in the selection and distribution of religious traditions; it is obvious that these processes—along with reflective cognitive processes—contribute to the rise of conscious religious concepts in memory (note that real-life religious concepts are not simply intuitive *or* reflective; Pyysiäinen 2004a: 127, 136). However, the intuitive knowledge obtained through practice is also a relevant issue in the study of human religiosity in general and ritual behaviour in particular (Whitehouse 2004a). As will be argued in this chapter, rituals can generate and convey bodily knowledge that is not consciously reflected upon by participants. The intuitive knowledge generated by means of ritual practices should therefore be included in the concept of 'religious knowledge' examined in this chapter (cf. also section 3.5 above).

## 6.2 THREE COGNITIVE APPROACHES TO RITUAL KNOWLEDGE

Theorists of religion have advanced a host of approaches to account for how ritual and religious knowledge are interrelated. In this chapter, the discussion is limited to three cognitive themes:

- Rituals generate *embodied* knowledge.
- Rituals generate *common* (shared) knowledge.
- Rituals accommodate *extended* knowledge.

These themes, especially the first and the third, draw closely on a field of cognitive science known as *embodied cognition*. The field is not easy to describe precisely. Representatives of the embodiment movement have very different backgrounds in various fields and disciplines, including among others cognitive psychology, philosophy of mind, and linguistics, and the approaches applied and the topics discussed in embodied cognition are necessarily vast. For our purposes, the description given by Glenberg et al. in a 2013 review article is helpful,

> [T]he fundamental tenet of embodied cognition research is that thinking is not something that is divorced from the body; instead, thinking is an activity strongly influenced by the body and the brain interacting with the environment. To say it differently, how we think depends on the sorts of bodies we have. Furthermore, the reason why cognition depends on the body is becoming clear: Cognition exists to guide action. We perceive in order to act (and what we perceive depends on how we intend to act); we have emotions to guide action; and understanding even the most abstract cognitive processes (e.g. the self, language) is benefited by considering how they are grounded in action. This concern for action contrasts with standard cognitive psychology that, for the most part, considers action and the body as secondary to cognition. (Glenberg et al. 2013: 573; for a partially overlapping description, see Shapiro 2011: 4–5)

The last point in the quotation, the criticism of 'standard cognitive psychology' (or 'standard cognitive science'), is a commonplace in the embodied cognition literature. The identity of the movement is based, in part at least, on drawing boundaries against certain classic ideas in cognitive science, such as computational and representational theories of the mind. The latter theories are often associated with what has been referred to as the modularity of mind hypothesis (see also section 2.2).[1] From the point of view of the present analysis, such large issues in cognitive science or in the philosophical debate over consciousness need not be decisive, for two reasons. First, CSR—at least in the broad sense described in Chapter Two—is not committed to computationalism (see also Pyysiäinen 2001: 5–8); scholars of religion may be able to draw more eclectically on different models of the mind in developing theories of religious behaviour and transmission than actual cognitive scholars or philosophers of the mind. Second, in spite of their critique of the standard model, a number of representatives of embodied cognition recognize that many embodied approaches can ultimately be reconciled with the 'standard' models of cognitive science, and that the results achieved in the field of embodied cognition may well be complementary rather than competing (Chemero 2009: 16; Clark 2011: 219; see also Shapiro 2011). As argued earlier in this volume, theoretical pluralism is the best strategy in applying cognitive approaches in Biblical Studies or in the History of Religion (section 2.5); perhaps this is the case for various fields applying cognitive science approaches more generally.[2]

An important point in Glenberg and his collaborators' description is their definition of cognition as fundamentally grounded in bodily actions and in the body interacting with the environment. The relationship between thinking and bodily actions (and the environment) immediately evokes the question, what light does embodied cognition research shed on the relationship between religious knowledge and ritual? It is in fact surprising that embodied cognition theorists only seldom focus their analysis on ritual activities.[3] A few cognitive scholars of religion, however, have begun to think about the implications of embodied cognition research for the study of religion,

---

[1] A classic work laying a ground for the computational model and the modularity of mind is Fodor 1975. To put it simply, the 'computational model' of cognition means that the mind is literally a computer. The computational model also involves the idea that thinking is the manipulation of complex symbols, i.e. language-like activity—hence it assumes a representational model of cognition.

[2] Note that cognitive scientists have begun to entertain the possibility that there will be no unified approach to cognitive science (Dale 2008).

[3] It is telling that none of the indices of the following recent book-length introductions to embodied (situated) cognition contains the entry 'ritual' or related descriptors, R. A. Wilson 2004; Gallagher 2005; Gibbs 2005; Chemero 2009; Clark 2011; Shapiro 2011.

drawing inferences for ritual behaviour (most prominently Geertz 2010). I follow this track, asking how embodied cognition can contribute to understanding the role of ritual in the transmission of religious knowledge and how some of its insights might be integrated into ritual theory more generally.

### 6.3 RITUALS GENERATE EMBODIED KNOWLEDGE

Embodiment is obviously a central theme in Ritual Studies (Bell 1992: 94–117). Mary Douglas' ideas concerning the correlation between the physical body and the social one, entailing typologies of different kinds of societies, have been highly influential (Douglas 1973). Feminist scholars and scholars interested in gender have focused on 'women's lived experience', at the centre of which is the body and bodily practices (Bell 1992: 96; K. Davies 1997). Pierre Bourdieu's theory of practice, emphasizing the importance of the body and bodily practices in the social world, has been developed and applied to Ritual Studies by Bell. At the heart of Bell's approach to ritual are 'ritualized bodies', which both (re)produce and are (re)produced by the process of ritualization 'through the interaction of the body with a structuring and structured environment' (Bell 1992: 96). Although Bell's approach is in many respects opposed to theories relying on empirical-scientific research (see Bell 2005: 7849 and section 1.6 above), the theme of embodiment can be seen as a link, weak as it may yet be, creating a common ground between cultural and cognitive approaches.

A linguistic branch of embodied cognition emphasizes the key role played by the body in the emergence of metaphorical thinking and human conceptualization (Lakoff 1987; Lakoff and Johnson 2003 [1980]). Another version of the linguistic approach to embodied cognition focuses on conceptual blending, which is argued as being based on simple bodily experiences (Fauconnier and Turner 2002). Blending theory and other cognitive linguistic approaches have been applied by a number of biblical scholars, casting new light on the interpretation of ancient texts and on the interaction between texts and readers (Howe and Green 2014). In the analysis of ritual, a cognitive linguistic reading of biblical texts can be informative in determining the interrelation of language, experience, and ritual performance (Tappenden 2013).

In cognitive psychology, embodied cognition research has provided robust evidence that activity of the body affects cognition and that cognition (or experiences of the body) and bodily actions interact in a number of ways. The importance of action is a central theme in embodied cognition. For one thing, embodied cognition researchers criticize traditional models which consider perception to be independent or prior to action—which is what we often intuitively think is happening when we react to our environment. Rather, they argue, action should be considered an intricate part of perception (Glenberg et al. 2013: 576). While these claims were originally made in connection with the processing of sensory information, such as the visual system (see Shapiro 2011: 28–50), they have been extended to cognitive processes more generally. Glenberg et al. (2013: 576) even maintain that 'activity in the body and sensorimotor cortices of the brain not only contribute to cognition—that activity is cognition'. This may be an extreme statement; but it accurately reflects the ethos among embodied cognition researchers.

The emphasis on interaction between cognition and bodily actions assumes a reciprocal view of thinking about cognitive performance, a 'form of causality in which every part of a system is always present in each behaviour of that system' (Gibbs 2005: 281). Such a dynamic systems (connectionist) approach to cognition may be at odds with the modularity of the mind, that is, the theory according to which the mind is made up of genetically designed ('hard-wired'), independently functioning modules, such as those responsible for vision, motor actions, language, folk psychology, and intuitive physics (Fodor 1983).[4] Many cognitive scholars of religion have relied on modularity theory in their search for the (intuitive) cognitive systems that contribute to religious thinking and behaviour (for example, Sperber 1994; Boyer 2002; Boyer and Liénard 2006; Tremlin 2006: 56–64; McCauley 2011).[5]

---

[4] Evolutionary psychologists have developed a theory of mind that is sometimes called 'massive modularity'. They argue that the human mind is composed of numerous, perhaps hundreds of, specialized mental modules, each which evolved to respond to some distinct challenge in the ancestral environment (see e.g. Tooby and Cosmides 1992; for a recent review of the evolutionary psychological research program, see Confer et al. 2010). See also section 2.2 in this volume.

[5] It is worth noting, however, that cognitive scholars of religion do not strictly follow either the Fodorian concept of modularity (involving, among other things, informational encapsulation) or the evolutionary psychological hypothesis of massive modularity (see e.g. McCauley 2011: 44–61). For a less strict understanding of modularity, see H. C. Barrett and Kurzban 2006.

## Ritual and Religious Knowledge 161

While I have made use of these findings in this book, we should not commit ourselves to an epistemology that would prevent us from exploring the potential of embodiment research for the study of early Christian rituals.

Lawrence Barsalou and collaborators have conveniently collected experimental evidence for embodied theories of knowledge (Barsalou et al. 2005; see also Glenberg et al. 2013 and Gibbs 2005: 142–51, for embodiment and memory). I list a few examples that seem to be of particular pertinence for Ritual Studies:

- *Changes in the body produce changes in cognition*, e.g. blocking the use of the corrugator (frowning) muscle by the cosmetic use of Botox slows the processing of sentences describing angry and sad events but not happy events (Havas et al. 2010).
- *Embodied states affect social information processing.* In one type of research, participants have been induced to perform various head movements, for example either nodding their heads forward and backward or shaking their heads sideways, believing that they were trying to dislodge headphones from their heads (Tom et al. 1991). Nodding action led participants to later rate messages heard during the experiment as more compelling. Furthermore, upright posture affects participants' confidence in their task performance and their pride in it (Riskind and Gotay 1982; Stepper and Strack 1993).
- *Social information processing produces embodied states*, e.g. activating knowledge about a stereotype (such as the ELDERLY) generates associated bodily states. In one experience subjects were primed to words like grey, bingo, and Florida to activate the ELDERLY stereotype. Once the stereotype became active, people walked more slowly to the elevator when the experiment was over, compared to when no stereotype was activated (Bargh et al. 1996).
- *Memory is partly based on embodied activity* (Gibbs 2005: 142–4). Studies comparing novice and expert bartenders, for example, show that expert skill involves an adept interplay between internal and external factors which simplifies the task confronting the body in action (Beach 1988). According to one study, people recalled objects in a room on the basis of their physical proximity to each other as the observer moved through the room, rather than in terms of the semantic relatedness of

the objects (Gibbs 2005: 143). A large body of research has demonstrated that actually performing an action helps people to remember a description of the action at a later time (Zimmer 2001; Barsalou et al. 2005; Gibbs 2005: 148–51). People recall phrases that they have enacted better than they do phrases that they have watched other people enact (Hornstein and Mulligan 2001). In general, motor actions enhance both short-term and long-term memory (Barsalou et al. 2005; Gibbs 2005).

These and other similar findings lend striking support to the claim that embodiment plays a critical role in the emergence of knowledge, including religious knowledge. Changes in the body, as well as bodily movements and postures, have a causal impact on cognitive processing, for example slowing down a process or affecting people's emotional attitudes. On the other hand, social information also generates embodied states, such as bodily postures, giving evidence for a reciprocal relationship between embodiment and cognition. Motor actions play a crucial role in remembering. Together, these studies indicate a tight coupling between the motor systems and information processing (Barsalou et al. 2003).

We are only slowly beginning to understand how deeply and pervasively activation in the body is associated with cognition, including religious knowledge. Embodiment research may thus have a significant bearing on determining how rituals affect religious belief and cognition, and how the ritual–religious knowledge interface works. Not only do our beliefs (or religious cognition more generally) influence what kinds of rituals we perform, but rituals also contribute to mental states and to the control of the mind. If nodding the head in the context of a short experiment produces measurable changes in people's judgements, one might expect that lifelong embodied ritual practices would bring about much deeper and more permanent effects on cognition. To be sure, we should be careful not to draw overly hasty conclusions, extending the findings of research conducted in experimental settings to real-life cultural practices, which are perhaps best studied using the ethnographic method of participant observation (Bloch 2012).[6] But here ethnography and cognitive

---

[6] Some research has been done on the long-term impact of meditative practices on the brain and behaviour (see e.g. Lutz et al. 2008). Moreover, a focus on procedural memory, which allows us to learn skills and acquire habits, promises to contribute to our understanding of the effects of long-lasting ritual activities on cognition.

psychology corroborate each other, rather than offering competing explanations. The capacity of ritual to imprint religious knowledge deeply on people's minds is in line with a number of ethnographies and social-scientific theories; see, for example, Whitehouse's work on the millenarian cult of the Pomio Kivung (1995, 2000) and Connerton's idea of communal memory preserved in bodily practices (1989), to mention but a few.[7] It may not be an exaggeration to say that rituals are one of the most powerful ways to change and direct our minds (Geertz 2010: 307).

## 6.4 EMBODIED COGNITION AND EARLY CHRISTIAN BAPTISM

How do these insights translate into an analysis of early Christian rituals? There are a number of directions in which the analysis can be pursued. Embodied cognition research holds the promise of new insights into many aspects of early Christian ritual life, including but not limited to ascetic practices, meditation, emerging prayer practices, and the use of music (for the last, see Weimer 2015). Here I discuss just one example, related to embodied religious knowledge conveyed by early Christian baptismal practice.

---

Whitehouse has done pioneering work on this topic, drawing attention to procedural knowledge in frequently performed, routinized rituals (Whitehouse 2004a: 87–104). He builds on the neuropsychologist Annette Karmiloff-Smith's theory of representational redescription, an account of learning as a recursive process in which internal cognitive processes progressively produce more explicit and consciously accessible understandings (Karmiloff-Smith 1992). According to Whitehouse, routinized rituals first give rise to what Karmiloff-Smith calls 'behavioural mastery', encoded in implicit memory; this later triggers quasi-theoretical knowledge concerning ritual processes, and, if supported by external teaching, propositional (doctrinal) knowledge as well.

[7] Embodied knowledge transmitted through rituals bears some similarity to Rappaport's idea of 'self-referential messages', i.e. the kind of information that the participants transmit 'concerning their own current physical, physic and social states to themselves and to other participants' (cf. 'canonical messages' that 'cannot in themselves represent the performers' contemporary states'; Rappaport 1999: 52–8, esp. 52). Rappaport's discussion, however, relates more closely to what we have called the coordinative aspect of ritual behaviour (cf. section 5.1 above). Moreover, Peirce's semiotic system (symbol, icon, index) may not be easily reconciled with cognitive theories of *implicit* knowledge.

Previously we have several times noted the ritual structure of early Christian baptism, which goes back to the ritual innovation by John the Baptist. In terms of Ritual Competence Theory, baptism is a special agent ritual, in which counterintuitive agents are primarily associated with the agent of the ritual (Lawson and McCauley 1990; McCauley and Lawson 2002; see also section 1.6); this kind of ritual structure does not seem to be common in Second-Temple or later Judaism (see Biró 2013 for the latter). Drawing on Lawson and McCauley, I formulated a hypothesis that special agent rituals are intuitively sensed as more powerful than rituals with other structural profiles (i.e. special instrument and special patient rituals; see section 3.5 above). The reshaping of Jewish purification with water into a rite in which a ritual agent (baptizer) acts for a ritual patient (baptizand) is an important part of the story of early Christian baptism.

An interesting question in this context is whether the specific structure of early Christian baptism, in which a ritual agent acts on behalf of a counterintuitive agent for an unclothed ritual patient, carries a particular kind of embodied religious knowledge in the minds of the participants, knowledge about counterintuitive agents working through human agents. Of course this is a very general kind of knowledge, which can be found in most religious traditions; it would be a mistake to argue that the other cults and traditions at the time of early Christianity were somehow lacking it.[8] But by making a special agent ritual a central rite of its cultic life, early Christianity placed particular emphasis on a knowledge of God's working mediated in and through ritual bodies. This opens up intriguing questions with regard to embodied knowledge transmitted through early Christian baptisms. We can ask, for example, whether this ritual design contributed to or interacted with the hierarchical structures in the early Churches and to the rise of the institution of the monarchical bishop? The latter claim is probably impossible to verify, but in view of the above evidence we should be open to the possibility that the form of baptismal rite, in addition to all the explicit knowledge attached to the baptismal process, conveyed in itself another mode of knowledge, one that may be related, among other things, to hierarchy and power (see Connerton 1989: 73 for the related idea that bodily postures express rank and power).

---

[8] To pick just one example, oracular persons and prophets are found in all the cultural traditions of the ancient Mediterranean world (Aune 1983).

The implicit ritual knowledge transmitted in and through the baptismal practices is of course difficult to identify. However, implicit knowledge must sometimes surface in explicit comments on early Christian baptism in our sources (remember that real-life religious concepts are always generated by intuitive *and* reflective processes). It is worth noting that power relations crop up occasionally in early reports of baptism, providing some support for the above hypothesis. For example, the peculiar but probably archaic formula attached to the baptismal act in some New Testament passages, baptism 'into (Greek *eis*) the name of Lord Jesus' (Acts 8:16; 19:5; cf. also 1 Cor. 1:13; Matt. 28:19; for a detailed analysis, see Hartman 1997), can be interpreted as carrying the idea of moving the baptized person 'into the ownership' of Jesus (the Greek phrase is used in commercial documents); alternatively it may refer to the intention or purpose of the act, sometimes used in cultic settings (an act of worship toward another; cf. Hebrew *lšm* and Aramaic *lšwm*). Such verbal formulas emphasizing a baptism into the name of Jesus or into some other entity (cf. 1 Cor. 12:3; Rom 6:3) may thus evoke connotations of placing a person in a relationship of belonging to a cultic deity, which is of course a power relationship.

That this kind of language could also be used for the relationship between a ritual agent and a ritual patient is supported by Paul's comments on dissensions within the Corinthian Church (1 Cor. 1:10–20). Paul criticizes the Christians of Roman Corinth for being divided into rival groups expressing allegiance to different early Christian leaders, that is, Paul, Apollos, and Cephas; some even claiming that 'they belong to Christ'. In his response (1:17–20), Paul makes several references to baptism, he asks, ironically, whether the Corinthians have been baptized 'into Paul' (echoing the baptismal formula) and says he is thankful for having personally baptized only a few members of the community. These comments would make sense if the allegiances appealed to in Corinth had to do with the ritual authority exerted by early Christian leaders.[9]

---

[9] It is also interesting that in a number of pictorial representations of baptism in early Christian iconography (especially those representing the baptism of Jesus) the baptizand is shown as a small youth being baptized by a large adult (Snyder 1985: 57). Such images can be taken as cognitive tools (see below, section 6.6), priming ritual participants for power relationships. I owe this point to Rikard Roitto.

To be sure, later early Christian theologians were not unanimous as to how tightly baptism should be connected to ecclesiastical authority. Ignatius of Antioch, writing in the early second century, famously argued that 'it is not permissible either to baptize or to hold a lovefeast without the bishop' (*Smyrn.* 8.2; trans. Holmes 2002). On the other hand, the Church Fathers sometimes express views that baptism administered by someone not belonging to the clergy should be accepted as valid as long as it was done in the correct form.[10] Nevertheless, regardless of differing theological interpretations, the broad picture is that ritual agency and leadership roles developed hand in hand in the history of early Christianity. This involved the emergence of a guild of ritual specialists and church leaders, entailing a sophisticated hierarchy of religious authority.

Knowledge about power relations is of course not the only kind of embodied knowledge that was transmitted by means of the baptismal ritual. We may ask, for example, how the bodily experience of movement into and out of the water influenced theological thinking concerning the meaning of baptism.[11]

In the course of time baptism became a synthetic ritual, comprising a multitude of individually administered rites involving the human body, preliminary ascetic practices, exorcistic rites such as blowing on the candidates (exsufflation), the giving of salt and signing with the cross, as well as prebaptismal and postbaptismal anointing, stripping, and reclothing with white garments, the threefold immersion (sometimes sprinkling), the imposition of hands, and (in some places) foot washing (R. M. Jensen 2012). Such bodily experiences interacted with

---

[10] See e.g. the story about Athanasius' childhood, relating his mimicking a bishop and the things done in church (Rufinus, *Hist.* 10.15). Rufinus' story assumes that a baptism performed by someone not himself clergy (indeed by a child) but in correct form was accepted as valid; see Ferguson 2009: 457–8. In the terms of Lawson and McCauley, such an interpretation of baptism in effect makes the rite a special instrument ritual. Maxwell Johnson argues that there was a fundamental distinction between the Christian East and certain Churches within the Christian West with regard to the necessity of the physical presence of the Bishop consecrating the chrism or presiding over certain rites of the baptismal process; Johnson 1999: 123–4.

[11] Rikard Roitto's ongoing project, 'The Cultural Evolution of Baptism: Ritual Practice and Theological Imagination', combines theories and insights from cultural evolution and embodied cognition to account for the development of baptismal practices and baptismal theology during the first five Christian centuries. For a summary of the project, see <http://blogs.helsinki.fi/ritual-earlychristianity/the-cultural-evolution-of-baptism/> accessed 30 June 2015.

explicit teaching about the meaning of these actions, and had a good chance of leaving a lasting mark on the memory.

## 6.5 RITUALS GENERATE COMMON KNOWLEDGE

In order to coordinate individual actions, which is fundamental for a religious community or in fact for any society, knowledge must be shared or common knowledge. This kind of knowledge involves not only that x and y know the same thing, but that x knows that y knows, y knows that x knows, x knows that y knows that x knows, and so on. In other words, shared knowledge is *recursive*, everyone has to know that everyone knows that everyone knows, etc. While the concept of recursion is a bone of contention among linguists and cognitive scientists,[12] it seems obvious that the ability to create a representation of someone else's mental representation (or one's own earlier representation), or what Tomasello (2014: 38) has called 'recursive mind reading', is a significant ingredient in all human cooperation.[13] This knowledge, the shared 'common ground' among human individuals, is what makes joint intentions possible and also distinguishes humans from the other big apes (Tomasello 2014). As Pyysiäinen puts it, 'society simply cannot function (or even exist) without common knowledge concerning human relationships' (2004b: 142).

In a compact and clearly argued book *Rational Ritual: Culture, Coordination, and Common Knowledge* (2001), the political scientist Michael Chwe has put forward the theory that collective rituals can be understood as practices that generate common knowledge. Chwe draws on rational choice and game-theoretical perspectives; he contends that the ubiquity of public rituals in human societies need not be explained by the heightened emotion (cf. Durkheim's 'effervescence') they induce or the symbolic meanings they convey, but by the capacity of rituals to create common knowledge. He offers instances

---

[12] Corballis (2011) provides a popular introduction to the issue. Recursion is central to the new version of the universal grammar hypothesis developed by Chomsky together with Marc Hauser and Tecumseh Fitch (Hauser et al. 2002).

[13] This does not necessarily mean an infinite back-and-forth of us thinking about one another's thinking, but rather that people simply recognize the common ground that they share with others (Tomasello 2014: 38). For a much stronger claim about the role of recursion in the evolution of human cognition, see Corballis 2011.

of rituals across history and cultures, for example from the French Revolution, from the modern media, and from films.

Pyysiäinen, taking a cue from Chwe, has suggested that the efficacy of rituals can at least partly be explained by the fact that rituals generate common knowledge (Pyysiäinen 2004b: 135–46; see also 2011b). Rituals can be efficacious only to the extent that everybody agrees on their efficacy. Or, to put it somewhat differently, rituals are efficacious because they generate common knowledge (for example, about changes in social status). A secret ceremony that no one has had an opportunity to witness or to hear about cannot really 'make' a man and a woman a married couple, while a public ceremony manifesting the social agreement that a couple is man and wife can turn the man and woman into a couple (cf. Pyysiäinen 2004b: 142–3). One can of course argue that all that is needed is a social agreement as to the efficacy of a wedding ritual, not the common knowledge created by the performance of a collective ritual; but this begs the question why rites of passages, such as weddings, are universally celebrated collectively, not in privacy.

Early Christian baptism was not a public event comparable to civic rituals in the Greco-Roman world, but it was a collective ritual. The sources reveal very little about the physical spaces where baptisms were administered, but a number of New Testament passages indicate that the whole household was baptized at the same time.[14] This could suggest that during the earliest phase of the Christian movement baptism was typically performed in a household setting, although baptisms were probably also held in outdoor contexts (cf. Justin's attestation that the baptismal candidates 'are brought by us where there is water'; *1 Apol.* 61).[15] Baptism inside a private home may have required a *domus* (a type of Roman house occupied by upper-class families), which had running water and bathing facilities.[16] Wherever

---

[14] See e.g. Acts 10:34–48; 16:13–15, 33; 18:8; 1 Cor. 1: 16; cf. also 2 Tim. 1: 16; 4:19.
[15] See also Tertullian, *Bapt.* 4, 'It makes no difference whether a man be washed in a sea or a pool, a stream or a fount, a lake or a trough' (trans. *The Ante-Nicene Fathers*, Roberts and Donaldson 1885, repr. 1994). L. Michael White suggests that until the middle of the second century Christians may have performed baptisms, among other places, in Roman *balinea* or (public) baths (see note 16 below).
[16] We have very little evidence as to where early Christians performed baptism before they started to renovate existing buildings in order to transform them for Christian social and liturgical purposes. White (2000: 710) concludes that 'there was no special place for baptism' in that period (cf. Justin's general reference to a place 'where there is water'). Another piece of literary evidence from the middle of the

baptism was performed, it is evident that it was a communal ritual which was normally witnessed by other adherents, in addition to the baptizer and the baptizand. In this connection, it is worth noting that Jesus' baptism by John the Baptist, which served as the prototype of all subsequent baptisms in early Christian teaching and art (R. M. Jensen 2012: 15), is described as a public event by the Synoptic Gospel authors.[17]

Thus, as in the case of many other collective rituals, the efficacy of the baptismal ritual is connected to the fact that it generated shared knowledge about the ritual candidate's incorporation into the Christian community. Baptism does not leave any bodily mark—in this regard, it is different from the circumcision of male converts to Judaism.[18] New Testament authors noted the parallelism between baptism and circumcision, and appealed to the tradition that emphasizes the ethical meaning of circumcision (Col. 2:11–12; Rom. 2:25–29; cf. Philo, *Migr*. 92, who accepts the spiritual sense but condemns those who reject the actual practice). Other early Christians vehemently denied that baptism replaces circumcision and demanded that newly converted males should receive the basic ethnic marker of Judaism (Gal. 5:2–11). As a ritual of conversion or an initiatory rite, baptism was not universally accepted in the earliest communities (DeMaris 2008). With regard to the larger public it remained a secret rite, those who received it were initiated into an exclusive community, comparable to many other private associations in the Greco-Roman world (R. M. Jensen 2012: 63). With the growth of the Christian movement, however, the baptismal ritual gradually

---

second century (*Passio sancti Justini et socii* 3) suggests that Justin's own assembly met up in an apartment 'above the baths of so-and so' (unfortunately the text is corrupt at the point where the name of or the owner of the baths are mentioned). Tying together Justin's own reference and the mention of baths in the *Martyrdom of Justin*, White conjectures that baptism in Justin's congregation might well have been performed downstairs at the baths (White 1996: 110; for a private bath as a possible place of baptism, see also Brandt 2011: 1589–60). In a Jewish setting, baptism may have been performed in a ritual bath or *miqveh* (for the presence of many such pools in Roman Palestine, see Adler 2013).

[17] There is, however, a difference with regard to the question whether Jesus' vision and the voice from heaven are described as a revelation that was experienced by Jesus alone (Mark 1:1–11) or as a public event (Matt. 3:16–17; Luke 3:21–22).

[18] It is not, however, certain how common such conversions were at the time of Christian beginnings; see M. Goodman 1994.

evolved into a complex ritual process which involved effective mechanisms for generating shared religious knowledge.

## 6.6 RITUALS ACCOMMODATE EXTENDED KNOWLEDGE

As noted in the beginning of this chapter, the embodied cognition school emphasizes that 'thinking is an activity strongly influenced by the body and the brain *interacting with the environment*' (Glenberg et al. 2013: 573, my italics). The latter half of this description brings us to the partly overlapping areas of research that have been called enactivism or embedded cognition or extended (distributed) cognition. In its broader sense, embodied cognition argues that cognitive activity is not only embodied, but also 'embedded' (i.e. it uses the structure of the environment) and 'extended' (i.e. cognition extends beyond the boundaries of individual organisms). These three theses can be grouped under the umbrella term 'situated cognition' (Robbins and Aydede 2009b), but the usage is not standard (Robbins and Aydede 2009a). 'Embodied cognition' is also often used as a general term for an approach to cognitive science which, in addition to the embodied mind, embraces (or at least considers) the views of both embedded and extended cognition (Shapiro 2011; Glenberg et al. 2013).

The idea of extended (or distributed) cognition is a hotly debated issue in cognitive science. Is it really possible to argue that cognition somehow extends beyond the boundaries of individual organisms? Would it make sense to contend that, especially in the present-day world, external tools are so important for human thinking that we have literally become cyborgs, partly constituted by technologies (for the latter argument, see Clark 2003)? The debate between representatives of 'contingent intracranialism' and those of 'contingent transcranialism' involves an interesting philosophical issue, and probably represents more than merely a terminological dispute over how to use the word 'cognition' (F. Adams and Aizawa 2009).[19] For the purposes

---

[19] Adams and Aizawa make two main points against transcranialism. First, they argue that transcranialists are guilty of what they call the 'coupling-constitution fallacy'. This fallacious pattern means that one draws attention to cases in which some object or process is coupled in some way to some cognitive agent and then jumps to the

## Ritual and Religious Knowledge 171

of my argument in this chapter, it is not necessary to settle the issue of whether the human cognitive processes in reality extend from the brain into the physical and social world. My claim is that rituals accommodate extended knowledge, which can be illustrated without assuming a hypothesis of 'cognition beyond skin and skull' (for arguments that this indeed is the case, see Clark and Chalmers 1998; R. A. Wilson 2004; Clark 2011; but compare F. Adams and Aizawa 2009). We can equally well presuppose that the extended knowledge accommodated by ritual activities is a matter of the mind strongly *interacting* with the environment (cf. Glenberg et al. 2013)— the claim accepted by both intracranialists and transcranialists—even if we rely on insights from embodied or situated cognition. Thus, insofar as we can state that extended knowledge is maintained by *extended cognition*, the use of the latter term can be taken as being analogical to such terms as 'external memory' or 'social memory' vs. memory within the brain.

The idea that cognition interacts between brain, body, and the physical and social environment is important for a ritual analysis of early Christianity. Rituals convey knowledge in themselves, often non-verbal (cf. above, section 6.4), but they also accommodate practices of interpretation, teaching and cultural technologies, that is, what we can call extended knowledge. This form of knowledge should not be excluded from the cognitive study of early Christian ritual.

One ritual theory that focuses on extended knowledge is Whitehouse's Modes of Religiosity. As already noted several times in this book, this theory highlights two types of mechanism in the emergence of religious knowledge: imagistic rituals, as cognitive puzzles, evoke spontaneous exegetical reflections encoded in episodic memory, whereas routinized doctrinal rituals, accompanied by frequent interpretations and sermons by religious authorities, generate verbally codified and systematic religious knowledge, which will be encoded in the participants' semantic memory. Part of this theory (especially the idea of spontaneous exegetical reflection) has proved helpful in analysing the traditions concerning John's ritual invention (see section 3.2). Whitehouse's modal dichotomy, however, even if it were

conclusion that the object or process constitutes part of the agent's cognitive apparatus (F. Adams and Aizawa 2010: 67–8). Second, they draw attention to the existence of distinctive causal processes that take place intracranially. For example, the human memory appears to show primacy and recency effects unlike those that occur in computer hard drives or pen and paper (F. Adams and Aizawa 2009: 92).

understood as two attractor positions (see Whitehouse 2004a: 74), does not seem to resonate with much of the early Christian evidence, where we find constant interplay between imagistic and doctrinal practices.[20]

Whitehouse's model is in line with the standard position in cognitive science, in that it assumes that spontaneous interpretations or systematic teachings by religious authorities are simply stored in the memory systems of the brain.[21] Closer to the embodied/situated cognition stance would be a view according to which various structured learning environments, symbolic technologies, images, the use of music, architecture, etc. work as cognitive tools for 're-engineering' cognition (M. Wilson 2010). As applied to religious knowledge generated in and through rituals, this perspective suggests a two-way traffic between cognitive processes and the cultural embeddings of ritual practices.

Extensive symbolic technologies and systems of knowledge grew up around early Christian baptism. These can be analysed as cognitive tools that interact with and influence religious cognition.

*The catechumenate.* A powerful institution which evolved for the production and maintaining of religious knowledge, a period of preparation from enrolment to the threshold of immersion, during which the baptismal candidate (catechumen) was encultured into the Christian doctrines, scriptures and way of life. The catechumenate flourished from the late first to the fifth century (Dujarier 1979; Brakmann 2004). While the length of this baptismal preparation varied from weeks to several years, it universally involved, at least from the third century onward, instruction, testing, exorcisms (see section 4.6), praying, and fasting (Finn 1992). The catechumenal practices of the early Church have not received particularly close scholarly attention, but the evidence supports the claim that early Christianity placed much emphasis on combining the ritual process of initiation with the teaching of religious knowledge. According to

---

[20] See Uro 2007, for an argument that early Christianity needed imagistic practices and that various second-century movements arose to fill this need. This view is in accord with Whitehouse's ethnography, which focused on one high-arousal splinter group among the Pomio Kivung. Whitehouse found that splinter-group activities in the traditional millennial Kivung cult tended to recur every few years (1995: 65).

[21] Note however that in his 2004 book, Whitehouse developed his model by considering the role of procedural memory in routinized rituals (Whitehouse 2004a; see note 6 in this chapter).

Finn, the early Christian conviction was that 'conversion to Christ was a long, collaborative ritual process through which catechumens gradually acquired the freedom to break the powerful hold of an old way of life and to embrace the new' (Finn 1992: 7). This process of reshaping and manipulating the minds of new members of the movement is a striking example of a 'cognitive re-tooling' of the individual's cognitive phenotype (M. Wilson 2010).

*Credal formulae and creeds.* In relation to the above point, historians of Christian doctrine have suggested that credal formulae and creeds developed in close connection with baptismal teaching. According to Trevor Hart, the origin of declaratory creeds 'seems to have been as learning aids within the lengthy and careful catechetical preparation of candidates for baptism' (Hart 2000: esp. 647). The ritual setting of the threefold credal structure can be found already in some early references to baptism in the New Testament and the *Apostolic Fathers* (Matt. 28:19; *Did.* 7), as well as in Justin Martyr's *First Apology* (61). In the *Apostolic Tradition,* we find a practice of the baptismal *interrogationes de fide* (an interrogation and response model of baptism), based on the threefold structure of the Apostles' Creed (*Trad. ap.* 21.12–18). Liturgical scholars and scholars of Christian doctrine have used this as evidence for the view that the declaratory use of the Apostles' Creed—and early Christian creeds more generally—emerged later and various formal creeds developed in interaction with the ritual process of baptism. We have no evidence for the declaratory form until the middle of the fourth century. This would support an approach to the history of early Christian doctrine that draws on embodied cognition research. The emergence of explicit confessional formulae and creeds is closely intertwined with bodily ritual practices.

*Stories and pictorial representations of Jesus' baptism* work as cognitive instruments for generating extended knowledge. In his pioneering work on early Christian archaeology, Graydon Snyder notes that during the third and fourth century one of the most popular biblical scenes was the baptism of Jesus (Snyder 1985: 57). These early pictures often portray Jesus as a small nude youth being baptized by a very large adult, John the Baptist, who stands above the small Jesus and is laying a hand on his head.[22] A dove usually hovers over the

---

[22] Jensen points out that John's gesture, placing his right hand on Jesus' head, suggests either the baptizer's pressing the candidate under the water or the imposition of hands (R. M. Jensen 2012: 14).

scene. As already noted, according to Jensen (2012: 15) the image reflects the fact that early Christians saw Jesus' baptism as the prototype for all subsequent baptisms. She comments that 'depicting the recipient as a child is not a departure from the narrative tradition but rather shows the newly baptized as having regained a childlike innocence through the remission of sins' (2012: 16). From the embodied cognition perspective, these artistic representations did not merely *reflect* early Christian experience; they functioned as cognitive tools, influencing the content of the experience at the same time that they expressed how baptism was experienced by early Christians. Barsalou et al. (2005) describe how religious art may contribute content to religious experience such as visions. As people view images, their visual systems are driven into neural states that represent them. Association areas then capture these states, which can later pop up in the form of a religious vision. Barsalou and his colleagues note that people who view a religious image tend to situate its *content personally*, rather than simulating the image per se (2005: 38). Although their point is to explain religious visions, further research on this and related cognitive processes may shed light on the dual image of Jesus and a neophyte (the small unclothed youth) in early Christian art.

Not only visual images but also *physical and architectural environments of baptism* provide cognitive embeddings for religious cognition. Although we have very little evidence as to where early Christians performed baptisms before they started to renovate existing buildings and construct new ones for liturgical purposes, archaeological research on domestic baths and public water systems in Greek and Roman cities may help us to imagine various options for ritual spaces in the earliest phase of the movement.[23] Catacombs as a place of baptism constitute a special environment, which certainly influenced the cognitive landscape of ritual participants. Baptismal architecture, such as baptisteries and baptismal fonts, began to evolve only from the fourth century onwards (Brandt 2011). The form[24] and capacity of baptismal fonts have given rise to discussion as to how physical structures reflected and reinforced the meaning of the ritual (R. M. Jensen 2012: 165–70), and whether early Christian baptism took place through immersion of the whole person or by the pouring

---

[23] For an analysis of the light cast upon early Christian baptismal practices by water systems in Roman Corinth, see DeMaris 2008: 37–56.
[24] Fonts could be built to resemble tombs, cruces, or wombs.

of water over the recipients (Stommel 1959). The interpretation of the archaeological record both informs and benefits from new insights into embodied/extended cognition.

These cognitive embeddings and technologies of knowledge are ripe for further research on the development of early Christian thinking from the perspective of ritual. A consideration of these and other cultural elements are crucial for a cognitive history of early Christian ritual. They are more than just 'ethnographic icing on the computational cake' or 'thin cultural "wrap arounds" that dress up the *real* cognitive processes going on underneath' (M. Day 2004: 116). We do not need to commit ourselves to the most radical claims of extended cognition in order to realize the importance of material culture and structured environments for religious cognition. Cognition may still be regarded as being 'in the head', even if one gives a greater role to culture and embodiment than they have in certain other approaches to cognitive science. The so-called 'standard' theories in CSR are promising new tools for analysing and explaining the role of ritual in the rise of the Christian movement, as has been demonstrated in previous chapters, but these should be supplemented by a consideration of the embodied and extended perspective on cognition (cf. also Geertz 2010). It would be unreasonable to assume that the massive and varied symbolic technologies and learning environments that accumulated around what originated as a relatively simple immersion rite failed to exert a vital impact on the cognitive landscape of ritual participants, even though the ritual profile of the core rite (immersion by a ritual agent) remained the same.

## 6.7 WHY (LITURGICAL) HISTORY NEEDS COGNITIVE SCIENCE

The focus on the extended knowledge conveyed in and through the baptismal ritual may raise the question of what difference it makes to analyse manifold institutions and ritual frames from the point of view of embodied or situated cognition. A great deal of research has been done on the above-listed topics from traditional historical perspectives and from that of the history of liturgy. In the preceding paragraph I argued that cognitive science needs an analysis of cultural embeddings of cognition. But what is the pay-off from applying cognitive science approaches to cultural and historical analyses? One of my aims in this book is to give an answer to this question. Here, as a conclusion, I focus on three points that are relevant to the issues discussed in this chapter.

First, enriching traditional historiography with approaches and findings from cognitive science is important and beneficial because such an interdisciplinary method creates a bridge between experimental research and historical studies. Maurice Bloch has made a similar case for integrating anthropology with cognitive science (Bloch 2012). His insights are relevant for the historian of religion as well.[25]

Bloch notes how anthropologists, working with the method of participatory observation, hope to find information about a deeper level of implicit and unexpressed knowledge by examining explicit forms of knowledge as these unfold in the institutions, practices, and discourses of the peoples they study. Cognitive psychologists, on the other hand, do not focus on the 'surface' level of knowledge, that is, what people say and do in a natural setting; they believe that the most reliable information about the rationale and the cognitive underpinnings of the minds of the people can be obtained by experimental methods and by the use of laboratory tests. The problem, according to Bloch, is that both sides assume that what they know is sufficient for inferring knowledge about some basic determinants of the human mind (2012: 106). He argues that we should not respond to this discrepancy by letting 'the different disciplines get on with their own thing', since both parts want ultimately to speak about the same subject (2012: 137). A much more fruitful strategy is to apply, to use the term introduced in section 2.5, 'explanatory pluralism' to complement anthropology—or, in this case, history of religion—with approaches and theories from cognitive science. In this chapter, we have made an attempt to integrate experimental research from embodied cognition to the question of how rituals generate and transmit religious knowledge. A leap from laboratory experiments to historical developments may be risky, but the risk is perhaps offset by considering evidence gleaned from multiple disciplines and approaches.

Second, for the historian of religion to ignore the cognitive challenge would be to miss an opportunity. Even if CSR can no longer be

---

[25] According to Bloch, the work of the anthropologist comes close to that of the historian.

seen as a unified research project (if indeed it ever has been such), there is general agreement that research on the cognitive architecture of the mind offers tools for the analysis of religious traditions (including ancient religions), helping to explain the spread of religious ideas. There are differing views as to the question of how much emphasis should be placed on intuitive processes (see section 2.2); whether to rely on 'natural selectionist' (cultural-evolutionary) or 'cognitive attractionist' models (Luther H. Martin 2011; see also section 2.2); and whether cognition should be seen as somehow extending beyond the boundaries of individual organisms. The embodied or situated cognition perspective discussed here is often described as an approach which is opposed to or competing with standard cognitive science. My argument has been that the embodied approach can offer complementary tools for the analysis of both implicit *and* explicit religious knowledge generated by ritual practices. The embodiment approach can thus be seen as a link creating a common ground between cultural and cognitive approaches.

Lastly, a rejection of the cognitive challenge would in effect mean that the scholar of religion subscribes to the view that nature and culture are fundamentally distinct or opposed. Such a dualistic view of humanity is simply no longer possible. Much more in line with our hugely increased knowledge concerning the evolutionary and cognitive roots of human thinking is the position recently strongly advocated by Bloch (2012: 52), '... when thinking of human beings we are dealing with a single process occurring within a single organism. "Culture" and "nature" may be distinguishable analytically but it is important not to mistake the heuristic separation for an empirical one.' Culture and history can of course for many practical reasons be studied without considering findings in cognitive and evolutionary sciences. Such analyses, however, should not be based on a dichotomous understanding, positing a fundamental opposition between culture and cognition. At a deeper level culture is, as Donald succinctly puts it, 'a gigantic cognitive web, defining and constraining the parameters of memory, knowledge, and thought in its members, both as individuals and as a group' (Donald 2001: xiv). This also applies, as I have shown, to knowledge transmitted in and through ritual practices.

# Concluding Remarks

I began this book by asking why Christianity happened. That provocative question cannot, of course, be answered comprehensively in one single book focusing on one particular aspect, the role of ritual in the emergence of the Christian movement. For one thing, the question can refer to a number of different issues. We need to specify: is the explanandum the development of the movement around Jesus of Nazareth into a vital religious cult in the Greco-Roman world, or Christianity's becoming the state religion of the Roman Empire, or its growth into a global religion with two billion adherents? Furthermore, even if we chose one of these specific questions, say, the first one—our examples would not provide evidence for the latter two—nothing even close to a complete answer would be possible. Explaining *why* early Christianity took place means finding causal connections that account for the occurrence of the particular series of events that led to the rise of the movement to the exclusion of other connections. The number of forces at work, and their interactions in this (or any other) historical development, are so complex that no theory—or even a set of complementary theories—can provide the necessary tools allowing us to explain it in full.

I have, however, argued in the preceding chapters that explanatory theories are helpful in the study of Christian beginnings, and have insisted that ritual theory is relevant to explaining the emergence of early Christian religion. I have done so because I believe that partial explanations are useful in the understanding of historical processes, and that a partial explanation focusing on the role of ritual should receive much more attention than it has had in previous scholarship. Most accounts of Christian origins have ignored ritual, and have thus overlooked one of the central driving forces of religious movements. A partial explanation that adds to other valid accounts, and that is solidly grounded in theory and empirical evidence, is thus relevant, even if it does not capture the whole complex chain and interaction of causal factors involved in the rise of Christianity.

The application of explanatory theories to historical events can be criticized on the ground that such an account merely gives 'a just-so story to explain with hindsight that the outcome was inevitable' (cf. Harari 2011: 238). The approach taken in this work, however, does not suggest that the factors identified led deterministically to the outcome that we all know, that is, the rise and success of the Christian movement. Instead, it highlights certain general social and psychological mechanisms, which in turn facilitate cross-cultural comparisons and shed light on the historical development under scrutiny. Ultimately, thus, such an approach does not make a clear-cut distinction between questions of 'why' and 'how'. Historical descriptions can be enriched by cognitive explanatory theories, while cognitive theories are also helpful in cases where the evidence does not allow rigorous testing of a theory (cf. my comments on the use of Pauline Christianity as a test case in section 5.3). This is not to say that early Christian scholars and historians of religion should not strive toward a more formalized application of cognitive theory or scientific modelling to the historiography of ancient religions.[1] But there is also a place for the kind of dialogue between cognitive and more traditional (or non-cognitive) social-scientific approaches promoted in this book.

As I explained in Chapter One, the study of Christian beginnings from a ritual point of view is still at an experimental and embryonic stage. A comprehensive critical study of early Christian rituals and their role in the formation of the movement probably remains years ahead. The test cases analysed in this book, however, do allow certain tentative conclusions. I briefly summarize three central ways in which the above analyses contribute to the scholarship on Christian beginnings.

The first has to do with the concept of ritual invention, discussed particularly in Chapter Three (3.2). Although the importance of John

---

[1] An example of the application of more formalized modelling to the study of ancient religions is the 'Generative Historiography of Religion Project' (GEHIR; 2015–17), launched at Masaryk University, Brno (Principal Investigator Aleš Chalupa). The project 'applies innovative methods used in the study of the dynamics of complex systems (mathematical and computational modelling, network science) to the historiography of ancient Graeco-Roman religions' (see http://gehir.phil.muni.cz/, accessed 26 June 2015).

the Baptist to the rise of the Jesus movement is recognized both by the Gospel authors and by modern scholars, the issue of ritual innovation has been almost universally ignored. John was a ritual inventor who developed (or disseminated) a powerful new version of the Jewish purificatory immersion, and his movement revolved heavily around this invention. Previous scholars have not been able to see the significance of John's innovation because they have not been interested in the process of ritualization in the rise of the biblical movements. Moreover, they have not focused on a structural analysis of John's ritual performance, nor have they made its ritual profile a point of departure for comparative studies. Testing the Ritual Competence Theory against the historical evidence concerning John's immersion rite helped to identify one important explanatory factor, and to ask further questions as to the role of ritual in the rise of Christianity. But theories of ritual invention and ritualization can be applied to other early Christian rituals as well. The most obvious topic for such an analysis is the early Christian meal tradition, in which we have, as Burton Mack puts it, 'a wonderfully elongated process of ritualization on our hands' (Mack 1996: 256).[2]

The second point highlighting the contribution of this volume relates to the ways in which cognitive theory can enrich and to some degree correct previous research, based on social-scientific theories and models. The socio-cognitive approach applied here enabled us to work across the hierarchies of disciplines and to integrate findings from the cognitive and evolutionary sciences into the study of the emergence of the Christian movement. Traditional social-scientific interpretations and explanations have not fostered such a multilevel analysis but have operated at a social level, which has also been the most common domain of theories of religion.[3]

The socio-cognitive approach to the healing activities of Jesus and the early Christians, carried out in Chapter Four, underlined certain problems that have plagued earlier studies. Healings are often discussed under the general rubric of 'miracles', and the latter have been

---

[2] Vojtěch Kaše's dissertation project (University of Helsinki, Masaryk University, Brno) focuses on the process of ritualization of early Christian meal practices, drawing on cognitive and experimental research.

[3] Note, however, that some recent work in Social Scientific Interpretation has successfully used insights from social psychology, in particular Social Identity Theory (Esler 2003; Tucker and Baker 2014), which has a cognitive dimension relying on research on perception and categorization (Luomanen et al. 2007a: 21-6).

seen as one cause for the victory of Christianity ever since Gibbon's *History of the Decline and Fall of the Roman Empire* (1994 [1776]: 471–5). This discussion, however, has often been burdened by theological (emic) ideas of the unique nature of Jesus' healings, or by the cultural relativistic models applied by many New Testament scholars. I have contended that a consideration of cognitive mechanisms leads to a more realistic picture of ritual healing and spirit possession in the formation of the early Christian movement. Similarly, I demonstrated in Chapter Five (5.2) that evolutionary-based theories of religious ritual behaviour, such as the Commitment Signalling Theory, can contribute to our understanding of the social life in the earliest Christian 'house churches', which have often been described in quite idealized terms.

Finally this book champions a new theoretical insight into Christian beginnings. This insight not only challenges the overwhelming emphasis in previous scholarship on the ideological aspects of early Christian religion, but also attempts to model the functioning of ritual as a conveyor of early Christian (shared) beliefs, and the profound interaction between body and cognition in that process. Scholars usually think that ritual practices reflect the ideological content of early Christianity (focusing, for example, on baptismal *theology*) or alternatively draw on insights from social theory to explain how bodily actions reflect or generate the social world. What has been missing is a theory that accommodates the profound and pervasive nature of the interaction between ritual and religious knowledge.[4] Not only do our beliefs influence what kinds of rituals we perform; rituals also contribute to our mental states and our thinking. Ritual is indeed a powerful tool for controlling people's minds. To argue that ritual (more accurately 'ritualization') is 'a rather blunt tool' (cf. Bell 1992: 212, 222) means to ignore the growing amount of empirical research showing how fundamentally our thinking is dependent on the body and on bodily actions (a few examples of this research were introduced in section 6.3). Any description of early Christian worldviews would thus require a consideration of this powerful interface between ritual and religious knowledge, just as a comprehensive investigation of early Christian rituals cannot ignore the capacity of ritual to convey both intuitive and explicit knowledge.

---

[4] Cf. Rikard Roitto's ongoing project, 'The Cultural Evolution of Baptism: Ritual Practice and Theological Imagination' (see section 6.4, note 11).

Research into embodied and situated cognition opens up exciting prospects for integrating empirical studies with the history of early Christianity. Drawing on both Ritual Competence Theory and embodied cognition insights, I hypothesized in Chapter Six (6.4) that the introduction of a baptism, with particular emphasis on the liturgical role of the agent of the ritual, might have contributed to the emergence and maintenance of leadership structures in the early Church. But it is not difficult to envision other promising topics for the employment of embodied cognition in the study of early Christianity: ascetic practices, meditation, emerging prayer practices, the use of music in ritual contexts, and so on. Moreover, the idea that cognition is dependent not only on bodily actions but also on *the body interacting with the environment* is suggestive of a new approach, taking the cultural embeddings of early Christian rituals, such as the Catechumenate, creeds, art, and physical constructions, as cognitive tools that influence and interact with human thinking. Ritual thus becomes a window onto a much larger world than the analysis of ritual actions—our point of departure—would suggest.

I hope I have been able to demonstrate that the socio-cognitive approach to early Christian ritual is capable both of generating new questions and of enriching old ones, as well as giving rise to an entirely new way of thinking. My aspiration is that this book will stimulate further hypotheses and studies on the role of ritual in the rise of early Christianity.

# References

Abbink, Jon. 1995. 'Ritual and Environment: the *Mosit* Ceremony of the Ethiopian Me'en People'. *Journal of Religion in Africa* 25: pp. 163–90.
Adams, Edward. 2013. *The Earliest Christian Meeting Places: Almost Exclusively Houses?* Library of New Testament Studies 450. London: Bloomsbury T&T Clark.
Adams, Fred and Ken Aizawa. 2009. 'Why the Mind Is Still in the Head'. In *Cambridge Handbook of Situated Cognition*, edited by Philip Robbins and Murat Aydede, pp. 78–95. Cambridge: Cambridge University Press.
Adams, Fred and Ken Aizawa. 2010. 'Defending the Bounds of Cognition'. In *The Extended Mind*, edited by Richard Menary, pp. 67–80. Cambridge, MA: MIT Press.
Adler, Yonatan. 2013. 'Religion, Judaism: Purity in the Roman Period'. In *The Oxford Encyclopedia of the Bible and Archaeology*, edited by Daniel Master, Vol. 2, pp. 240–9. Oxford: Oxford University Press.
Albera, Dionigi. 2006. 'Anthropology of the Mediterranean: Between Crisis and Renewal'. *History and Anthropology* 17 (2): pp. 109–33.
Albl, Martin C. 2002. '"Are Any among You sick?" The Health Care System in the Letter of James'. *Journal of Biblical Literature* 121 (1): pp. 123–43.
Alcorta, Candace S. and Richard Sosis. 2005. 'Ritual, Emotion, and Sacred Symbols'. *Human Nature* 16 (4): pp. 323–59.
Alexander, Philip S. 1999. 'The Demonology of the Dead Sea Scrolls'. In *The Dead Sea Scrolls after Fifty Years*, edited by Peter W. Flint, James C. VanderKam, and Andrea E. Alvarez, pp. 331–53. Leiden: Brill.
Alexander, Philip S. 2003. 'Contextualizing the Demonology of the Testament of Solomon'. In *Die Dämonen—Demons*, edited by Armin Lange, Hermann Lichtenberger, and K. F. Diethard Römheld, pp. 613–35. Tübingen: Mohr Siebeck.
Alikin, Valeriy A. 2010. *The Earliest History of the Early Christian Gathering: Origin, Development and Content of the Christian Gathering in the First to Third Centuries*. Supplements to Vigiliae Christianae 102. Leiden: Brill.
Allison, Dale C. 2003. 'The Continuity Between John and Jesus'. *Journal for the Study of the Historical Jesus* 1 (1): pp. 6–27.
Anshel, Anat and David A. Kipper. 1988. 'The Influence of Group Singing on Trust and Cooperation'. *Journal of Music Therapy* 25 (3): pp. 145–55.
Ascough, Richard S. 1998. *What Are They Saying About the Formation of Pauline Churches?* New York: Paulist Press.
Ashton, John. 2000. *The Religion of Paul the Apostle*. New Haven, CT: Yale University Press.

# References

Atkinson, Jane Monnig. 1989. *The Art and Politics of Wana Shamanship*. Berkeley, CA: University of California Press.

Atkinson, Quentin and Harvey Whitehouse. 2011. 'The Cultural Morphospace of Ritual Form'. *Evolution of Human Behavior* 32 (1): pp. 50–62.

Atran, Scott. 2002. *In Gods We Trust: The Evolutionary Landscape of Religion*. Oxford: Oxford University Press.

Atran, Scott and Ara Norenzayan. 2004. 'Religion's Evolutionary Landscape: Counterintuition, Commitment, Compassion, Communion'. *Behavioral and Brain Sciences* 27: pp. 713–70.

Aune, David E. 1980. 'Magic in Early Christianity'. In *Aufstieg und Niedergang der römischen Welt* 2.23.2, edited by Hildegard Temporini and Wolfgang Haase, pp. 1507–57. Berlin: de Gruyter.

Aune, David E. 1983. *Prophecy in Early Christianity and the Ancient Mediterranean World*. Grand Rapids, MI: Eerdmans.

Avemarie, Friedrich. 1999. 'Ist die Johannestaufe ein Eisdruck von Tempelkritik? Skizze eines methodischen Problems'. In *Gemeinde ohne Tempel— Community without Temple: Zur Substituierung un Transformation des Jerusalemer Tempels und seines Kults im Alten Testament, antiken Judentum und frühen Christentum*, edited by Beate Ego, Armin Lange, and Peter Pilhofer, pp. 395–410. Tübingen: Mohr Siebeck.

Bainbridge, William Sims. 2014. 'Artificial Intelligence Models and Religious Evolution'. In *Evolution, Religion, and Cognitive Science: Critical and Constructive Essays*, edited by Fraser Watts and Léon Turner, pp. 219–37. Oxford: Oxford University Press.

Baird, William. 2003. *History of New Testament Research: Volume Two: From Jonathan Edwards to Rudolf Bultmann*. Minneapolis, MN: Fortress.

Bargh, John A., Mark Chen, and Lara Burrows. 1996. 'Automacy of Social Behavior: Direct Effects of Trait Construct and Stereotype Activation in Action'. *Journal of Personality and Social Psychology* 71: pp. 230–44.

Barkow, Jerome H., Leda Cosmides, and John Tooby, eds. 1992. *The Adapted Mind: Evolutionary Psychology and the Generation of Culture*. New York: Oxford University Press.

Barnard, Leslie William, ed. 1997. *St. Justin Martyr: The First and Second Apologies*. Translation with Introduction and Notes by Leslie William Barnard. Ancient Christian Writers 56. New York: Paulist Press.

Barrett, H. Clark and Robert Kurzban. 2006. 'Modularity in Cognition: Framing the Debate'. *Psychological Review* 113 (3): pp. 628–47.

Barrett, Justin L. 1999. 'Theological Correctness: Cognitive Constraint and the Study of Religion'. *Method and Theory in the Study of Religion* 11: pp. 325–39.

Barrett, Justin L. 2004a. 'The Naturalness of Religious Concepts: An Emerging Cognitive Science of Religion'. In *New Approaches to the Study of Religion*. Vol 2: *Textual, Comparative, Sociological and Cognitive*

*Approaches*, edited by Peter Antes, Armin W. Geertz, and Randi R. Warne, pp. 401–18. Berlin: de Gruyter.

Barrett, Justin L. 2004b. *Why Would Anyone Believe in God?* Cognitive Science of Religion Series. Lanham, MD: AltaMira.

Barrett, Justin L. 2007. 'Cognitive Science of Religion'. *Religion Compass* 1: pp. 1–19.

Barrett, Justin L. 2008a. 'Why Santa Claus is not God'. *Journal of Cognition and Culture* 8: pp. 149–61.

Barrett, Justin L. 2008b. 'Keeping "Science" in the Cognitive Science of Religion'. In *The Evolution of Religion: Studies, Theories and Critiques*, edited by Joseph Bulbulia, et al., pp. Santa Margarita, CA: Collis Foundation.

Barrett, Justin L. 2011. 'Cognitive Science of Religion: Looking Back, Looking Forward'. *Journal for the Scientific Study of Religion* 50 (2): pp. 229–39.

Barrett, Justin L. and Frank C. Keil. 1996. 'Conceptualizing a Nonnatural Entity: Anthropomorphism in God Concepts'. *Cognitive Psychology* 31: pp. 219–47.

Barrett, Justin L. and E. Thomas Lawson. 2001. 'Ritual Intuitions: Cognitive Contributions to Judgments of Ritual Efficacy'. *Journal of Cognition and Culture* 1 (2): pp. 183–201.

Barrett, Justin L. and Melanie A. Nyhof. 2001. 'Spreading Non-Natural Concepts: The Role of Intuitive Conceptual Structures in Memory and Transmission of Cultural Materials'. *Journal of Cognition and Culture* 1 (1): pp. 69–100.

Barrett-Lennard, R. J. S. 1994. *Christian Healing After New Testament: Some Approaches to Illness in the Second, Third, and Fourth Centuries*. Lanham, MD: University Press of America.

Barsalou, Lawrence W., W. Kyle Simmons, Aron K. Barbey, and Christine D. Wilson. 2003. 'Grounding Conceptual Knowledge in Modality-Specific Systems'. *Trends in Cognitive Science* 7 (2): pp. 84–91.

Barsalou, Lawrence W., Aron K. Barbey, W. Kyle Simmons, and Ava Santos. 2005. 'Embodiment in Religious Knowledge'. *Journal of Cognition and Culture* 5 (1–2): pp. 14–55.

Bauer, Walter. 1988. *Griechisch-deutsches Wörterbuch zu den Schriften des Neuen Testaments und der frühchristlichen Literatur*. 6th rev. edition, edited by K. Aland and B. Aland. Berlin: de Gruyter.

Baumstark, Anton. 1953. *Liturgie comparée: principes et méthodes pour l'étude historique des liturgies chrétiennes*. 3. éd., revue par Dom Bernard Botte. Collection Irénikon. Chevetogne: Éditions de Chevetogne.

Baumstark, Anton. 1958. *Comparative Liturgy*. Revised by Bernard Dotte; English edition by F. L. Cross. London: Mowbray.

Beach, K. 1988. 'The Role of External Mnemonic System in Acquiring an Occupation'. In *Practical Aspects of Memory*, edited by M. Gruneberg and P. Morris, pp. 342–46. Oxford: Wiley.

Becker, Jürgen. 1972. *Johannes der Täufer und Jesus von Nazareth*. Biblische Studien 63. Neukirchen-Vluyn: Neukirchener Verlag.
Bell, Catherine. 1992. *Ritual Theory—Ritual Practice*. Oxford: Oxford University Press.
Bell, Catherine. 1997. *Ritual: Perspectives and Dimensions*. Oxford: Oxford University Press.
Bell, Catherine. 2005. 'Ritual (Further Considerations)'. In *Encyclopedia of Religion*: 2nd edn, edited by Lindsay Jones, Vol. 11, pp. 7848–56. Detroit, MI: Macmillan.
Bell, Catherine, ed. 2007. *Teaching Ritual*. Oxford: Oxford University Press.
Bellah, Robert N. 2005. 'Durkheim and Ritual'. In *The Cambridge Companion to Ritual*, edited by J. C. Alexander and P. Smith, pp. 183–201. Cambridge: Cambridge University Press.
Berger, Peter L. and Thomas Luckmann. 1967. *The Social Construction of Reality: A Treatise in the Sociology of Knowledge*. London: Allen Lane.
Betz, Hans Dieter, ed. 1992. *The Greek Magical Papyri in Translation*. 2nd edn, Chicago: The University of Chicago Press.
Betz, Hans Dieter. 2011a. 'History of Religions School'. In *Religion: Past and Present*, edited by Hans Dieter Betz, et al. <http://referenceworks.brillonline.com/entries/religion-past-and-present/history-of-religions-school-COM_024585>. Accessed 27 March 2015.
Betz, Hans Dieter. 2011b. 'Jesus' Baptism and the Origins of Christian Ritual'. In *Ablution, Initiation, and Baptism: Late Antiquity, Early Judaism, and Early Christianity*, Vol 1, edited by David Hellholm, et al., pp. 377–96. Berlin: De Gruyter.
Bianchi, Ugo. 1975. *The History of Religions*. Leiden: Brill.
Biró, Tamás. 2013. 'Is Judaism Boring? On the Lack of Counterintuitive Agents in Jewish Rituals'. In *Mind, Morality, and Magic: Cognitive Science Approaches in Biblical Studies*, edited by István Czachesz and Risto Uro, pp. 120–42. Durham: Acumen.
Blasi, Anthony, Jean Duhaime, and Paul-André Turcotte, eds. 2002. *Handbook of Early Christianity: Social Science Approaches*. Walnut Creek, CA: AltaMira.
Blass, Friedrich, Albert Debrunner, and Friedrich Rehkopf. 1979. *Grammatik des neutestamentlichen Griechisch*. 15. Aufl. Göttingen: Vandenhoeck & Ruprecht.
Blatty, William Peter. 1971. *The Exorcist*. New York: Harper & Row.
Bloch, Maurice. 2012. *Anthropology and the Cognitive Challenge*. New Departures in Anthropology. Cambridge: Cambridge University Press.
Bloom, Paul. 2004. *Descartes' Baby: How the Science of Child Development Explains What Makes Us Human*. New York: Basic Books.
Boda, Mark J., Daniel K. Falk, and Rodney A. Werline, eds. 2007. *Seeking the Favor of God*, Vol 2: *The Development of Penitential Prayer in Second*

*Temple Judaism*. Early Judaism and its Literature. Atlanta, GA: Society of Biblical Literature.
Boddy, Janice. 1994. 'Spirit Possession Revisited: Beyond Instrumentality'. *Annual Review of Anthropology* 23: pp. 407–34.
Bohak, Gideon. 2008. *Ancient Jewish Magic: A History*. Cambridge: Cambridge University Press.
Bormann, Lukas. 2015. 'Das Abendmahl: Kulturanthropologische, kognitionswissenschaftliche und ritualwissenschaftliche Perspektiven'. In *Sacred Meal, Communal Meal, Table Fellowship, and the Eucharist*, edited by David Hellholm, pp. 1081–118. Göttingen: Mohr Siebeck.
Boster, James S., Richard R. Hudson, and Steven J. C. Gaulin. 1998. 'High Paternity Certainties of Jewish Priests'. *American Anthropologist* 100 (4): pp. 967–71.
Botte, Bernard. 1958. 'Foreword to the Third Edition'. In *Comparative Liturgy* by Anton Baumstark, edited by Bernard Botte and F. L. Cross, pp. vii–xi. London: Mowbray.
Boudon, Raymond. 1991. 'What Middle-Range Theories Are?'. *Contemporary Sociology* 20: pp. 519–22.
Bousset, Wilhelm. 1921. *Kyrios Christos: Geschichte des Christusglaubens von den Anfängen des Christentums bis Irenäus*. Zweite umgearbeitete Auflage. Forschungen zur Religion und Literatur des Alten und Neuen Testament 4. Göttingen: Vanhoeck & Ruprecht.
Bousset, Wilhelm. 1970. *Kyrios Christos: A History of the Belief in Christ from the Beginnings of Christianity to Irenaeus*. Trans. John E. Steely. Nashville, TN: Abingdon.
Boyd, Robert and Peter J. Richerson. 1985. *Culture and the Evolutionary Process*. Chicago, IL: University of Chicago Press.
Boyer, Pascal. 1994a. *The Naturalness of Religious Ideas: A Cognitive Theory of Religion*. Berkeley, CA: University of California Press.
Boyer, Pascal. 1994b. 'Cognitive Constraints on Cultural Representations: Natural Ontologies and Religious Ideas'. In *Mapping the Mind: Domain Specificity in Cognition and Culture*, edited by L. A. Hirschfeld and S. A. Gelman, pp. 391–411. Cambridge: Cambridge University Press.
Boyer, Pascal. 2002. *Religion Explained: The Human Instincts that Fashion Gods, Spirits and Ancestors*. London: Vintage.
Boyer, Pascal. 2005. 'A Reductionist Model of Distinct Modes of Religious Transmission'. In *Mind and Religion: Psychological Foundations of Religiosity*, edited by Harvey Whitehouse and Robert N. McCauley, pp. 3–29. Walnut Creek, CA: AltaMira.
Boyer, Pascal, ed. 2008. *Cognitive Aspects of Religious Symbolism*. Cambridge: Cambridge University Press.
Boyer, Pascal and Pierre Liénard. 2006. 'Why Ritualized Behavior? Precaution Systems and Action Parsing in Developmental, Pathological

and Cultural Rituals'. *Behavioral and Brain Sciences* 29 (6): pp. 595–650.
Boyer, Pascal and Charles Ramble. 2001. 'Cognitive Templates for Religious Concepts: Cross-cultural Evidence for Recall of Counter-intuitive Representations'. *Cognitive Science* 25: pp. 535–64.
Bradshaw, Paul F. 2002. *The Search for the Origins of Christian Worship: Sources and Methods for the Study of Early Liturgy*. 2nd edn. London: SPCK.
Bradshaw, Paul F. and Katharine E. Harmon. 2013. 'Ritual'. In *The Study of Liturgy and Worship: An Alcuin Guide*, edited by Juliette Day and Benjamin Gordon-Taylor, pp. 21–32. London: SPCK.
Bradshaw, Paul F., Maxwell E. Johnson, and L. Edward Phillips. 2002. *The Apostolic Tradition: A Commentary*. Hermeneia: A Critical and Historical Commentary on the Bible. Minneapolis, MN: Fortress.
Brakke, David. 2006. *Demons and the Making of the Monk: Spiritual Combat in Early Christianity*. Cambridge, MA: Harvard University Press.
Brakmann, Heinzgerd. 2004. 'Katechumenat'. In *Reallexikon für Antike und Christentum*, edited by Georg Schöllgen, et al., Vol. 20, pp. 497–574. Stuttgart: Anton Hiersemann.
Brandt, Olof. 2011. 'Understanding the Structures of Early Christian Baptisteries'. In *Ablution, Initiation, and Baptism: Late Antiquity, Early Judaism, and Early Christianity*, edited by David Hellholm, et al., Vol. 2, pp. 1587–609. Berlin: De Gruyter.
Brody, Howard. 2010. 'Ritual, Medicine, and the Placebo Response'. In *The Problem of Ritual Efficacy*, edited by Willam S. Sax, Johannes Quack, and Jan Weinhold, pp. 151–67. Oxford: Oxford University Press.
Brown, Peter. 1971. 'The Rise and Function of the Holy Man in Late Antiquity'. *Journal of Roman Studies* 61: pp. 80–101.
Bulbulia, Joseph. 2004. 'Religious Costs as Adaptations that Signal Altruistic Intention'. *Evolution and Cognition* 10 (1): pp. 19–42.
Bulbulia, Joseph. 2009a. 'Religion as Evolutionary Cascade'. In *Contemporary Theories of Religion: A Critical Companion*, edited by Michael Stausberg, pp. 156–72. London: Routledge.
Bulbulia, Joseph. 2009b. 'Charismatic Signalling'. *Journal for the Study of Religion, Nature and Culture* 3 (4): pp. 518–51.
Bulbulia, Joseph. 2013. 'Why "Costly-Signalling" Models of Religion Require Cognitive Psychology?'. In *Origins of Religion, Cognition, and Culture*, edited by Armin W. Geertz, pp. 71–81. London: Routledge.
Bulbulia, Joseph and Andrew Mahoney. 2008. 'Religious Solidarity: The Hand Grenade Experiment'. *Journal of Cognition and Culture* 8: pp. 295–320.
Bulbulia, Joseph and Paul Reddish. 2013. 'Explaining Effervescence'. In *A New Science of Religion*, edited by Gregory W. Dawes and James Mclaurin, pp. 43–64. London: Routledge.

Bulbulia, Joseph and Richard Sosis. 2011. 'Signalling Theory and the Evolution of Religious Cooperation'. *Religion* 41 (3): pp. 363–88.
Bulbulia, Joseph, et al. 2013. 'The Cultural Evolution of Religion'. In *Cultural Evolution: Society, Technology, Language, and Religion*, edited by Peter J. Richerson and Morten H. Christiansen, pp. 381–404. Cambridge, MA: The MIT Press.
Bulbulia, Joseph, Quentin Atkinson, Russell Gray, and Simon Greenhill. 2013. 'Why Do Religious Cultures Evolve Slowly? The Cultural Evolution of Cooperative Calling and the Historical Study of Religions'. In *Mind, Morality and Magic: Cognitive Science Approaches in Biblical Studies*, edited by István Czachesz and Risto Uro, pp. 197–211. Durham: Acumen.
Bulkeley, Kelly. 2003. 'Review of *Religion Explained: The Evolutionary Origins of Religious Thought*, by Pascal Boyer and *How Religion Works: Towards a New Cognitive Science of Religion*, by Ilkka Pyysiäinen'. *Journal for the American Academy of Religion* 71 (3): pp. 671–74.
Burke, Peter. 1987. *The Historical Anthropology of Early Modern Italy: Essays on Perception and Communication.* Cambridge: Cambridge University Press.
Buss, David M. 1999. *Evolutionary Psychology: The New Science of Mind.* Boston: Allyn and Bacon.
Cameron, Ron and Merrill P. Miller, eds. 2004. *Redescribing Christian Origins.* Society of Biblical Literature Symposium Series. Atlanta, GA: Society of Biblical Literature.
Cameron, Ron and Merrill P. Miller, eds. 2011. *Redescribing Paul and the Corinthians.* Early Christianity and Its Literature 5. Atlanta, GA: Society of Biblical Literature.
Carney, Thomas F. 1975. *The Shape of the Past: Models and Antiquity.* Lawrence KS: Coronado Press.
Carruthers, Peter. 2006. *The Architecture of the Mind: Massive Modularity and the Flexibility of Thought.* Oxford: Clarendon.
Casey, Maurice. 2010. *Jesus of Nazareth: An Independent Historian's Account of His Life and Teaching.* London: T&T Clark.
Casey, R. P., ed. 1934. *The Excerpta ex Thedoto of Clement of Alexandria*, trans. and notes by R. P. Casey. London: Christophers.
Chalcraft, David J., ed. 2007. *Sectarianism in Early Judaism: Sociological Advances.* London: Equinox.
Charlesworth, James H., ed. 1985. *Old Testament Pseudepigrapha*: Vol. 2: *Expansions of the 'Old Testament' and Legends, Wisdom and Philosophical Literature, Prayers, Psalms, and Odes, Fragments of Lost Judeo-Hellenistic Works.* London: Darton, Longman & Todd.
Chemero, Anthony. 2009. *Radical Embodied Cognitive Science.* Cambridge, MA: The MIT Press.
Chupungco, Anscar J., ed. 1998. *Handbook for Liturgical Studies.* Collegeville, MN: Liturgical Press.

Chwe, Michael Suk-Young. 2001. *Rational Ritual: Culture, Coordination, and Common Knowledge*. Princeton, NJ: Princeton University Press.

Clark, Andy. 2003. *Natural Born Cyborgs*. New York: Oxford University Press.

Clark, Andy. 2011. *Supersizing Mind: Embodiment, Action and Cognitive Extension*. New York: Oxford University Press.

Clark, Andy and David Chalmers. 1998. 'The Extended Mind'. *Analysis* 58: pp. 10–23.

Cloutier, Jasmin and C. Neil Macrae. 2008. 'The Feeling of Choosing: Self-Involvement and the Cognitive Status of Things Past'. *Consciousness and Cognition* 17: pp. 125–35.

Cohen, Emma. 2007. *The Mind Possessed: The Cognition of Spirit Possession in an Afro-Brazilian Religious Tradition*. Oxford: Oxford University Press.

Cohen, Emma. 2008. 'What is Spirit Possession? Defining, Comparing, and Explaining Two Possession Forms'. *Ethnos* 73 (1): pp. 101–26.

Cohen, Emma and Justin L. Barrett. 2008a. 'Conceptualizing Spirit Possession: Ethnographic and Experimental Evidence'. *Ethos* 36 (2): pp. 246–67.

Cohen, Emma and Justin L. Barrett. 2008b. 'When Minds Migrate: Conceptualizing Spirit Possession'. *Journal of Cognition and Culture* 8: pp. 23–48.

Collins, Billie Jean, Bob Buller, and Johh F. Kutsko, eds. 2014. *The SBL Handbook of Style*: 2nd edn. Atlanta, GA: SBL Press.

Confer, Jaime C., et al. 2010. 'Evolutionary Psychology: Controversies, Questions, Prospects, and Limitations'. *American Psychologist* 65 (2): pp. 110–26.

Connerton, Paul. 1989. *How Societies Remember*. Cambridge: Cambridge University Press.

Corballis, Michael C. 2011. *The Recursive Mind: The Origins of Human Language, Thought, and Civilization*. Princeton, NJ: Princeton University Press.

Craffert, Pieter F. 2008. *The Life of a Galilean Shaman: Jesus of Nazareth in Anthropological-Historical Perspective*. Matrix: The Bible in Mediterranean Context. Eugen, OR: Cascade Books.

Craver, Carl F. 2007. *Explaining the Brain: Mechanisms and the Mosaic Unity of Neuroscience*. Oxford: Oxford University Press.

Cronk, Lee. 1994. 'Evolutionary Theories of Morality and the Manipulative Use of Signals'. *Zygon* 29 (1): pp. 81–101.

Crossan, John Dominic. 1991. *The Historical Jesus: The Life of a Mediterranean Jewish Peasant*. San Francisco, CA: Harper.

Cuneo, Michael W. 2001. *American Exorcism: Expelling Demons in the Land of Plenty*. London: Bantam Books.

Czachesz, István. 2010. 'Long-term, Explicit Memory in Rituals'. *Journal of Cognition and Culture* 10: pp. 321–33.

Czachesz, István. 2011. 'Explaining Magic: Earliest Christianity as a Test Case'. In *Past Minds: Studies in Cognitive Historiography*, edited by Luther H. Martin and Jesper Sørensen, pp. 141-65. London: Equinox.

Czachesz, István. 2012a. 'Filled with New Wine? Neuroscientific Correlates of Religious Experience in the New Testament'. In *Experientia, Volume 2*, edited by Colleen Shantz and Rodney A. Werline, Early Judaism and Its Literature 35, pp. 71-90. Atlanta, GA: Society of Biblical Literature.

Czachesz, István. 2012b. 'Women, Charity, and Mobility in Early Christianity: Weak Links and the Historical Transformation of Religions'. In *Changing Minds: Religion and Cognition through the Ages*, edited by István Czachesz and Tamás Biró, pp. 129-54. Leuven: Peeters.

Czachesz, István. 2013a. 'A Cognitive Perspective on Magic in the New Testament'. In *Mind, Morality and Magic: Cognitive Science Approaches in Biblical Studies*, edited by István Czachesz and Risto Uro, pp. 164-79. Durham: Acumen.

Czachesz, István. 2013b. 'Rethinking Biblical Transmission: Insights from the Cognitive Neuroscience of Memory'. In *Mind, Morality and Magic: Cognitive Science Approaches in Biblical Studies*, edited by István Czachesz and Risto Uro, pp. 43-61. Durham: Acumen.

Czachesz, István. 2013c. 'Jesus' Religious Experience in the Gospels: Toward a Cognitive Neuroscience Approach'. In *Jesus—Gestalt und Gestaltungen: Rezeption des Galiläers in Wissenshaft, Kirche und Gesellschaft: Festschrift für Gerd Theissen zum 70. Geburtstag*, edited by Petra von Gemünden, David G. Horrell, and Max Küchler, pp. 569-96. Göttingen: Vandenhoeck & Ruprecht.

Czachesz, István and Anders Lisdorf. 2013. 'Computer Modeling of Cognitive Processes in Biblical Studies: The Primacy of Urban Christianity as a Test Case'. In *Mind, Morality and Magic: Cognitive Science Approaches in Biblical Studies*, edited by István Czachesz and Risto Uro, pp. 77-97. Durham: Acumen.

Czachesz, István and Risto Uro, eds. 2013. *Mind, Morality, and Magic: Cognitive Science Approaches in Biblical Studies*. Durham: Acumen.

Dale, Rick. 2008. 'The Possibility of a Pluralistic Cognitive Science'. *Journal of Experimental and Theoretical Artificial Intelligence* 20 (3): pp. 155-79.

Davies, Douglas J. 2011. *Emotion, Identity, and Religion: Hope, Reciprocity, and Otherness*. Oxford: Oxford University Press.

Davies, Kathy, ed. 1997. *Embodied Practices: Feminist Perspectives on the Body*. London: SAGE.

Davies, Stevan L. 1983. 'John the Baptist and Essene Kashruth'. *New Testament Studies* 29: pp. 569-71.

Davies, Stevan L. 1995. *Jesus the Healer: Possession, Trance, and the Origins of Christianity*. London: SCM.

Day, Juliette. 2011. 'Review of *Baptism in the Early Church*. *History, Theology, and Liturgy in the First Five Centuries*, by Everett Ferguson. Grand Rapids, MI—Cambridge: Eerdmans, 2009'. *The Journal of Ecclesiastical History* 62 (2): pp. 349–51.

Day, Juliette and Benjamin Gordon-Taylor, eds. 2013. *The Study of Liturgy and Worship: An Alcuin Guide*. London: SPCK.

Day, Matthew. 2004. 'Religion, Off-Line Cognition and the Extended Mind'. *Journal of Cognition and Culture* 4 (1): pp. 101–21.

Deacon, Terrence W. 1997. *The Symbolic Species: The Co-evolution of Language and the Brain*. New York: Norton & Company.

della Porta, Donatella and Michael Keating. 2008. 'How Many Approaches in the Social Sciences: An Epistemological Introduction'. In *Approaches and Methodologies in the Social Sciences: A Pluralistic Perspective*, edited by Donatella della Porta and Michael Keating, pp. 19–39. Cambridge: Cambridge University Press.

DeMaris, Richard E. 1999. 'Funerals and Baptisms, Ordinary and Otherwise: Ritual Criticism and Corinthian Rites'. *Biblical Theology Bulletin* 29 (1): pp. 23–34.

DeMaris, Richard E. 2002. 'The Baptism of Jesus: A Ritual-Critical Approach'. In *The Social Setting of Jesus and the Gospels*, edited by Wolfgang Stegemann, Bruce J. Malina, and Gerd Theissen, pp. 137–57. Minneapolis, MN: Fortress.

DeMaris, Richard E. 2008. *The New Testament in Its Ritual World*. London: Routledge.

Dibelius, Martin and Heinrich Greeven. 1976. *James: A Commentary on the Epistle of James*. Hermeneia. Philadelphia, PA: Fortress.

Dix, Gregory. 2005. *The Shape of the Liturgy*. New edition with an introduction by Dr Simon Jones. London: Continuum.

Dölger, Franz Joseph. 1909. *Der Exorzismus im altchristlichen Taufritual: Eine religionsgeschictliche Studie*. Studien zur Geschichte und Kultur des Altertums 3: 1–2. Paderborn: Ferdinand Schöningh.

Donald, Merlin. 2001. *A Mind So Rare: The Evolution of Human Consciousness*. New York: W.W. Norton.

Douglas, Mary. 1973. *Natural Symbols: Explorations in Cosmology*. 2nd edn. London: Barrie & Jenkins.

Driver, Tom F. 1991. *The Magic of Ritual: Our Need for Liberating Rites that Transform Our Lives and Communities*. New York: Harper San Francisco.

Driver, Tom F. 2007. 'Review of *A Sociological History of Christian Worship*, by Martin D. Stringer, Cambridge: Cambridge University Press 2005'. *Church History* 76 (3): pp. 682–5.

DuBois, Thomas A. 2009. *An Introduction to Shamanism*. Cambridge: Cambridge University Press.

Dujarier, Michele. 1979. *A History of the Catechumenate: The First Six Centuries*. New York: Sadlier.
Dulaney, Siri and Alan Page Fiske. 1994. 'Cultural Rituals and Obsessive-Compulsive Disorder: Is There a Common Psychological Mechanism?'. *Ethos* 22 (3): pp. 243–83.
Dunderberg, Ismo. 2008. *Beyond Gnosticism: Myth, Lifestyle, and Society in the School of Valentinus*. New York: Columbia University Press.
Durkheim, Émile. 1912. *Les formes élémentaires de la vie religieuse: Le systéme totémique en Australie*. Paris: Quadrige/PUF.
Durkheim, Émile. 2001. *The Elementary Forms of Religious Life*. Trans. Carol Cosman. Oxford World's Classics. Oxford: Oxford University Press.
Eberhart, Christian A., ed. 2011. *Ritual and Metaphor: Sacrifice in the Bible*. Resources for Biblical Study 68. Atlanta, GA: Society of Biblical Literature.
Ebertz, Michael N. 1987. *Das Charisma des Gekreuzigten. Zur Soziologie der Jesusbewegung*. WUNT. Tübingen: Mohr Siebeck.
Ego, Beate, Armin Lange, and Peter Pilhofer, eds. 1999. *Gemeinde ohne Tempel—Community without Temple: Zur Substituierung und Transformation das Jerusalemer Tempels und seines Kults im Alten Testament, antiken Judentum and frühen Christentum*. Wissenshaftliche Unersuchungen zum Neuen Testament 118. Tübingen Mohr Siebeck.
Eichorn, Albert. 1898. *Das Abendmahl im Neuen Testament*. Hefte zur 'Christlichen Welt' 36. Leibzig: Mohr Siebeck.
Eliade, Mircae. 1964. *Shamanism: Archaic Techniques of Ecstacy*. Trans. Willard R. Trask. Princeton, NJ: Princeton University Press.
Elliott, John H. 1981. *A Home for the Homeless: A Social-Scientific Criticism of 1 Peter, Its Situation and Strategy*. Minneapolis, MN: Fortress.
Elliott, John H. 1986. 'Social-Scientific Criticism of the New Testament: More on Methods and Models'. *Semeia* 35: pp. 1–33.
Elliott, John H. 1993. *What Is Social-Scientific Criticism?* Guides to Biblical Scholarship. Minneapolis, MN: Fortress.
Emmons, Robert A. and Patrick McNamara. 2006. 'Sacred Emotions and Affective Neuroscience: Gratitude, Costly Signaling, and the Brain'. In *Where Science and God Meets: How Brain and Evolutionary Studies Alter Our Understanding of Religion*, edited by Patrick McNamara, Vol. 1, pp. 12–30. Wesport, CT: Praeger.
Engler, Steven and Mark Quentin Gardiner. 2009. 'Religion as Superhuman Agency'. In *Contemporary Theories of Religion: A Critical Companion*, edited by Michael Stausberg, pp. 22–38. London: Routledge.
Enslin, Morton S. 1975. 'John and Jesus'. *Zeitschrift für die neutestamentliche Wissenschaft und die Kunde der älteren Kirche* 66: pp. 1–18.
Ernst, Josef. 1989. *Johannes der Täufer. Interpretation—Geschichte—Wirkungsgeschichte*. Berlin: de Gruyter.

Eshel, Esther. 2003. 'Genres of Magical Texts in the Dead Sea Scrolls'. In *Die Dämonen—Demons*, edited by Armin Lange, Hermann Lichtenberger, and K. F. Diethard Römheld, pp. 395–415. Tübingen: Mohr Siebeck.

Esler, Philip F. 1994. *The First Christians in Their Social Worlds: Social-Scientific Approaches to New Testament Interpretation*. London: Routledge.

Esler, Philip F. 1995a. 'Introduction'. In *Modelling Early Christianity*, edited by Philip F. Esler, pp. 1–22. London: Routledge.

Esler, Philip F., ed. 1995b. *Modelling Early Christianity: Social Scientific Studies of the New Testament in Its Context*. London: Routledge.

Esler, Philip F. 2000. 'Models in New Testament Interpretation: A Reply to David Horrell'. *Journal for the Study of the New Testament* 78: pp. 107–13.

Esler, Philip F. 2003. *Conflict and Identity in Romans: The Social Setting of Paul's Letter*. Minneapolis, MN: Fortress.

Estrada, Nelson P. 2004. *From Followers to Leaders: The Apostles in the Ritual Status Transformation in Acts 1–2*. Journal for the Study of the New Testament: Supplement Series 255. London: T&T Clark International.

Evans, Graig E. 1999. 'Authenticating the Activities of Jesus'. In *Authenticating the Activities of Jesus*, edited by Bruce Chilton and Graig E. Evans, pp. 3–30. Leiden: Brill.

Eve, Eric. 2009. *The Healer from Nazareth: Jesus' Miracles in the Historical Context*. London: SPCK.

Fauconnier, Gilles and Mark Turner. 2002. *The Way We Think: Conceptual Blending and the Mind Hidden Complexities*. New York: Basic Books.

Feldman, Louis H., trans., ed. 1965. *Josephus: Jewish Antiquites*, books xviii–xix, vol 9. Loeb Classical Library 433. Cambridge, MA: Harvard University Press.

Ferguson, Everett. 2009. *Baptism in the Early Church: History, Theology, and Liturgy in the First Five Centuries*. Grand Rapids, MI: Eerdmans.

Ferngren, Gary B. 2009. *Medicine and Health Care in Early Christianity*. Baltimore, ML: The John Hopkins University Press.

Finn, Thomas M. 1992. *Early Christian Baptism and the Catechumenate: West and East Syria*. Message of the Fathers of the Church 5. Collegeville, MN: The Liturgical Press.

Fiske, Alan Page and Nick Haslam. 1997. 'Is Obsessive Compulsive Disorder a Pathology of the Human Disposition to Perform Socially Meaningful Rituals? Evidence of Similar Content'. *The Journal of Mental Disease* 185 (4): pp. 211–22.

Fodor, Jerry A. 1975. *The Language of Thought*. Cambridge, MA: Harvard University Press.

Fodor, Jerry A. 1983. *Modularity of the Mind*. Cambridge, MA: MIT Press.

Forbes, Christopher. 1995. *Prophecy and Inspired Speech in Early Christianity and Its Hellenistic Environment*. Wissenshaftliche Untersuchungen zum Neuen Testament 2. Tübingen: Mohr Siebeck.

Franek, Juraj. 2014. 'Has the Cognitive Science of Religion (Re)defined "Religion"?'. *Religio: Revue pro religionistiku* 22 (1): pp. 3–27.
Freud, Sigmund. 1963. 'Obsessive Acts and Religious Practices'. In *Character and Culture*, edited by Philip Rieff, pp. 17–26. New York: Collier.
Freyne, Seán. 2011. 'Jewish Immersion and Christian Baptism: Continuity on the Margins?' In *Ablution, Initiation, and Baptism: Late Antiquity, Early Judaism, and Early Christianity*, vol. 1, edited by David Hellholm, et al., Beihefte zur Zeitschrift für die neutestamentliche Wissenschaft und die Kunde der älteren Kirche 176: I, pp. 221–53. Berlin: De Gruyter.
Furseth, Inger and Pål Repstad. 2006. *An Introduction to the Sociology of Religion: Classical and Contemporary Perspectives*. Hants: Ashgate.
Gager, John G. 1975. *Kingdom and Community: The Social World of Early Christianity*. Englewood Cliffs, NJ: Prentice Hall.
Gallagher, Shaun. 2005. *How the Body Shapes the Mind*. Oxford: Clarendon Press.
Gane, Roy E. 2004. *Ritual Dynamic Structure*. Piscataway, NJ: Gorgias.
Gärdenfors, Peter. 2006. *How Homo Became Sapiens: On the Evolution of Thinking*. Oxford: Oxford University Press.
Geertz, Armin W. 2010. 'Brain, Body, and Culture: A Biocultural Theory of Religion'. *Method and Theory in the Study of Religion* 22: pp. 304–21.
Gervais, Will M. and Joseph Henrich. 2010. 'The Zeus Problem: Why Representational Content Biases Cannot Explain Faith in Gods'. *Journal of Cognition and Culture* 10: pp. 383–9.
Gervais, Will M., Ayana K. Willard, Ara Norenzayan, and Joseph Henrich. 2011. 'The Cultural Transmission of Faith: Why Innate Intuitions Are Necessary, But Insufficient, to Explain Religious Belief'. *Religion* 41 (3): pp. 389–410.
Gibbon, Edward. 1994 [1776]. *The History of the Decline and Fall of the Roman Empire*, Vol. 1, edited by David Womersley. London: Allen Lane.
Gibbs, Raymond W., Jr. 2005. *Embodiment and the Cognitive Science*. Cambridge: Cambridge University Press.
Glenberg, Arthur M., Jessica K. Witt, and Janet Metcalfe. 2013. 'From the Revolution to Embodiment: 25 Years of Cognitive Psychology'. *Perspectives on Psychological Science* 8 (5): pp. 573–85.
Goodman, Felicitas D. 2005. 'Glossolalia'. In *Encyclopedia of Religion*: 2nd edn, edited by Lindsay Jones, Vol. 5, pp. 3504–47. Detroit, MI: Macmillan.
Goodman, Martin. 1994. *Mission and Conversion: Proselytizing in the Religious History of the Roman Empire*. Oxford: Clarendon Press.
Gorman, Frank H., Jr. 1990. *The Ideology of Ritual: Space, Time and Status of Priestly Theology*. Supplements to Journal for the Study of the Old Testament 91. Sheffield: JSOT Press.
Gorman, Frank H., Jr. 1995. 'Ritual Studies and Biblical Studies: Assessment of the Past, Prospects for the Future'. In *Transformation, Passages and*

*Processes: Ritual Approaches to Biblical Texts*, edited by Mark McVann, Semeia 67, pp. 13–36. Atlanta, GA: Scholars Press.

Grabbe, Lester L. 2000. *Judaic Religion in the Second Temple Period: Belief and Practice from the Exile to Yavneh*. London: Routledge.

Grimes, Ronald L. 1985. *Research in Ritual Studies: A Programmatic Essay and Bibliography*. Atla Bibliography Series 14. Metuchen, NJ: The American Theological Library/Scarecrow.

Grimes, Ronald L. 1995. *Beginnings in Ritual Studies*: Revised Edition. Columbia, SC: University of South Carolina Press.

Grimes, Ronald L. 2000. *Deeply into the Bone: Re-inventing Rites of Passage*. Berkeley, CA: University of California Press.

Grimes, Ronald L. 2008. 'Performance Theory and the Study of Ritual'. In *New Approaches to the Study of Religion*. Vol. 2: *Textual, Comparative, Sociological, and Cognitive Approaches*, edited by Peter Antes, Armin W. Geertz, and Randi R. Warni, pp. 109–38. Berlin: de Gruyter.

Grimes, Ronald L. 2014. *The Craft of Ritual Studies*. Oxford: Oxford University Press.

Griswold, Charles L. and David Konstan, eds. 2012. *Ancient Forgiveness: Classical, Judaic, and Christian*. Cambridge: Cambridge University Press.

Grudem, Wayne A. 1982. *The Gift of Prophecy in 1 Corinthians*. Lanham, MD: University Press of America.

Gruenwald, Ithamar. 2003. *Rituals and Ritual Theory in Ancient Israel*. The Brill Reference Library of Judaism. Leiden: Brill.

Gudme, Anne Katrine de Hemmer. 2013. 'A Kind of Magic: The Law of Jealousy in Numbers 5:11–31 as Magical Ritual and as Ritual Text'. In *Studies on Magic and Divination in the Biblical World*, edited by Anne Katrine de Hemmer Gudme and Helen Jacobus, pp. 149–67. Piscataway, NJ: Gorgias Press.

Gunkel, Hermann. 1927. 'The "Historical Movement" in the Study of Religion'. *The Expository Times* 38: pp. 532–6.

Guthrie, Stewart E. 1980. 'A Cognitive Theory of Religion'. *Current Anthropology* 21 (2): pp. 181–203.

Guthrie, Stewart E. 1993. *Faces in the Clouds: A New Theory of Religion*. New York: Oxford University Press.

Guthrie, Stewart E. 2007. 'Opportunity, Challenge, and a Definition of Religion'. *Journal for the Study of Religion, Nature and Culture* 1 (1): pp. 58–67.

Hacking, Ian. 1999. *The Social Construction of What?* Cambridge, MA: Harvard University Press.

Hägerland, Tobias. 2006. 'Jesus and the Rites of Repentance'. *New Testament Studies* 52: pp. 166–87.

Hägerland, Tobias. 2012. *Jesus and the Forgiveness of Sins: An Aspect of His Prophetic Mission*. Society for New Testament Studies: Monograph Series 150. Cambridge: Cambridge University Press.

Handelman, Don and Galina Lindquist, eds. 2005. *Ritual in Its Own Right: Exploring Dynamics of Transformation*. New York: Berghahn Books.

Harari, Yuval Noah. 2011. *Sapiens: A Brief History of Humankind*. London: Vintage books.

Harland, Philip A. 2009. *Dynamics of Identity in the World of the Early Christians: Associations, Judeans, and Cultural Minorities*. London: T & T Clark.

Harmon-Jones, Eddie and Piotr Winkielman. 2007. *Social Neuroscience: Integrating Psychological and Biological Explanations of Social Behavior*. New York: Guilford Press.

Hart, Trevor. 2000. 'Creeds, Councils and Doctrinal Development'. In *The Early Christian World*, Vol. 1, edited by Philip F. Esler, pp. 639–59. London: Routledge.

Hartin, Patrick J. 1999. *A Spirituality of Perfection: Faith in Action in the Letter of James*. Collegeville, MN: The Liturgical Press.

Hartman, Lars. 1997. *'Into the Name of the Lord': Baptism in the Early Church*. Studies of the New Testament and Its World. Edinburgh: T&T Clark.

Harvey, Graham, ed. 2005. *Ritual and Religious Belief: A Reader*. London: Equinox.

Hauser, Marc, Noam Chomsky, and W. Tecumseh Fitch. 2002. 'The Faculty of Language: What Is It, Who Has It, and How Did It Evolve?'. *Science* 298: pp. 1569–79.

Havas, David A., et al. 2010. 'Cosmetic Use of Botulinium Toxin-A Affects Processing of Emotional Language'. *Psychological Science* 21: pp. 895–900.

Hawking, Stephen and Leonard Mlodinow. 2010. *The Grand Design: New Answers to the Ultimate Questions of Life*. London: Bantam.

Hedström, Peter and Richard Swedberg. 1998a. 'Social Mechanisms: An Introductory Essay'. In *Social Mechanisms: An Analytical Approach to Social Theory*, edited by Peter Hedström and Richard Swedberg, pp. 1–31. Cambridge: Cambridge University Press.

Hedström, Peter and Richard Swedberg, eds. 1998b. *Social Mechanisms: An Analytical Approach to Social Theory*. Studies in Rationality and Social Change. Cambridge: Cambridge University Press.

Hedström, Peter and Petri Ylikoski. 2010. 'Causal Mechanisms in the Social Sciences'. *The Annual Review of Sociology* 36: pp. 49–67.

Heimola, Mikko. 2012. 'Religious Rituals and Social Norms in the Making of Adaptive Systems: Empirical and Theoretical Synthesis on Revivals in the 19th Century Finland'. PhD Diss. University of Helsinki.

Heitmüller, Wilhelm. 1903. *Taufe und Abendmahl bei Paulus: Darstellung und religionsgeschichtliche Beleuchtung*. Göttingen: Vandenhoeck & Ruprecht.

Hellholm, David, Tor Vegge, Øyvind Norderval, and Christer Hellholm, eds. 2011. *Ablution, Initiation, and Baptism: Late Antiquity, Early Judaism,* and *Early Christianity*. Beihefte zur Zeitschrift für die neutestamentliche Wissenschaft 176: 1–3. Berlin: Walter de Gruyter.

Hendel, Ronald S. 2012. 'Away from Ritual: The Prophetic Critique'. In *Social Theory and the Study of Israelite Religion: Essays in Retrospect and Prospect*, edited by Saul M. Olyan, Resources for Biblical Study 71, pp. 59–79. Atlanta, GA: Society of Biblical Literature.

Henrich, Joseph. 2009. 'The Evolution of Costly Displays, Cooperation and Religion: Credibility Enhancing Displays and Their Implications for Cultural Evolution'. *Evolution and Human Behavior* 30: pp. 244–60.

Hollenbach, Paul W. 1981. 'Jesus, Demoniacs, and Public Authorities: A Socio- Historical Study'. *Journal for the American Academy of Religion* 49: pp. 567–88.

Hollenbach, Paul W. 1982. 'The Conversion of Jesus: From Jesus the Baptizer to Jesus the Healer'. In *Aufstieg und Niedergang der römishcen Welt* 2.25.1, edited by Hildegard Temporini and Wolfgang Haase, pp. 196–219. Berlin: de Gruyter.

Hollenbach, Paul W. 1993. 'Help for Interpreting Jesus' Exorcisms'. *Society of Biblical Literature 1993 Seminar Papers* 32: pp. 119–28.

Holmén, Tom. 2001. *Jesus and Jewish Covenant Thinking*. Biblical Interpretation Series 55. Leiden: Brill.

Holmes, Michael W., ed. 2002. *The Apostolic Fathers: Greek Texts and English Translations*. 2nd edn. Grand Rapids, MI: Baker.

Holtzmann, Heinrich Julius. 1897. *Lehrbuch des neutestamentlichen Theologie*. Freiburg: Mohr.

Hornstein, Susan L. and Neil W. Mulligan. 2001. 'Memory of Action Events: The Role of Objects in Memory of Self- and Other-Performed Tasks'. *American Journal of Psychology* 114 (2): pp. 119–217.

Horrell, David G. 1996. *The Social Ethos of the Corinthian Correspondence: Interests and Ideology from 1 Corinthians to 1 Clement*. Studies of the New Testament and Its World. Edinburgh: T&T Clark.

Horrell, David G. 2000. 'Models and Methods in Social-Scientific Interpretation: A Response to Philip Esler'. *Journal for the Study of the New Testament* 78: pp. 83–105.

Horrell, David G. 2002. 'Social Sciences Studying Formative Christian Phenomena: A Creative Movement'. In *Handbook of Early Christianity: Social Science Approaches*, edited by Anthony J. Blasi, Jean Duhaime, and Paul-André Turcotte, pp. 3–28. Walnut Creek, CA: AltaMira.

Horrell, David G. 2004. 'Domestic Space and Christian Meetings at Corinth: Imagining New Contexts and the Buildings East of the Theatre'. *New Testament Studies* 50: pp. 349–69.

Horrell, David G. 2008. 'Pauline Churches or Early Christian Churches: Unity, Disagreement, and the Eucharist'. In *Einheit der Kirche im Neuen Testament*, edited by Anatoly A. Alexeev, Christos Karakolis, and Ulrich

Luz, Wissenshaftliche Untersuchungen zum Neuen Testament 218, pp. 185–203. Tübingen: Mohr Siebeck.

Horrell, David G. and Edward Adams, eds. 2004. *Christianity at Corinth: The Quest for the Pauline Church*. Louisville, KY: Westminster John Knox.

Horsley, R. A. 1987. *Jesus and the Spiral of Violence. Popular Jewish Resistance in Roman Palestine*. San Francisco: Harper & Row.

Horst, Steven. 2007. *Beyond Reduction: Philosophy of Mind and Post-Reductionist Philosophy of Science*. Oxford: Oxford University Press.

Howe, Bonnie and Joel B. Green, eds. 2014. *Cognitive Linguistic Explorations in Biblical Studies*. Berlin: de Gruyter.

Humphrey, Caroline and James Laidlaw. 1994. *The Archetypal Actions of Ritual: A Theory of Ritual Illustrated by the Jain Rite of Worship*. Oxford: Clarendon.

Hurtado, Larry W. 2003. *Lord Jesus Christ: Devotion to Jesus in Earliest Christianity*. Grand Rapids, MI: Eerdmans.

Hüsken, Ute and Frank Neubert, eds. 2012. *Negotiating Rites*. New York: Oxford University Press.

Iannaccone, Laurence R. 1994. 'Why Strict Churches Are Strong'. *American Journal of Sociology* 99 (5): pp. 1180–211.

Irons, William. 2001. 'Religion as a Hard-to-fake Sign of Commitment'. In *Evolution and the Capacity for Commitment*, edited by Randolph N. Nesse, pp. 292–309. New York: Russell Sage Foundation.

Jablonka, Eva and Marion J. Lamb. 2005. *Evolution in Four Dimensions: Genetic, Epigenetic, Behavioral, and Symbolic Variation in the History of Life*. Life and Mind. Cambridge, MA: MIT Press.

Jensen, Jeppe Sinding. 2009. 'Religion as the Unintended Product of Brain Functions in the "Standard Cognitive Science of Religion Model"'. In *Contemporary Theories of Religion: A Critical Companion*, edited by Michael Stausberg, pp. 129–55. London: Routledge.

Jensen, Robin M. 2011. *Living Water: Images, Symbols, and Settings of Early Christian Baptism*. Supplements to Vigiliae Christianae 101. Leiden: Brill.

Jensen, Robin M. 2012. *Baptismal Imagery in Early Christianity: Ritual, Visual, and Theological Dimensions*. Grand Rapids, MI: Baker Academic.

Johnson, Maxwell E. 1999. *The Rites of Christian Initiation: Their Evolution and Interpretation*. Collegeville, MN: The Liturgical Press.

Johnson, Maxwell E. 2013. 'Initiation'. In *The Study of Liturgy and Worship: An Alcuin Guide*, edited by Juliette Day and Benjamin Gordon-Taylor, pp. 125–34. London: SPCK.

Jokiranta, Jutta. 2013. 'Ritual System in the Qumran Movement: Frequency, Boredom and Balance'. In *Mind, Morality and Magic: Cognitive Science Approaches in Biblical Studies*, edited by István Czachesz and Risto Uro, pp. 144–63. Durham: Acumen.

Kapferer, Bruce. 1983. *A Celebration of Demons: Exorcism and the Aesthetics of Healing in Sri Lanka*. Bloomington, IN: Indiana University Press.
Kärkkäinen Terian, Sara. 2004. 'Crisis Rituals'. In *The Routledge Encyclopedia of Religious Rites, Rituals, and Festivals*, edited by Frank A. Salamone, pp. 101–3. New York: Routledge.
Karmiloff-Smith, Annette. 1992. *Beyond Modularity: A Developmental Perspective on Cognitive Science*. Cambridge, MA: MIT Press.
Kaše, Vojtěch. 2014. 'Early Christians in the Machine: How Does a Belief in Supernatural Efficacy of a Ritual Emerge?' Poster in the IACSR Meeting and General Assembly, Brno, Czech Republic, 20–22 June 2014.
Kazen, Thomas. 2002. *Jesus and Purity Halakhah: Was Jesus Indifferent to Impurity?* Coniectanea biblica. Stockholm: Almqvist & Wiksell.
Kazen, Thomas. 2011. *Emotions in Biblical Law: A Cognitive Science Approach*. Hebrew Bible Monographs 36. Sheffield: Sheffield Phoenix Press.
Kelhoffer, James A. 2005. *The Diet of John the Baptist: 'Locusts and Wild Honey' in Synoptic and Patristic Interpretation*. Wissenshafttliche Untersuchungen zum Neuen Testament 176. Tübingen: Mohr Siebeck.
Kelly, Henry Ansgar. 1985. *The Devil at Baptism: Ritual, Theology, and Drama*. Ithaca, NY: Cornell University Press.
Ketola, Kimmo. 2007. 'A Cognitive Approach to Ritual Systems in First-Century Judaism'. In *Explaining Early Judaism and Christianity: Contributions from Cognitive and Social Science*, edited by Petri Luomanen, Ilkka Pyysiäinen, and Risto Uro, Biblical Interpretation 89, pp. 95–114. Leiden: Brill.
Ketola, Kimmo. 2008. *The Founder of the Hare Krishnas as Seen by Devotees: A Cognitive Study of Religious Charisma*. Numen Book Series 120. Leiden: Brill.
King, Karen L. 2003. *What Is Gnosticism?* Cambridge, MA: The Belknap Press of Harvard University Press.
Klawans, Jonathan 2006. *Purity, Sacrifice, and the Temple: Symbolism and Supersessionism in the Study of Ancient Judaism*. Oxford: Oxford University Press.
Klingbeil, Gerald A. 1998. *A Comparative Study of the Ritual of Ordination as Found in Leviticus 8 and Emar 369*. Lewiston, NY: Edwin Mellen.
Klingbeil, Gerald A. 2007. *Bridging the Gap: Ritual and Ritual Texts in the Bible*. Bulletin for Biblical Research Supplements 1. Winona Lake, IN: Eisenbrauns.
Klinghardt, Matthias. 1996. *Gemeinschaft und Mahlgemeinschaft: Soziologie und Liturgie Früchristlicher Mahlfeiern*. Tübingen: Francke Verlag.
Klutz, Todd. 1999. 'The Grammar of Exorcism in the Ancient Mediterranean World'. In *Jewish Roots of Christological Monotheism: Papers from the St. Andrews Conference on the Historical Origins of the Worship on Jesus*,

edited by Carey C. Newman, James R. Davila, and Gladys S. Lewis, Journal for the Study of Judaism in the Persian, Hellenistic, and Roman Periods: Supplement Series 63, pp. 156–65. Leiden: Brill.

Klutz, Todd. 2004. *The Exorcism Stories in Luke-Acts*. Society for New Testament Studies Monograph Series 129. Cambridge: Cambridge University Press.

Knust, Jennifer Wright and Zsuzsanna Várhelyi, eds. 2011. *Ancient Mediterranean Sacrifice*. Oxford: Oxford University Press.

Kollmann, Bernd. 1996. *Jesus und die Christen als Wundertäter: Studien zu Magie, Medizin und Shamanismus in Antike und Christentum*. Forschungen zur Religion und Literatur des Alten und Neuen Testaments 170. Göttingen: Vandenhoeg & Ruprecht.

Konstan, David. 2010. *Before Forgiveness: The Origins of a Moral Idea*. Cambridge: Cambridge University Press.

Konvalinka, Ivana, et al. 2011. 'Synchronized Arousal Between Performers and Related Spectators in a Fire-Walking Ritual'. *Proceedings of the National Academy of Sciences* 108 (20): pp. 8514–19.

Kreinath, Jens. 2008. 'Semiotics'. In *Theorizing Rituals: Issues, Topics, Approaches, Concepts*, edited by Jens Kreinath, Jan Snoek, and Michael Stausberg, Numen Book Series 114: 1, pp. 429–70. Leiden: Brill.

Kreinath, Jens, Jan Snoek, and Michael Stausberg. 2007. *Theorizing Rituals: Annotated Bibliography of Ritual Theory, 1966–2005*. Numen Book Series 114: 2. Leiden: Brill.

Kreinath, Jens, Jan Snoek, and Michael Stausberg. 2008a. 'Ritual Studies, Ritual Theory, Theorizing Rituals: An Introductory Essay'. In *Theorizing Rituals: Issues, Topics, Approaches, Concepts*, edited by Jens Kreinath, Jan Snoek, and Michael Stausberg, Numen Book Series 114: 1, pp. xv–xxvii. Leiden: Brill.

Kreinath, Jens, Jan A. M. Snoek, and Michael Stausberg, eds. 2008b. *Theorizing Rituals: Issues, Topics, Approaches, Concepts*. Numen Book Series 114: 1. Leiden: Brill.

Kudlien, Fridolf. 1978. 'Beichte und Heilung'. *Medizin Historisches Journal* 13: pp. 1–14.

Laderman, Carol and Marina Roseman, eds. 1996. *The Performance of Healing*. New York: Routledge.

Laidlaw, James. 2007. 'A Well-Disposed Social Anthropologist's Problems with the "Cognitive Science of Religion"'. In *Religion, Anthropology and Cognitive Science*, edited by Harvey Whitehouse and James Laidlaw, pp. 211–46. Durham, NC: Carolina Academic Press.

Laidlaw, James and Caroline Humphrey. 2008. 'Action'. In *Theorizing Rituals: Classical Topics, Theoretical Approaches, Analytical Concepts*, edited by Jens Kreinath, Jan Snoek, and Michael Stausberg, Numen Book Series 114: 1, pp. 265–84. Leiden: Brill.

Lakoff, George. 1987. *Woman, Fire and Dangerous Things: What Categories Reveal about the Mind*. Chicago, IL: University of Chicago Press.

Lakoff, George and Mark Johnson. 2003. *Metaphors We Live By*. A new afterword 2003. Chicago: The University of Chicago Press.

Laland, Kevin N., Kim Sterelny, John Odling-Smee, William Hoppitt, and Tobias Uller. 2011. 'Cause and Effect in Biology Revisited: Is Mayr's proximate-ultimate dichotomy still useful?'. *Science* 334 (6062): pp. 1512–16.

Lamoreaux, Jason T. 2013. *Ritual, Women, and Philippi: Reimagining the Early Philippian Community*. Matrix: The Bible in Mediterranean Context Series 8. Eugene, OR: Cascade Books.

Lampe, Peter. 1994. 'The Eucharist: Identifying with Christ on the Cross'. *Interpretation* 48 (1): pp. 36–49.

Lawrence, Jonathan D. 2006. *Washing in Water: Trajectories of Ritual Bathing in the Hebrew Bible and Second Temple Literature*. Society of Biblical Literature: Academia Biblica 23. Atlanta, GA: Society of Biblical Literature.

Lawrence, Louise J. 2009. 'Ritual and the First Urban Christians: Boundary Crossings of Life and Death'. In *After the First Urban Christians: The Social-Scientific Study of Pauline Christianity Twenty-Five Years Later*, edited by Todd D. Still and David G. Horrell, pp. 99–115. London: T&T Clark.

Lawson, E. Thomas. 2008. 'Cognitive Categories, Cultural Forms and Ritual Structures'. In *Cognitive Aspects of Religious Symbolism*, edited by Pascal Boyer, pp. 188–206. Cambridge: Cambridge University Press.

Lawson, E. Thomas and Robert N. McCauley. 1990. *Rethinking Religion: Connecting Cognition and Culture*. Cambridge: Cambridge University Press.

Lawson, E. Thomas and Robert N. McCauley. 2002. 'The Cognitive Representation of Religious Ritual Form: A Theory of Participant's Competence of the Religious Ritual System'. In *Current Approaches in the Cognitive Science of Religion*, edited by Ilkka Pyysiäinen and Veikko Anttonen, pp. 154–77. London: Continuum.

Leeper, Elisabeth A. 1990. 'From Alexandria to Rome: The Valentinian Connection to the Incorporation of Exorcism as a Prebaptismal Rite'. *Vigiliae christianae* 44 (1): pp. 6–24.

Lehmkühler, Karsten. 1996. 'Die Beteutung des Kultus für das Christentum der Moderne: Eine Discussion zwischen Wilhelm Bousset und Ernst Troelsch'. In *Die Religionsgeschichtliche Schule: Facetten eines theologischen Umbruchs*, edited by Gerd Lüdemann, Studien und Texter zur Religionsgeschichtliche Schule 1, pp. 207–24. Frankfurt am Main: Peter Lang.

Levenson, Robert W. 2003. 'Blood, Sweat and Fears: The Autonomic Architecture of Emotion'. In *Emotions Inside Out*, edited by P. Ekman,

J. J. Campos, R. J. Davidson, and F. B. M. de Waal, pp. 358–66. New York: New York Academy of Sciences.

Lewis, I. M. 1971. *Ecstatic Religion: An Anthropological Study of Spirit Possession and Shamanism*. Middlesex: Penguin.

Liénard, Pierre and Pascal Boyer. 2006. 'Whence Collective Rituals? A Cultural Selection Model of Ritualized Behavior'. *American Anthropologist* 108 (4): pp. 814–27.

Liénard, Pierre and E. Thomas Lawson. 2008. 'Evoked Culture, Ritualization and Religious Rituals'. *Religion* 38: pp. 157–71.

Lietzmann, Hans. 1979. *Mass and Lord's Supper: A Study in the History of the Liturgy*. Trans. Dorothea H. G. Reeve. With introduction and further inquiry by Robert Douglas Richardson. Leiden: Brill.

Linnemann, Eta. 1973. 'Jesus und der Täufer'. In *Festschrift für Ernst Fuchs*, edited by G. Ebeling, E. Jüngel, and G. Schunack, pp. 219–36. Tübingen: Mohr Siebeck.

Lucia, Amanda J. 2014. *Reflections of Amma: Devotees in a Global Embrace*. Oakland, CA: University of California Press.

Luomanen, Petri. 2007. 'The Sociology of Knowledge, the Social Identity Approach and the Cognitive Science of Religion'. In *Explaining Christian Origins and Early Judaism: Contributions from Cognitive and Social Science*, edited by Petri Luomanen, Ilkka Pyysiäinen, and Risto Uro, Biblical Interpretation Series 89, pp. 199–230. Leiden: Brill.

Luomanen, Petri. 2013. 'How Religions Remember: Memory Theories in Biblical Studies and in the Cognitive Study of Religion'. In *Mind, Memory and Magic: Cognitive Science Approaches in Biblical Studies*, edited by István Czachesz and Risto Uro, pp. 24–42. Durham: Acumen.

Luomanen, Petri, Ilkka Pyysiäinen, and Risto Uro. 2007a. 'Introduction: Social and Cognitive Perspectives in the Study of Christian Origins and Early Judaism'. In *Explaining Early Judaism and Christianity: Contributions from Cognitive and Social Science*, edited by Petri Luomanen, Ilkka Pyysiäinen, and Risto Uro, Biblical Interpretation 89, pp. 1–33. Leiden: Brill.

Luomanen, Petri, Ilkka Pyysiäinen, and Risto Uro, eds. 2007b. *Explaining Christian Origins and Early Judaism: Contributions from Cognitive and Social Science*. Biblical Interpretation Series 89. Leiden: Brill.

Lupieri, Edmondo F. 1993. 'John the Baptist in New Testament Traditions and History'. In *Aufstieg und Niedergand der römischen Welt* 2.26.1, edited by Hildegard Temporini and Wolfgang Haase, pp. 430–61. Berlin: de Gruyter.

Lutz, Antoine, Heleen A. Slagter, John D. Dunne, and Richard J. Davidson. 2008. 'Attention Regulation and Monitoring in Meditation'. *Trends in Cognitive Science* 12 (4): pp. 163–9.

Lüdemann, Gerd and Martin Schröder. 1987. *Die Religionsgeschichtliche Schule in Göttingen: Eine Dokumentation*. Göttingen: Vandenhoeck & Ruprecht.

McCauley, Robert N. 1996. 'Explanatory Pluralism and the Co-evolution of Theories in Science'. In *The Churchlands and Their Critics*, edited by Robert N. McCauley, pp. 17–47. Cambridge, MA: The MIT Press.

McCauley, Robert N. 2007. 'Reduction: Models of Cross-Scientific Relations and Their Implications for the Psychology-Neuroscience Interface'. In *Philosophy of Psychology and Cognitive Science*, edited by Paul Thagard, Handbook of the Philosophy of Science, pp. 105–58. Amsterdam: North Holland.

McCauley, Robert N. 2011. *Why Religion is Natural and Science is Not*. New York: Oxford University Press.

McCauley, Robert N. 2013. 'Explanatory Pluralism and the Cognitive Science of Religion: Why Scholars in Religious Studies Should Stop Worrying about Reductionism'. In *Mental Culture: Classical Social Theory and the Cognitive Science of Religion*, edited by Dimitris Xygalatas and William W McCorkle, Jr, pp. 11–32. Durham: Acumen.

McCauley, Robert N. and William Bechtel. 2001. 'Explanatory Pluralism and Heuristic Identity Theory'. *Theory and Psychology* 11 (6): pp. 737–60.

McCauley, Robert N. and Emma Cohen. 2010. 'Cognitive Science and the Naturalness of Religion'. *Philosophy Compass* 5 (9): pp. 779–92.

McCauley, Robert N. and E. Thomas Lawson. 2002. *Bringing Ritual to Mind: Psychological Foundations of Cultural Forms*. Cambridge: Cambridge University Press.

McClenon, James. 2002. *Wondrous Healing: Shamanism, Human Evolution, and the Origin of Religion*. DeKalb, IL: Northern Illinois University Press.

McCutcheon, Russell T. 1997. *Manufacturing Religion: The Discourse on Sui Generis Religion and the Politics of Nostalgia*. New York: Oxford University Press.

MacDonald, Margaret Y. 1988. *The Pauline Churches: A Socio-Historical Study of Institutionalization in the Pauline and Deutero-Pauline Writings*. Society of New Testament Studies Monograph Series 60. Cambridge: Cambridge University Press.

McGowan, Andrew B. 1999. *Ascetic Eucharists: Food and Drink in Early Christian Ritual Meals*. Oxford: Oxford University Press.

McGowan, Andrew B. 2014. *Ancient Christian Worship: Early Church Practices in Social, Historical, and Theological Perspective*. Grand Rapids, MI: Baker Academic.

Mack, Burton L. 1988. *A Myth of Innocence: Mark and Christian Origins*. Philadelphia, PA: Fortress.

Mack, Burton L. 1996. 'On Redescribing Christian Origins'. *Method and Theory in the Study of Religion* 8 (3): pp. 247–69.

Mack, Burton L. 2001. *The Christian Myth: Origins, Logic, and Legacy*. New York: Continuum.

MacMullen, Ramsey. 1984. *Christianizing the Roman Empire (A.D. 100–400)*. New Haven, CT: Yale University Press.
McNeill, William H. 1995. *Keeping Together in Time: Dance and Drill in Human History*. Cambridge, MA: Harvard University Press.
McVann, Mark. 1995. 'Reading Mark Ritually: Honor-Shame and the Ritual of Baptism'. In *Transformations, Passages, and Processes: Ritual Approaches to Biblical Texts*, edited by Mark McVann, Semeia 67, pp. 179–98. Atlanta, GA: Scholars Press.
Malina, Bruce J. 1981. *The New Testament World: Insights from Cultural Anthropology*. London: SCM.
Malina, Bruce J. 1985. 'Review of Wayne Meeks, *The First Urban Christians*, New Haven: Yale University Press, 1983'. *Journal of Biblical Literature* 104: pp. 346–9.
Malina, Bruce J. 1986. *Christian Origins and Cultural Anthropology: Practical Models for Biblical Interpretation*. Atlanta; GA: John Knox.
Malina, Bruce J. 1999. 'Assessing the Historicity of Jesus' Walking on the Sea'. In *Authenticating the Activities of Jesus*, edited by Bruce Chilton and Graig E. Evans, pp. 351–72. Leiden: Brill.
Malley, Brian and Justin L. Barrett. 2003. 'Does Myth Inform Ritual? A Test of the Lawson–McCauley Hypothesis'. *Journal of Ritual Studies* 17: pp. 1–14.
Marjanen, Antti. 2008. 'Montanism: Egalitarian Ecstatic "New Prophecy"'. In *A Companion to Second-Century Christian 'Heretics'*, edited by Antti Marjanen and Petri Luomanen, pp. 185–212. Leiden: Brill.
Martin, Dale B. 1995. *The Corinthian Body*. New Haven: Yale University Press.
Martin, Dale B. 1999. 'Social-Scientific Criticism'. In *To Each Its Own Meaning: An Introduction to Biblical Criticisms and Their Application*, edited by Steven L. McKenzie and Stephen R. Haynes, pp. 125–41. Louisville, KY: Westminster John Knox.
Martin, Luther H. 2000. 'Of Religious Syncretism, Comparative Religion and Spiritual Quests'. *Method and Theory in the Study of Religion* 12: pp. 277–86.
Martin, Luther H. 2011. 'Evolution, Cognition, and History'. In *Studies in Cognitive Historiography*, edited by Luther H. Martin and Jesper Sørensen, pp. 1–10. London: Equinox.
Martin, Luther H. and Jesper Sørensen, eds. 2011. *Past Minds: Studies in Cognitive Historiography*. Religion, Cognition and Culture. London: Equinox.
Mayr, Ernst. 1961. 'Cause and Effect in Biology: Kinds of Causes, Predictability, and Teleology Are Viewed by a Practising Biologist'. *Science* 134 (10): pp. 1501–6.
Meeks, Wayne A. 1972. 'The Man From Heaven in Johannine Sectarianism'. *Journal of Biblical Literature* 91: pp. 44–72.

Meeks, Wayne A. 1983. *The First Urban Christians: The Social World of the Apostle Paul.* New Haven, CT: Yale University Press.
Meeks, Wayne A. 2005. 'Why Study the New Testament?'. *New Testament Studies* 51 (2): pp. 155–70.
Meier, John P. 1994. *A Marginal Jew: Rethinking the Historical Jesus.* New York: Doubleday.
Merton, Robert K. 1949. *Social Theory and Social Structure.* Glencoe, IL: Free Press.
Merton, Robert K. 1967. 'On Sociological Theories of the Middle Range'. In *On Theoretical Sociology*, edited by Robert K. Merton, pp. 39–72. New York: The Free Press.
Mesoudi, Alex. 2011. *Cultural Evolution: How Darwinian Theory Can Explain Human Culture and Synthesize the Social Sciences.* Chicago, IL: University of Chicago Press.
Meyer, Marvin W. and Richard Smith, eds. 1994. *Ancient Christian Magic: Coptic Texts of Ritual Power.* San Francisco, CA: HarperSanFrancisco.
Meyers, Eric M. 2002. 'Aspects of Everyday Life in Roman Palestine with Special Reference to Private Domiciles and Ritual Baths'. In *Jews in the Hellenistic and Roman Cities*, edited by John R. Bartlett, pp. 193–220. London: Routledge.
Mitchell, Margaret M. 1991. *Paul and the Rhetoric of Reconciliation: An Exegetical Investigation of the Language and Composition of 1 Corinthians.* Hermeneutische Untersuchungen zur Theologie; 28. Tübingen: Mohr Siebeck.
Mitchell, Nathan D. 1999. *Liturgy and the Social Sciences.* Collegeville, MN: Liturgical Press.
Mithen, Steven J. 1996. *The Prehistory of the Mind: The Cognitive Origins of Art and Science.* London: Thames & Hudson.
Morgan, Michael L. 2012. 'Mercy, Repentance, and Forgiveness in Ancient Judaism'. In *Ancient Forgiveness: Classical, Judaic, and Christian*, edited by Charles L. Griswold and David Konstan, pp. 137–57. Cambridge: Cambridge University Press.
Muir, Edward. 1997. *Ritual in Early Modern Europe.* New Approaches to European History. Cambridge: Cambridge University Press.
Murray, Michael and Lyn Moore. 2009. 'Costly Signaling and the Origin of Religion'. *Journal of Cognition and Culture* 9: pp. 225–45.
Naveh, Shakeh and Shaul Shaked, eds. 1985. *Amulets and Magic Bowls: Aramaic Incantations of Late Antiquity.* Jerusalem: The Magnes Press.
Nemeroff, Carol and Paul Rozin. 2000. 'The Making of the Magical Mind: The Nature and Function of Sympathetic Magical Thinking'. In *Imagining the Impossible: Magical, Scientific, and Religious Thinking in Children*, edited by Karl S. Rosengren, Carl N. Johnson, and Paul L. Harris, pp. 1–34. Cambridge: Cambridge University Press.

Neyrey, Jerome H. 1986a. 'Body Language in 1 Corinthians: The Use of Anthropological Models for Understanding Paul and His Opponents'. *Semeia* 35: pp. 129-70.

Neyrey, Jerome H. 1986b. 'The Idea of Purity in Mark's Gospel'. *Semeia* 35: pp. 91-128.

Neyrey, Jerome H. 1988. *An Ideology of Revolt: John's Christology in Social-Science Perspective*. Philadelphia, MN: Fortress.

Neyrey, Jerome H. and Eric C. Stewart, eds. 2008. *The Social World of the New Testament: Insights and Models*. Peabody, MA: Hendrickson.

Nikolsky, Ronit, Fred Tappenden, Tamas Biró, and István Czachesz, eds. forthcoming. *Cognitive Science and Biblical Interpretation*. Sheffield: Sheffield Phoenix Press.

Nissinen, Martti. 2013. 'Prophecy as Construct: Ancient and Modern'. In *'Thus Speaks Ishtar of Arbeal': Prophecy in Israel, Assyria, and Egypt in the Neo-Assyrian Period*, edited by Robert P. Gordon and Hans M. Barstad, pp. 11-36. Winona Lake, IN: Eisenbrauns.

Ochs, Vanessa L. 2007. *Inventing Jewish Ritual*. Philadelphia, PA: The Jewish Publication Society.

Olyan, Saul M. 2004. *Biblical Mourning: Ritual and Social Dimensions*. Oxford: Oxford University Press.

Ortner, Sherry B. 1973. 'On Key Symbols'. *American Anthropologist* 75 (5): pp. 1338-46.

Osiek, Carolyn and David L. Balch. 1997. *Families in the New Testament World: Household and House Churches*. The Family, Religion, and Culture. Louisville: Westminster John Knox.

Pals, Daniel L. 1996. *Seven Theories of Religion*. New York: Oxford University Press.

Pearson, James L. 2002. *Shamanism and the Ancient Mind: A Cognitive Approach to Archaeology*. Walnut Creek, CA: AltaMira.

Penner, Hans H. 1971. 'The Poverty of Functionalism'. *History of Religions* 11: pp. 91-7.

Penney, Douglas A. and Michael O. Wise. 1994. 'By the Power of Beelzebub: An Aramaic Incantation Formula from Qumran'. *Journal of Biblical Literature* 113 (4): pp. 627-50.

Petersen, Anders Klostergaard. 1998. 'Shedding New Light on Paul's Understanding of Baptism: A Ritual-theoretical Approach to Romans 6'. *Studia Theologica—Nordic Journal of Theology* 52 (1): pp. 3-28.

Petersen, Anders Klostergaard. 2011. 'Rituals of Purification, Rituals of Initiation: Phenomenological, Taxonomical and Culturally Evolutionary Reflections'. In *Ablution, Initiation, and Baptism: Late Antiquity, Early Judaism, and Early Christianity*, edited by Christer Hellholm, et al., Beihefte zur Zeitschrift für die neutestamentliche Wissenshaft 176:1, pp. 3-40. Berlin: De Gruyter.

## References

Pettazzoni, Raffaele. 1954. *Essays in the History of Religions*. Studies in the History of Religions 1. Leiden: Brill.
Pilch, John J. 1993. 'Visions in Revelation and Alternate Consciousness: A Perspective from Cultural Anthropology'. *Society of Biblical Literature 1993 Seminar Papers* 32: pp. 154–77.
Pilch, John J. 1998. 'Appearances of the Risen Jesus in Cultural Context: Experiences of Alternate Reality'. *Biblical Theology Bulletin* 28: pp. 52–60.
Pilch, John J. 2000. *Healing in the New Testament: Insights from Medical and Mediterranean Anthropology*. Minneapolis, MN: Fortress.
Pinker, Steven. 2002. *The Blank Slate: The Modern Denial of Human Nature*. New York: Penguin Books.
Prentiss, Karen Pechilis. 1999. *The Embodiment of Bhakti*. New York: Oxford University Press.
Pyysiäinen, Ilkka. 2001. *How Religion Works: Towards a New Cognitive Science of Religion*. Cognition and Culture 1. Leiden: Brill.
Pyysiäinen, Ilkka. 2004a. 'Intuitive and Explicit in Religious Thought'. *Journal of Cognition and Culture* 4 (1): pp. 123–49.
Pyysiäinen, Ilkka. 2004b. *Magic, Miracles, and Religion: A Scientist's Perspective*. Walnut Creek, CA: AltaMira.
Pyysiäinen, Ilkka. 2009. *Supernatural Agents: Why We Believe in Souls, Gods, and Buddhas*. London: Oxford University Press.
Pyysiäinen, Ilkka. 2011a. 'Reduction and Explanatory Pluralism in the Cognitive Science of Religion'. In *Changing Minds: Religion and Cognition through the Ages*, edited by István Czachesz and Tamás Bíró, pp. 15–29. Leuven: Peeters.
Pyysiäinen, Ilkka. 2011b. 'Believing and Doing: How Ritual Action Enhances Religious Belief'. In *Religious Narrative, Cognition and Culture*, edited by Armin W. Geertz and Jeppe Sinding Jensen. Religion, Cognition and Culture, pp. 147–62. London: Equinox.
Pyysiäinen, Ilkka. 2012a. 'Religion: From Mind to Society and Back'. In *Grounding Social Sciences in Cognitive Sciences*, edited by Ron Sun, pp. 239–64. Cambridge, MA: The MIT Press.
Pyysiäinen, Ilkka. 2012b. 'Cognitive Science of Religion: State -of-the-Art'. *Journal for the Cognitive Science of Religion* 1 (1): pp. 5–28.
Pyysiäinen, Ilkka. 2014. 'The Cognitive Science of Religion'. In *Evolution, Religion and Cognitive Science*, edited by Fraser Watts and Léon Turner, pp. 21–37. Oxford: Oxford University Press.
Pyysiäinen, Ilkka and Veikko Anttonen, eds. 2002. *Current Approaches in the Cognitive Science of Religion*. London: Continuum.
Pyysiäinen, Ilkka and Marc Hauser. 2010. 'Religion as Evolved Adaptation or By-Product?' *Trends in Cognitive Sciences* 14 (3): pp. 104–9.
Räisänen, Heikki. 2001. *Challenges to Biblical Interpretation: Collected Essays, 1991–2001*. Biblical Interpretation 59. Leiden: Brill.

Räisänen, Heikki. 2010. *The Rise of Christian Beliefs: The Thought World of Early Christians.* Minneapolis, MN: Fortress.

Raj, Selva J. 2005. 'Passage to America: Ammachi on American Soil'. In *Gurus in America*, edited by Thomas A. Forsthoefel and Cynthia Ann Humes, SUNY Series in Hindu Studies, pp. Albany, NY: State University of New York Press.

Rappaport, Roy A. 1979. *Ecology, Meaning, and Religion.* Richmond, CA: North Atlantic Books.

Rappaport, Roy A. 1984. *Pigs for the Ancestors: Ritual in the Ecology of a New Guinea People.* 2nd edn. New Haven, CT: Yale University Press.

Rappaport, Roy A. 1999. *Ritual and Religion in the Making of Humanity.* Cambridge: Cambridge University Press.

Reddish, Paul, Joseph Bulbulia, and Ronald Fisher. 2014. 'Does Synchrony Promote Generalized Prosociality'. *Religion, Brain and Behavior* 4 (1): pp. 3–19.

Regev, Eyal. 2004. 'Moral Impurity and the Temple in Early Christianity in Light of Ancient Greek Practice and Qumranic Ideology'. *Harvard Theological Review* 97 (4): pp. 383–411.

Reitzenstein, Richard. 1921. *Das iranische Erlösungsmysterium: Religionsgeschichtliche Untersuchungen.* Bonn: A. Marcus & W. Weber.

Richerson, Peter J. and Robert Boyd. 2005. *Not by Genes Alone: How Culture Transformed Human Evolution.* Chicago, IL: The University of Chicago Press.

Riskind, John H. and Carolyn C. Gotay. 1982. 'Physical Posture: Could It Have Regulatory or Feedback Effects on Motivation and Emotion?' *Motivation and Emotion* 6: pp. 273–98.

Robbins, Philip and Murat Aydede. 2009a. 'A Short Primer on Situated Cognition'. In *The Cambridge Handbook of Situated Cognition*, edited by Philip Robbins and Murat Aydede, pp. 3–10. Cambridge: Cambridge University Press.

Robbins, Philip and Murat Aydede, eds. 2009b. *The Cambridge Handbook of Situated Cognition.* Cambridge: Cambridge University Press.

Roberts, Alexander and James Donaldson, eds. 1885, repr. 1994. *Ante-Nicene Fathers*, Vol. 3: *Latin Christianity: Its Founder, Tertullian, revised and chronologically arranged with brief prefaces and occasional notes by A. Cleveland Coxe.* Peabody, MA: Hendrickson.

Rohrbaugh, Richard, ed. 1996. *The Social Sciences and New Testament Interpretation.* Peabody, MA: Hendrickson.

Roitto, Rikard. 2011. *Behaving as a Christ-Believer: A Cognitive Perspective on Identity and Behavior Norms in Ephesians.* Winona Lake, IN: Eisenbrauns.

Roitto, Rikard. 2012. 'Practices of Confession, Intercession and Forgiveness in 1 John 1:9; 5:16'. *New Testament Studies* 58 (2): pp. 235–53.

Rotschild, Clare K. 2005. *Baptist Traditions and Q*. Wissenschaftliche Untersuchungen zum Neuen Testament 190. Tübingen Mohr Siebeck.
Rousseau, John J. 1993. 'Jesus, an Exorcist of a Kind'. *Society of Biblical Literature 1993 Seminar Papers* 32: pp. 129–53.
Rudolph, Kurt. 1991. 'Early Christianity as Religious-Historical Phenomenon'. In *The Future of Early Christianity: Essays in Honor of Helmut Koester*, edited by Birger A. Pearson, pp. 9–19. Minneapolis, MN: Fortress.
Ruffle, Bradley J. and Richard Sosis. 2007. 'Does It Pay To Pray? Costly Ritual and Cooperation'. *The B. E. Journal of Economic Analysis & Policy* 7 (1): article 18.
Russell, C. D. Arnold. 2006. *The Social Role of Liturgy in the Religion of the Qumran Community*. Studies on the Texts of the Desert of Judah. Leiden: Brill.
Salamone, Frank A., ed. 2004. *Encyclopedia of Religious Rites, Rituals and Festivals*. Routledge Encyclopedias of Religion and Society. New York: Routledge.
Sanders, E. P. 1985. *Jesus and Judaism*. London: SCM.
Sanders, E. P. 1992. *Judaism: Practice and Belief 63BCE-66CE*. London: SCM.
Sax, William S. 2010. 'Ritual and the Problem of Efficacy'. In *The Problem of Ritual Efficacy* edited by William S. Sax, Johannes Quack, and Jan Weinhold, Oxford Ritual Studies, pp. 3–16. Oxford: Oxford University Press.
Sax, William S., Johannes Quack, and Jan Weinhold, eds. 2010. *The Problem of Ritual Efficacy*. Oxford: Oxford University Press.
Schieffelin, Edward L. 2007. 'Introduction'. In *When Rituals Go Wrong: Mistakes, Failure and the Dynamics of Ritual*, edited by Ute Hüsken, Numen Book Series 115, pp. 1–20. Leiden: Brill.
Schjødt, Uffe, et al. 2013. 'Cognitive Resource Depletion in Religious Interactions'. *Religion, Brain and Behavior* 3 (1): pp. 39–86.
Seelig, Gerald. 2001. *Religionsgeschichtliche Methode in Vergangheit und Gegenwart: Studien zur Geschichte und Methode des religionsgeschichtlichen Vergleichs in der neutestamentlichen Wissenshaft*. Arbeiten zur Bible und ihrer Geschichte 7. Leipzig: Evangelische Verlaganstalt.
Segal, Robert A., ed. 1998. *The Myth and Ritual Theory: An Anthology*. Malden, MA: Blackwell.
Segal, Robert A. 2009. 'Religion as Ritual: Roy Rappaport's Changing Views from *Pigs for the Ancestors* (1968) to *Ritual and Religion in the Making of Humanity* (1999)'. In *Contemporary Theories of Religion: A Critical Companion*, edited by Michael Stausberg, pp. 66–82. London: Routledge.
Sered, Susan S. and Linda L. Barnes. 2007. 'Teaching Healing/Healing Rituals'. In *Teaching Ritual*, edited by Catherine Bell, AAR: Teaching Religious Studies, pp. 195–208. Oxford: Oxford University Press.
Shantz, Colleen. 2009. *Paul in Ecstasy: The Neurobiology of the Apostle's Life and Thought*. Cambridge: Cambridge University Press.

Shapiro, Lawrence. 2011. *Embodied Cognition*. London: Routledge.
Sharpe, Eric J. 1986. *Comparative Religion: A History*. Trowbridge: Duckworth.
Sidky, Homayan. 2010. 'On the Antiquity of Shamanism and its Role in Human Religiosity'. *Method and Theory in the Study of Religion* 22: pp. 68–92.
Slingerland, Edward. 2008. *What Science Offers to the Humanities: Integrating Body and Culture*. Cambridge: Cambridge University Press.
Slingerland, Edward and Mark Collard. 2012. 'Creating a Consilience: Toward a Second Wave'. In *Introduction: Creating a Consilience: Integration the Sciences and the Humanities*, edited by Edward Slingerland and Mark Collard, pp. 3–40. New York: Oxford University Press.
Slone, D. Jason. 2004. *Theological Incorrectness: Why Religious People Believe What They Shouldn't*. Oxford: Oxford University Press.
Smith, Dennis E. 2003. *From Symposium to Eucharist: The Banquet in the Early Christian World*. Minneapolis, MN: Fortress.
Smith, Dennis E. and Hal Taussig, eds. 2012. *Meals in the Early Christian World: Social Formation, Experimentation, and Conflict at the Table*. New York: Palgrave Macmillan.
Smith, Eric Alden. 2000. 'Three Styles in the Evolutionary Analysis of Human Behavior'. In *Adaptation and Human Behavior: An Anthropological Perspective*, edited by Lee Cronk, Napoleon Chagnon, and William Irons, pp. 27–46. New York: Aldine de Gruyter.
Smith, Jonathan Z. 1987. *To Take Place: Toward Theory in Ritual*. Chicago, IL: The University of Chicago Press.
Smith, Jonathan Z. 2009. 'Religion and the Bible'. *Journal of Biblical Literature* 128 (1): pp. 5–27.
Smith, Jonathan Z. 2011. 'Re: Corinthians'. In *Redescribing Paul and the Corinthians*, edited by Ron Cameron and Merrill P. Miller, Early Christianity and Its Literature 5, pp. 17–34. Atlanta, GA: Society of Biblical Literature.
Smith, Morton. 1973. *Clement of Alexandria and a Secret Gospel of Mark*. Cambridge, MA: Harvard University Press.
Smith, Morton. 1978. *Jesus the Magician*. San Francisco, CA: Harper & Row.
Smith, William Robertson. 2002 [1894]. *Religion of the Semites. With a New Introduction by Robert A. Segal*. New Brunswick, NJ: Transactions.
Snoek, Jan A. M. 2008. 'Defining "Rituals"'. In *Theorizing Rituals: Issues, Topics, Approaches, Concepts*, edited by Jens Kreinath, Jan Snoek, and Michael Stausberg, Numen Book Series 114:1, pp. 3–14. Leiden: Brill.
Snyder, Graydon F. 1985. *Ante Pacem: Archaeological Evidence of Church Life before Constantine*. Macon, GA: Mercer University Press.
Soler, Montserrat. 2008. 'Commitment Costs and Cooperation: Evidence from Cadomble, an Afro-Brazilian Religion'. In *The Evolution of Religion:*

*Studies, Theories & Critiques*, edited by Joseph Bulbulia, et al., pp. 167–74. Santa Margarita, CA: Collins Foundation Press.

Sorensen, Eric. 2002. *Possession and Exorcism in the New Testament and Early Christianity*. Wissenshchaftliche Untersuchungen zum Neuen Testament, 2. Reihe 157 Tübingen: Mohr Siebeck.

Sørensen, Jesper. 2005. 'Charisma, Tradition, and Ritual: A Cognitive Approach to Magical Agency'. In *Mind and Religion: Psychological and Cognitive Foundations of Religiosity*, edited by Harvey Whitehouse and Robert N. McCauley, pp. 167–85. Walnut Creek, CA: AltaMira.

Sosis, Richard. 2000. 'Religion and Intragroup Cooperation: Preliminary Results of a Comparative Analysis of Utopian Communities'. *Cross-Cultural Research* 34 (1): pp. 77–88.

Sosis, Richard. 2003. 'Why Aren't We All Hutteries: Costly Signaling Theory and Religious Behavior'. *Human Nature* 14 (2): pp. 91–127.

Sosis, Richard. 2004. 'The Adaptive Value of Religious Ritual'. *American Scientist* 92: pp. 166–72.

Sosis, Richard. 2006. 'Religious Behaviors, Badges, and Bans: Signaling Theory and the Evolution of Religion'. In *Where God and Science Meet: How Brain and Evolutionary Studies Alter Our Understanding of Religion?* Vol. One: *Evolution, Genes and the Religious Brain*, edited by Patrick McNamara, pp. 61–85. Westport, CT: Praeger.

Sosis, Richard. 2009. 'The Adaptionist-Byproduct Debate on the Evolution of Religion: Five Misunderstandings of the Adaptionist Program'. *Journal of Cognition and Culture* 9: pp. 315–32.

Sosis, Richard and Candace Alcorta. 2003. 'Signaling, Solidarity, and the Sacred: The Evolution of Religious Behavior'. *Evolutionary Anthropology* 12: pp. 264–74.

Sosis, Richard and E. R. Bressler. 2003. 'Cooperation and Commune Longevity: A Test of Costly Signaling Theory of Religion'. *Cross-Cultural Research* 37: pp. 211–39.

Sosis, Richard and Joseph Bulbulia. 2011. 'The Behavioral Ecology of Religion: The Benefits and Costs of One Evolutionary Approach'. *Religion* 41 (3): pp. 341–62.

Sosis, Richard and W. Penn Handwerker. 2011. 'Psalms and Coping with Uncertainty: Religious Israeli Women's Responses to the 2006 Lebanon War'. *American Anthropologist* 113 (1): pp. 40–55.

Sosis, Richard and Bradley J. Ruffle. 2003. 'Religious Ritual and Cooperation: Testing for a Relationship on Israeli Religious and Secular Kibbutzim'. *Current Anthropology* 44 (5): pp. 713–22.

Sosis, Richard and Bradley J. Ruffle. 2004. 'Ideology, Religion, and the Evolution of Cooperation: Field Experiments on Israeli Kibbutzim'. In *Socioeconomic Aspects of Human Behavioral Ecology*, edited by Michael Alvard, Research in Economic Anthropology 23, pp. 89–117. Greenwich, CT: Jai Press.

Sperber, Dan. 1974. *Rethinking Symbolism*. Cambridge: Cambridge University Press.
Sperber, Dan. 1994. 'The Modularity of Thought and the Epidemiology of Representations'. In *Mapping the Mind: Domain Specificity in Cognition and Culture*, edited by L. A. Hirschfeld and S. A. Gelman, pp. 39–67. Cambridge: Cambridge University Press.
Sperber, Dan. 1996. *Explaining Culture: A Naturalistic Approach*. Oxford: Blackwell.
Spinks, Bryan D. 2013. *Do This in Remembrance of Me: The Eucharist from the Early Church to the Present Day*. SCM Studies in Worship and Liturgy. London: SCM.
Staal, Frits. 1989. *Rules without Meaning: Ritual, Mantras and the Human Sciences*. Bern: Peter Lang.
Stausberg, Michael. 2008. '"Ritual": A Lexigraphich Survey of Some Related Terms from an Emic Perspective'. In *Theorizing Rituals: Issues, Topics, Approaches, Concepts*, edited by Jens Kreinath, Jan Snoek, and Michael Stausberg, Numen Book Series 114: 1, pp. 37–51. Leiden: Brill.
Stausberg, Michael. 2009. 'There is Life in the Old Dog Yet: An Introduction to Contemporary Theories of Religion'. In *Contemporary Theories of Religion: A Critical Companion*, edited by Michael Stausberg, pp. 1–21. London: Routledge.
Stegemann, Ekkehard and Wolfgang Stegemann. 1999. *The Jesus Movement: A Social History of its First Century*. Edinburgh: T&T Clark.
Stephenson, Barry. 2010. *Performing the Reformation: Public Ritual in the City of Luther*. Oxford Ritual Studies. Oxford: Oxford University Press.
Stephenson, Barry. 2015. *Ritual: A Very Short Introduction*. Oxford: Oxford University Press.
Stepper, Sabine and Fritz Strack. 1993. 'Proprioceptive Determinants of Emotional and Nonemotional Feelings'. *Journal of Personality and Social Psychology* 64: pp. 211–20.
Still, Todd D. and David G. Horrell, eds. 2009. *After the First Urban Christians: The Social-Scientific Study of Pauline Christianity Twenty-Five Years Later*. London: T&T Clark.
Stoller, Paul. 2004. *Stranger in the Village of the Sick: A Memoir of Cancer, Sorcery, and Healing*. Boston, MA: Beacon.
Stoller, Paul and Cheryl Olkes. 1987. *In Sorcery's Shadow: A Memoir of Apprenticeship among the Songhay of Niger*. Chicago, IL: University of Chicago Press
Stommel, Eduard. 1959. 'Christliche Taufriten und antike Badesitten'. *Jahrbuch für Antike und Christentum* 2: pp. 5–14.
Stowers, Stanley K. 1995. 'Greeks Who Sacrifice and Those Who Do Not: Toward an Anthropology of Greek Religion'. In *The Social World of the First Christians: Essays in Honor of Wayne Meeks*, edited by Michael

L. White and Larry O. Yarbrough, pp. 293–333. Minneapolis, MN: Fortress.

Stowers, Stanley K. 1996. 'Elusive Coherence: Ritual and Rhetoric in 1 Corinthians 10–11'. In *Rethinking Christian Origins: A Colloquium Honoring Burton L. Mack*, edited by Elisabeth A. Castelli and Hal Taussig, pp. 68–83. Valley Forge, PA: Trinity International.

Stowers, Stanley K. 2011a. 'The Religion of Plant and Animal Offerings Versus the Religion of Meanings, Essences and Textual Mysteries'. In *Ancient Mediterranean Sacrifice: Images, Acts, Meanings*, edited by Jennifer Knust and Zsuzsa Varhelyi, pp. 35–56. Oxford: Oxford University Press.

Stowers, Stanley K. 2011b. 'Kinds of Myth, Meals, and Power: Paul and the Corinthians'. In *Redescribing Paul and the Corinthians*, edited by Ron Cameron and Merrill P. Miller, Early Christianity and Its Literature 5, pp. 105–49. Atlanta, GA: Society of Biblical Literature.

Strecker, Christian. 1999. *Die liminale Theologie des Paulus: Zugänge zur paulinishcen Theologie aus kulturanthropologischer Perspektive*. Forschungen zur Religion und Literatur des Alten und Neuen Testaments 185. Göttingen: Vandenhoeck & Ruprecht.

Strecker, Christian. 2002. 'Jesus and the Demoniacs'. In *The Social Setting of Jesus and the Gospels*, edited by Wolfgang Stegemann, Bruce J. Malina, and Gerd Theissen, pp. 85–102. Minneapolis, MN: Fortress.

Strecker, Christian. 2011. 'Taufrituale in frühen Christentum und in der Alten Kirche'. In *Ablution, Initiation, and Baptism: Late antiquity, Early Judaism, and Early Christianity*, edited by Christer Hellholm, et al., Beihefte zur Zeitschrift für die neutestamentliche Wissenschaft 176: 2, 2, pp. 1383–440. Berlin: De Gruyter.

Stringer, Martin D. 2005. *A Sociological History of Christian Worship*. Cambridge: Cambridge University Press.

Stringer, Martin D. 2011. *Rethinking the Origins of the Eucharist*. SCM Studies in Worship and Liturgy. London: SCM.

Sun, Ron. 2012. 'Prolegomena to Cognitive Social Sciences'. In *Grounding Social Sciences in Cognitive Sciences*, edited by Ron Sun, pp. 3–32. Cambridge, MA: MIT Press.

Symons, Cynthia S. and Blair T. Johnson. 1997. 'The Self-reference Effect in Memory: A Meta-Analysis'. *Psychological Bulletin* 121 (3): pp. 371–94.

Taft, Robert F. 2001. 'Anton Baumstark's Comparative Liturgy Revisited'. In *Comparative Liturgy Fifty Years After Anton Baumstark (1872–1948)*, edited by Robert F. Taft and Gabriele Winkler, Orientalia Christiana Analecta 265, pp. 191–232. Rome: Pontificio Istituto Orientale.

Taft, Robert F. and Gabriele Winkler, eds. 2001. *Comparative Liturgy Fifty Years After Anton Baumstark*. Orientalia Christiana Analecta 265. Rome: Pontificio Istitutio Orientale.

## References 215

Tambiah, Stanley J. 1979. 'A Performative Approach to Ritual'. *Proceedings of the British Academy* 65: pp. 113–69.

Tappenden, Frederick S. 2013. 'Putting Practice into Words and Words into Practice: On the (Dis)Connection of Language and Experience in Romans 6:1–11'. Paper read at the SBL Annual Meeting, Baltimore, ML, 23–26 November 2013.

Taussig, Hal. 2009. *In the Beginning Was the Meal: Social Experimentation and Early Christian Identity*. Minneapolis, MN: Fortress.

Taylor, Joan E. 1997. *The Immerser: John the Baptist within Second Temple Judaism*. Grand Rapids, MI: Eerdmans.

Theissen, Gerd. 1979. *Studien zur Soziologie des Urchristentums*. Wissenchafliche Untersuchung zum Neuen Testament, 2. Reihe 19. Tübingen: Mohr Siebeck.

Theissen, Gerd. 1982. *The Social Setting of Pauline Christianity*. Trans. John H. Schütz. Edinburgh: T&T Clark.

Theissen, Gerd. 1983. *The Miracle Stories of the Early Christian Tradition*. Trans. S. F. McDonagh. Edinburgh: T&T Clark.

Theissen, Gerd. 1999. *A Theory of Primitive Christian Religion*. Trans. John Bowden. London: SCM.

Theissen, Gerd. 2004. *Die Jesusbewegung: Sozialgeschichte einer Revolution der Werte*. Gütersloh: Gütersloher Verlagshaus.

Theissen, Gerd. 2008. 'Rituale des Glaubens: Religiose Rituale im Licht akademischer Riten'. In *Die neue Kraft der Rituale*, edited by Axel Michaelis, Studium Generale der Ruprecht-Karsl-Universität Heidelberg, pp. 11–44. 2nd edn. Heidelberg: Universitätsverlag Winter.

Theissen, Gerd. 2010. 'Jesus and his Followers as Healers: Symbolic Healing in Early Christianity'. In *The Problem of Ritual Efficacy*, edited by William S. Sax, Johannes Quack, and Jan Weinhold, pp. 45–66. Oxford: Oxford University Press.

Theissen, Gerd. 2013. *Dinamica rituale dei sacramenti nel cristianesimo primitivo*. Leitourgia. Sezione antropologica. Milano: Cittadella.

Throop, C. Jason and Charles D. Laughlin. 2002. 'Ritual, Collective Effervescence and the Categories: Toward a Neo-Durkheimian Model of the Nature of Human Consciousness, Feeling and Understanding'. *Journal of Ritual Studies* 16 (1): pp. 40–63.

Tom, Gail, et al. 1991. 'The Role of Overt Head Movement in the Formation of Affect'. *Basic and Applied Social Psychology* 12: pp. 281–9.

Tomasello, Michael. 2014. *A Natural History of Human Thinking*. Cambridge, MA: Harvard University Press.

Tooby, John and Leda Cosmides. 1992. 'The Psychological Foundations of Culture'. In *The Adapted Mind: Evolutionary Psychology and the Generation of Culture*, edited by Jerome H. Barkow, Leda Cosmides, and John Tooby, pp. 19–136. Oxford: Oxford University Press.

Tremlin, Todd. 2005. 'Divergent Religion: A Dual-Process Model of Religious Thought, Behavior, and Morphology'. In *Mind and Religion: Psychological and Cognitive Foundations of Religiosity*, edited by Harvey Whitehouse and Robert N. McCauley, Cognitive Science of Religion Series, pp. 69–84. Walnut Creek, CA: AltaMira.

Tremlin, Todd. 2006. *Minds and Gods: The Cognitive Foundations of Religion*. Oxford: Oxford University Press.

Tucker, Brian J. and Coleman A. Baker, eds. 2014. *T&T Clark Handbook to Social Identity in the New Testament*. London: Bloomsbury.

Turley, Stephen Richard. 2013. 'Revealing Rituals: Washings and Meals in Galatians and 1 Corinthians'. PhD Diss. University of Durham.

Turley, Stephen Richard. 2015. *The Ritualized Revelation of the Messianic Age*. The Library of New Testament Studies 544. London: Bloomsbury T&T Clark.

Turner, Léon. 2014. 'Pluralism and Complexity in the Evolutionary Cognitive Science of Religion'. In *Evolution, Religion and Cognitive Science: Critical and Constructive Essays*, edited by Fraser Watts and Léon Turner, pp. 1–20. Oxford: Oxford University Press.

Turner, Victor. 1967. *The Forest of Symbols: Aspects of Ndembu Ritual*. Ithaca, NY: Cornell University Press.

Turner, Victor. 1969. *The Ritual Process: Structure and Anti-Structure*. Chicago: Aldine.

Turner, Victor. 1988. *The Anthropology of Performance*. New York: PAJ Publications.

Twelftree, Graham H. 1993. *Jesus the Exorcist. A Contribution to the Study of the Historical Jesus*. Wissenschaftliche Untersuchungen zum Neuen Testament, 2. Reihe 54 Tübingen: Mohr Siebeck.

Twelftree, Graham H. 2007a. 'Jesus the Exorcist and Ancient Magic'. In *A Kind of Magic: Understanding Magic in the New Testament and Its Religious Environment*, edited by Michael Labahn and Bert Jan Lietart Peerbolte, pp. 57–86. London: T&T Clark.

Twelftree, Graham H. 2007b. *In the Name of Jesus: Exorcism among Early Christians*. Grand Rapids, MI: Baker.

Unger, Domini J. ed. 1992. *St Irenaeus of Lyons: Against the Hereses*. Volume I, Book I. Translated and annotated by Dominic J. Unger with further revisions by John J. Dillon. Ancient Christian Writers 55. New York: The Newman Press.

Uro, Risto. 1987. *Sheep Among the Wolves: A Study on the Mission Instructions of Q*. Annales Academiae Scientiarum Fennicae. Dissertationes humanarum litterarum. Helsinki: Suomalainen tiedeakatemia.

Uro, Risto. 1995. 'John the Baptist and the Jesus Movement: What Does Q Tell Us?'. In *The Gospel Behind the Gospels: Current Studies on Q*, edited by Ronald A. Piper, Supplements to Novum Testamentum 75, pp. 231–55. Leiden: Brill.

Uro, Risto. 1998. 'Is Thomas an Encratite Gospel?' In *Thomas at the Crossroads: Essays on the Gospel of Thomas*, edited by Risto Uro, Studies in the New Testament and Its World, pp. 140–62. Edinburgh: T&T Clark.

Uro, Risto. 2007. 'A Cognitive Approach to Gnostic Rituals'. In *Explaining Christianity Origins and Early Judaism: Contributions from Cognitive and Social Science*, edited by Petri Luomanen, Ilkka Pyysiäinen, and Risto Uro, Biblical Interpretation 89, pp. 115–37. Leiden: Brill.

Uro, Risto. 2010. 'Ritual and Christian Origins'. In *Understanding the Social World of the New Testament*, edited by Dietmar Neufeld and Richard E. DeMaris, pp. 220–32. London: Routledge.

Uro, Risto. 2011a. 'Towards a Cognitive History of Early Christian Rituals'. In *Changing Minds: Religion and Cognition through the Ages*, edited by István Czachesz and Tamás Bíró, Groningen Studies in Cultural Changes., pp. 103–21. Leiden: Peeters.

Uro, Risto. 2011b. 'Ritual, Memory and Writing in Early Christianity'. *Temenos* 47 (2): pp. 159–82.

Uro, Risto. 2011c. 'Kognitive Ritualtheorien: Neue Modelle für die Analyse urchristliche Sakramente'. *Evangelische Theologie* 71 (4): pp. 272–88.

Uro, Risto. 2011d. 'Cognitive and Evolutionary Approaches to Ancient Rituals: Reflections on Recent Theories and Their Relevance for the Historian of Religion'. In *Mystery and Secrecy in Late Antique Thought and Praxis*, edited by John Turner, Christian H. Bull, and Liv Ingeborg Lied, Nag Hammadi and Manichaean Studies 76, pp. 487–510. Leiden: Brill.

Uro, Risto. 2012. 'Explaining Radical Family Ethos in the Synoptic Gospels: From Functionalist Accounts to Cognitive Theorizing'. In *Kari Syreeni FS*, edited by Sven-Olav Back and Matti Kankaanniemi, Studier i exegetik och judaistik utgivna av Teologiska fakulteten vid Åbo Akademi 11, pp. 251–376. Åbo: Åbo Akademi.

Uro, Risto. 2013. 'From Corpse Impurity to Relic Veneration: New Light from Cognitive and Psychological Studies'. In *Mind, Memory and Magic: Cognitive Science Approaches in Biblical Studies*, edited by István Czachesz and Risto Uro, pp. 180–96. Durham: Acumen.

Uro, Risto, Juliette Day, Richard E. DeMaris, and Rikard Roitto, eds. forthcoming. *The Oxford Hanbook of Early Christian Ritual*. Oxford: Oxford University Press.

Vaage, Leif. E. 1996. 'Bird-watching at the Baptism of Jesus: Early Christian Mythmaking in Mark 1:9-11'. In *Reimagining Christian Origins: A Colloquium Honoring Burton L. Mack*, edited by Elisabeth A. Castelli and Hal Taussig, pp. 280–94. Valley Forge, PA: Trinity Press International.

van Aarde, Andries. 2008. '"Anthropological Rabbits" and "Positivistic Ducks": An Experimental Reflection on Pieter Craffert's "Shamanic Jesus"'. *Hervormde Theologiese Studies* 64 (2): pp. 767–98.

van Baaren, Rick B., Rob W. Holland, Kerry Kawakami, and Ad van Knibbenberg. 2003. 'Mimicry and Prosocial Behavior'. *Psychological Science* 15 (1): pp. 71–4.
van Baaren, Rick B., Rob W. Holland, and Bregje Steenaert. 2004. 'Mimicry for Money: Behavioral Consequences of Imitation'. *Journal of Experimental Social Psychology* 39 (4): pp. 393–8.
van Gennep, Arnold. 1960. *The Rites of Passage*. Trans. M. B. Vizedom and G. L. Caffee. Chicago, IL: The University of Chicago Press.
Van Slyke, James A. 2011. *The Cognitive Science of Religion*. Ashgate Science and Religion Series. Farnham: Ashgate.
Vermes, Geza. 2012. *Christian Beginnings: From Nazareth to Nicaea*. London: Penguin.
Vial, Theodore M. 1999. 'Opposites Attract: The Body and Cognition in a Debate over Baptism'. *Numen* 46: pp. 121–45.
Vielhauer, Philipp. 1965. 'Tracht und Speise Johannes des Täufers'. In *Aufsätze zum Neuen Testament*, edited by Philipp Vielhauer, Theologische Bucherei 31, pp. 47–54. München: Chr. Kaiser.
Visala, Aku. 2011. *Naturalism, Theism and the Cognitive Study of Religion: Religion Explained?*. Ashgate Science and Religion Series. Farnham: Ashgate.
von Dobbeler, Stephanie. 1988. *Das Gericht un Erbarmen Gottes: Die Botschaft Johannes Täufers und ihre Rezeption bei den Johannesjüngern in Rahmen der Theologiegeschichte der Frühjudentums*. Bonner Biblischer Beiträge 70. Frankfurt am Main.
Vyse, Stuart A. 1997. *Believing in Magic: The Psychology of Superstition*. New York: Oxford University Press.
Wahlen, Clinton. 2004. *Jesus and the Impurity of Spirits in the Synoptic Gospels*. Wissenschaftliche Untersuchungen zum Neuen Testament, 2. Reihe 185. Tübingen: Mohr Siebeck.
Wallace, Daniel B. 1996. *Greek Grammar Beyond the Basics: An Exegetical Syntax of the New Testament*. Grand Rapids, MI: Zondervan.
Wassen, Cecilia. 2008. 'What Do the Angels Have Against the Blind and the Deaf? Rules of Exclusion in the Dead Sea Scrolls'. In *Common Judaism: Explorations in Second-Temple Judaism*, edited by Wayne McCready and Adele Reinhartz, pp. 109–24. Minneapolis, MN: Fortress.
Webb, Robert L. 1991. *John the Baptizer and Prophet. A Socio-Historical Study*. Journal for the Study of the New Testament: Supplement Series 62. Sheffield: Sheffield Academy Press.
Webb, Robert L. 1994. 'John the Baptist and His Relationship to Jesus'. In *Studying the Historical Jesus: Evaluations of the State of Current Research*, edited by Bruce D. Chilton and Craig A. Evans, New Testament Tools and Studies 19, pp. 179–230. Leiden: Brill.
Webb, Robert L. 2000. 'Jesus' Baptism: Its Historicity, and Implications'. *Bulletin for Biblical Research* 10 (2): pp. 261–309.

Wedderburn, A. J. M. 1987. *Baptism and Resurrection: Studies in Pauline Theology against Its Graeco-Roman Background*. Wissenschafliche Untersuchungen zum Neuen Testament 44. Tübingen: Mohr (Siebeck).
Wedderburn, A. J. M. 2002. 'Paul's Collection: Chronology and History'. *New Testament Studies* 48 (1): pp. 95–110.
Weimer, Jade Brooklyn. 2015. 'Musical Assemblies: How Early Christian Music Functioned as a Rhetorical *Topos*, a Mechanism of Recruitment, and a Fundamental Marker of and Emerging Christian Identity'. PhD Diss. University of Toronto.
West, Fritz. 1995. *The Comparative Liturgy of Anton Baumstark*. Alcuin/GROW Liturgical Study. Nottingham: Grove Books.
White, Michael L. 1996. *The Social Origins of Christian Architecture*. Vol. 1: *Building God's House in the Roman World: Architectural Adaptation among Pagans, Jews, and Christians*. Harvard Theological Studies 42. Valley Forge, PA: Trinity Press International.
White, Michael L. 2000. 'Architecture: The First Five Centuries'. In *The Early Christian World*, edited by Philip F. Esler, 2 Vols, pp. 693–746. London: Routledge.
Whitehouse, Harvey. 1995. *Inside the Cult: Religious Innovation and Transmission in Papua New Guinea*. Oxford: Clarendon.
Whitehouse, Harvey. 2000. *Arguments and Icons*. Oxford: Oxford University Press.
Whitehouse, Harvey. 2002. 'Modes of Religiosity: Towards a Cognitive Explanation of the Sociopolitical Dynamics of Religion'. *Method and Theory in the Study of Religion* 14 (3): pp. 293–315.
Whitehouse, Harvey. 2004a. *Modes of Religiosity: A Cognitive Theory of Religious Transmission*. Walnut Creek, CA: AltaMira.
Whitehouse, Harvey. 2004b. 'Modes of Religiosity and the Cognitive Science of Religion'. *Method and Theory in the Study of Religion* 16 (3): pp. 293–315.
Whitehouse, Harvey and James Laidlaw, eds. 2004. *Ritual and Memory: Toward a Comparative Anthropology of Religion*. Walnut Creek, CA: AltaMira.
Whitehouse, Harvey and Robert N. McCauley, eds. 2005. *Mind and Religion: Psychological and Cognitive Foundations of Religiosity*. Walnut Creek, CA: AltaMira.
Whitehouse, Harvey and Luther H. Martin, eds. 2004. *Theorizing Religions Past: Archeology, History, and Cognition*. Walnut Creek, CA: AltaMira.
Whitehouse, Harvey, Ken Kahn, Michael E. Hochberg, and Joanna J. Bryson. 2012. 'The Role of Simulations in Theory Construction for the Social Sciences: Case Studies concerning Divergent Modes of Religiosity'. *Religion, Brain and Behavior* 2 (3): pp. 182–224.

Williams, Ritva H. 2010. 'Purity, Dirt, Anomalies, and Abominations'. In *Understanding the Social World of the New Testament*, edited by Dietmar Neufeld and Richard E. DeMaris, pp. 207-19. London: Routledge.

Wilson, Margaret. 2010. 'The Re-Tooled Mind: How Culture Re-Engineers Cognition'. *Social Cognition and Affective Neuroscience* 5 (2-3): pp. 180-7.

Wilson, Robert A. 2004. *Boundaries of the Mind: The Individual in the Fragile Sciences—Cognition*. Cambridge: Cambridge University Press.

Wiltermuth, Scott S. and Chip Heath. 2009. 'Synchrony and Cooperation'. *Psychological Science* 20 (1): pp. 1-5.

Winkelman, Michael. 1986. 'Trance States: A Theoretical Model and Cross-Cultural Analysis'. *Ethos* 14 (2): pp. 174-203.

Winkelman, Michael. 1992. *Shamans, Priests, and Witches: A Cross-Cultural Study of Magico-Religious Practitioners*. Anthropological Research Papers 44. Tempe, AZ: Arizona State University.

Winkelman, Michael. 2000. *Shamanism: The Neural Ecology of Consciousness and Healing*. Westport, CT: Bergin and Carvey.

Winkelman, Michael. 2002. 'Shamanism and Cognitive Evolution'. *Cambridge Archaeological Journal* 12 (1): pp. 71-101.

Wright, N. T. 1996. *Jesus and the Victory of God*. Christian Origins and the Question of God 2. Minneapolis, MN: Fortress.

Xygalatas, Dimitris. 2013. *The Burning Saints: Cognition and Culture in the Fire-walking Rituals of the Anastenaria*. Religion, Cognition and Culture. Durham: Acumen.

Xygalatas, Dimitris, et al. 2013. 'Extreme Rituals Promote Prosociality'. *Psychological Science* 20 (10): pp. 1-4.

Yarbro Collins, Adela. 1989. 'The Origin of Christian Baptism'. *Studia Liturgica* 19: pp. 28-46.

Yarbro Collins, Adela. 2007. *Mark: A Commentary*. Hermeneia. Minneapolis, MN: Fortress.

Zahavi, Amotz and Avishag Zahavi. 1997. *The Handicap Principle: The Missing Piece of Darwin's Puzzle*. New York: Oxford University Press.

Zimmer, Hubert D. 2001. 'Why Do Actions Speak Louder than Words: Action Memory as a Variant of Encoding Manipulations or the Result of a Memory System'. In *Memory for Action: A Distinct Form of Episodic Memory*, edited by Hubert D. Zimmer, et al., pp. 151-98. New York: Oxford University Press.

Znamenski, Andrei A. 2007. *The Beauty of the Primitive: Shamanism and the Western Imagination*. Oxford: Oxford University Press.

# Index of Modern Authors

Abbink, Jon 59
Adams, Edward 129$n$, 139$n$, 140
Adams, Fred 170–1
Adler, Yonatan 80, 83, 169$n$
Albera, Dionigi 19
Albl, Martin C. 122
Alcorta, Candace S. 92, 133–4, 137, 139, 151–2
Alexander, Philip S. 118, 120
Alikin, Valeriy A. 148
Allison, Dale C. 98
Anshel, Anat 152
Anttonen, Veikko 44$n$
Ashton, John 103
Atkinson, Quentin 36, 60, 93, 133$n$
Atran, Scott 47, 48, 58, 134, 156
Aune, David E. 119, 120, 164$n$
Avemarie, Friedrich 81, 82
Aydede, Murat 51, 170

Bainbridge, William Sims 26$n$
Baird, William 9, 12
Baker, Coleman A. 180$n$
Balch, David L. 129$n$
Bargh, John A. 161
Barkow, Jerome H. 47
Barnard, Leslie William 121
Barnes, Linda L. 109, 111
Barrett, H. Clark 47
Barrett, Justin, L. 42–5, 47, 54, 57, 59, 87, 105, 116, 155–6, 160$n$
Barrett-Lennard, R. J. S. 121, 123, 125
Barsalou, Lawrence W. 161–2, 174
Bauer, Walter 72
Baumstark, Anton 14–15
Beach, K. 161
Bechtel, William 57
Becker, Jürgen 84
Bell, Catherine 8, 17, 25, 28–31, 34, 63, 73, 74, 100, 104, 130, 159, 181
Bellah, Robert N. 130
Berger, Peter L. 18, 43$n$, 105$n$
Betz, Hans Dieter 10, 72, 120
Bianchi, Ugo 12
Biró, Tamás 32, 59, 85, 88, 164

Blasi, Anthony 19
Blass, Friedrich 83$n$
Blatty, William Peter 105
Bloch, Maurice 19, 76, 89, 162, 176–7
Bloom, Paul 116
Boda, Mark J. 81
Boddy, Janice 104, 105, 114
Bohak, Gideon 120
Bormann, Lukas 28$n$
Boster, James S. 139
Botte, Bernard 15
Boudon, Raymond 54
Bousset, Wilhelm 9–12
Boyd, Robert 48–9, 91
Boyer, Pascal 34, 38$n$, 43–7, 49, 56$n$, 58, 68, 83$n$, 87, 125, 134, 137, 160
Bradshaw, Paul F. 12, 14, 15, 17$n$, 124
Brakke, David 121
Brakmann, Heinzgerd 172
Brandt, Olof 169n, 174
Bressler, E. R. 136, 140
Brody, Howard 114$n$
Brown, Peter 121
Bryson, Joanna J. 60
Bulbulia, Joseph 38, 49–50, 61, 92–3, 96–7, 132–7, 147, 151–2
Bulkeley, Kelly 56$n$
Buller, Bob 72
Burke, Peter 23
Burrows, Lara 161
Buss, David M. 47

Cameron, Ron 21, 140
Carney, Thomas F. 26, 27
Carruthers, Peter 48
Casey, Maurice 81, 108, 110, 112
Casey, R. P. 123
Chalcraft, David J. 84
Chalmers, David 171
Chalupa, Aleš 179$n$
Charlesworth, James H. 81
Chemero, Anthony 158
Chen, Mark 161
Chomsky, Noam 33, 58, 85, 167
Chupungco, Anscar J. 9

# Index of Modern Authors

Chwe, Michael Suk-Young 167–8
Clark, Andy 158, 170, 171
Cloutier, Jasmin 91
Cohen, Emma 104–5, 115–19, 125, 155
Collard, Mark 57
Collins, Billie Jean 72
Confer, Jaime C. 47
Connerton, Paul 163–4
Corballis, Michael C. 167$n$
Cosmides, Leda 47, 48, 160$n$
Craffert, Pieter F. 97$n$, 102–8, 110
Craver, Carl F. 55
Cronk, Lee 139
Crossan, John Dominic 80, 100, 102, 104
Cuneo, Michael W. 105, 106
Czachesz, István 26$n$, 32, 37, 42, 49$n$, 60, 66, 68, 90–1, 106, 112, 119, 129, 149–50, 153

Davies, Douglas J. 41
Davies, Kathy 159
Davies, Stevan L. 91, 97$n$, 102–4, 107
Day, Juliette 3$n$, 9, 17$n$, 27
Day, Matthew 175
Deacon, Terrence W. 132–3
Debrunner, Albert 83$n$
della Porta, Donatella 63
DeMaris, Richard E. 3$n$, 7, 17$n$, 19, 23, 26, 71$n$, 84, 97$n$, 145–6, 169, 174
Dibelius, Martin 122
Dix, Gregory 14
Dölger, Franz Joseph 123, 125
Donald, Merlin 51, 85, 177
Donaldson, James 168
Douglas, Mary 19, 159
Driver, Tom F. 17, 25
DuBois, Thomas A. 104, 115
Duhaime, Jean 19
Dujarier, Michele 172
Dulaney, Siri 125
Dunderberg, Ismo 123
Durkheim, Émile 5, 11, 66–7, 128–30, 131, 147, 167

Eberhart, Christian A. 143
Ebertz, Michael N. 98
Ego, Beate 82$n$
Eichorn, Albert 9, 11
Eliade, Mircea 115
Elliott, John H. 18–19, 26, 27, 31, 107
Emmons, Robert A. 151

Engler, Steven 35, 58, 61$n$
Enslin, Morton S. 71
Ernst, Josef 9, 18$n$, 72, 89, 91
Eshel, Esther 120
Esler, Philip F. 151, 180$n$
Estrada, Nelson P. 24
Evans, Graig E. 201
Eve, Eric 102, 104, 111, 118

Falk, Daniel K. 81
Fauconnier, Gilles 159
Feldman, Louis H. 82
Ferguson, Everett 16, 27, 72, 83–4, 93, 166$n$
Ferngren, Gary B. 120
Finn, Thomas M. 172–3
Fisher, Ronald 151–2
Fiske, Alan Page 38$n$, 125
Fitch, W. Tecumseh 167
Fodor, Jerry A. 158$n$, 160
Forbes, Christopher 151
Franek, Juraj 28, 155
Freud, Sigmund 125
Freyne, Seán 80, 83
Furseth, Inger 77

Gallagher, Shaun 158
Gane, Roy E. 23
Gardiner, Mark Quentin 35, 58, 61$n$
Gaulin, Steven J. C. 139
Geertz, Armin W. 51–2, 54$n$, 159, 163, 175
Gervais, Will M. 48–9, 156
Gibbon, Edward 181
Gibbs, Raymond W. Jr. 158$n$, 160–2
Glenberg, Arthur M. 51, 157–8, 160, 161, 170–1
Goodman, Martin 169$n$
Gordon-Taylor, Benjamin 9, 17$n$
Gorman, Frank H., Jr. 23
Gotay, Carolyn C. 161
Grabbe, Lester L. 144
Gray, Russell 93, 133$n$
Greenhill, Simon 93, 133$n$
Greeven, Heinrich 122
Grimes, Ronald L. 1, 8, 25, 27–30, 41, 55, 73–4, 129, 132
Griswold, Charles L. 95
Grudem, Wayne A. 149
Gruenwald, Ithamar 23–6
Gudme, Anne Katrine de Hemmer 3$n$, 32, 129

## Index of Modern Authors 223

Gunkel, Hermann 9
Guthrie, Stewart E. 28, 43, 44

Hacking, Ian 43n
Hägerland, Tobias 81, 98, 122
Handelman, Don 25
Handwerker, W. Penn 139
Harland, Philip A. 148
Harmon, Katharine E. 17n, 150
Harmon-Jones, Eddie 150
Hart, Trevor 173
Hartin, Patrick J. 123
Hartman, Lars 165
Harvey, Graham 154
Haslam, Nick 38n, 125
Hauser, Marc 134–5, 167
Havas, David A. 161
Hawking, Stephen 64
Heath, Chip 152
Hedström, Peter 54–5
Heimola, Mikko 92, 134, 136
Heitmüller, Wilhelm 9, 11
Hellholm, Christer 16
Hellholm, David 16
Hendel, Ronald S. 82n
Henrich, Joseph 24, 48–9, 68, 91, 108, 133n, 156
Hochberg, Michael E. 60
Holland, Rob W. 151
Hollenbach, Paul W. 98, 100, 102, 104
Holmén, Tom 81
Holmes, Michael W. 166
Holtzmann, Heinrich Julius 11
Hoppitt, William 136
Hornstein, Susan L. 162
Horrell, David G. 19n, 27, 140, 142n
Horst, Steven 52
Hudson, Richard R. 139
Humphrey, Caroline 35, 65–6, 68, 74–5, 79, 85, 89, 108
Hurtado, Larry W. 10n
Hüsken, Ute 41

Iannaccone, Laurence R. 94
Irons, William 50, 92, 134

Jablonka, Eva 48n, 85
Jensen, Jeppe Sinding 43, 46
Jensen, Robin M. 16–17, 166, 169, 173–4
Johnson, Blair T. 91
Johnson, Mark 159

Johnson, Maxwell E. 17, 124, 166
Jokiranta, Jutta 32, 37

Kahn, Ken 60
Kapferer, Bruce 104, 111
Karmiloff-Smith Annette 163
Kaše, Vojtěch 3n, 28n, 136n, 180n
Kawakami, Kerry 151
Kazen, Thomas 32, 104, 117
Keating, Michael 63
Keil, Frank C. 44
Kelhoffer, James A. 91
Kelly, Henry Ansgar 56n, 123–5
Ketola, Kimmo 32, 37, 59, 78, 79
King, Karen L. 12
Kipper, David A. 152
Klawans, Jonathan 82n
Klingbeil, Gerald A. 23, 26
Klinghardt, Matthias 147
Klutz, Todd 102–4, 112, 117, 120n
Knust, Jennifer Wright 81n
Kollmann, Bernd 102, 111, 121
Konstan, David 95
Konvalinka, Ivana 152
Kreinath, Jens 26, 55, 62, 73, 101, 154
Kudlien, Fridolf 94
Kurzban, Robert 47, 160n
Kutsko, Johh F. 72

Laderman, Carol 109n
Laidlaw, James 35, 37, 53, 60, 65–6, 68, 74–5, 79, 85, 89, 108
Lakoff, George 159
Laland, Kevin N. 136
Lamb, Marion J. 48n, 85
Lamoreaux, Jason T. 7
Lampe, Peter 129n, 148
Lange, Armin 82n
Lawrence, Jonathan D. 80
Lawrence, Louise J. 145
Lawson, E. Thomas 31, 33–5, 39, 42–5, 53, 57–61, 63, 65–6, 68, 77, 85–8, 99, 100, 114, 127, 129, 164, 166n
Leeper, Elisabeth A. 123
Lehmkühler, Karsten 10
Levenson, Robert W. 151
Lewis, I. M. 103–4, 114
Liénard, Pierre 38n, 83n, 100, 125, 137, 160
Lietzmann, Hans 12–13
Lindquist, Galina 25

Linnemann, Eta 98
Lisdorf, Anders 26n, 32
Lucia, Amanda J. 79, 84
Luckmann, Thomas 18, 43n, 105n
Lüdemann, Gerd 9
Luomanen, Petri 32, 37, 42, 43, 180n
Lupieri, Edmondo F. 84, 89
Lutz, Antoine 162n

McCauley, Robert N. 31, 33-5, 37, 39, 43-5, 47, 53-4, 57-61, 63, 65, 66, 75-7, 85-8, 99, 114, 127, 129, 155-6, 160, 164-6
McClenon, James 114, 115
McCutcheon, Russell T. 28
MacDonald, Margaret Y. 20, 145
McGowan, Andrew B. 14, 16
Mack, Burton L. 22, 25, 71, 102, 112, 143, 180
MacMullen, Ramsey 121
McNamara, Patrick 151
McNeill, William H. 133, 152
Macrae, C. Neil 91
McVann, Mark 24
Mahoney, Andrew 137
Malina, Bruce J. 18-20, 22, 105, 145
Malley, Brian 44n, 59, 87
Marjanen, Antti 119
Martin, Dale B. 27, 143, 150n
Martin, Luther H. 12, 32, 37, 42, 60, 177
Mayr, Ernst 136n
Meeks, Wayne A. 19-20, 24, 88n, 140, 144-7
Meier, John P. 81, 93, 110, 111
Merton, Robert K. 54
Mesoudi, Alex 48, 55, 140
Meyer, Marvin W. 120
Meyers, Eric M. 80, 83
Miller, Merrill P. 21, 140
Mitchell, Margaret M. 143
Mitchell, Nathan D. 17n
Mithen, Steven J. 44
Mlodinow, Leonard 64
Moore, Lyn 137
Morgan, Michael L. 96
Muir, Edward, 23
Mulligan, Neil W. 162
Murray, Michael 137

Naveh, Shakeh 120
Nemeroff, Carol 116

Neubert, Frank 41
Neyrey, Jerome H. 19
Nissinen, Martti 119
Norderval, Øyvind 16
Norenzayan, Ara 48, 134, 156
Nyhof, Melanie A. 44

Ochs, Vanessa L. 75
Odling-Smee, John 136
Olkes, Cheryl 106
Olyan, Saul M. 81
Ortner, Sherry B. 19
Osiek, Carolyn 129n

Pals, Daniel L. 46, 128
Pearson, James L. 115
Penner, Hans H. 136
Penney, Douglas A. 111n
Petersen, Anders Klostergaard 16, 24
Pettazzoni, Raffaele 94
Phillips, L. Edward 124
Pilch, John J. 104, 105
Pilhofer, Peter 82n
Pinker, Steven 48
Prentiss, Karen Pechilis 79
Pyysiäinen, Ilkka 8, 32, 42-6, 49n, 52, 56, 57, 61, 68, 87, 101n, 115, 128, 129, 134-6, 154-6, 158, 167-8, 180n

Quack, Johannes 35, 41, 66

Räisänen, Heikki 53, 144
Raj, Selva J. 79
Ramble, Charles 44
Rappaport, Roy A. 5, 25, 130-2, 138-9, 145n, 163n
Reddish, Paul 147, 151-2
Regev, Eyal 81
Rehkopf, Friedrich 83n
Reitzenstein, Richard 11
Repstad, Pål 77
Richerson, Peter J. 48-9, 91
Riskind, John H. 161
Robbins, Philip 51, 170
Roberts, Alexander 168
Rohrbaugh, Richard 19
Roitto, Rikard 3n, 17n, 32, 95-6, 123, 165n, 166n, 181n
Roseman, Marina 109
Rotschild, Clare K. 72, 83, 90, 93, 98
Rousseau, John J. 102, 112

# Index of Modern Authors

Rozin, Paul 116
Rudolph, Kurt 12
Ruffle, Bradley J. 134, 137
Russell, C. D. 23, 94

Salamone, Frank A. 73
Sanders, E. P. 71, 80, 102
Santos, Ava 161, 162, 174
Sax, William S. 28, 35, 41, 62, 66, 114
Schjødt, Uffe 52
Schröder, Marti 9
Seelig, Gerald 12
Segal, Robert A. 132$n$, 154
Sered, Susan S. 109, 111
Shantz, Colleen 32, 115$n$, 118, 149–50
Shaked, Shaul 120
Shapiro, Lawrence 157–8, 160, 170
Sidky, Homayan 115$n$
Simmons, W. Kyle 161–2, 174
Slingerland, Edward 42, 57, 141$n$
Slone, D. Jason 45
Smith, Dennis E. 16, 129$n$, 147, 148
Smith, Eric Alden 49, 50
Smith, Jonathan Z. 10, 21–2, 148, 149
Smith, Morton 80, 81, 102, 107
Smith, Richard 120
Smith, William Robertson 10
Snoek, Jan A. M. 26, 28, 55, 62, 73
Snyder, Graydon F. 165$n$, 173
Soler, Montserrat 137
Sorensen, Eric 111$n$, 118, 122
Sørensen, Jesper 32, 42, 75
Sosis, Richard 38, 39, 46, 49–50, 92, 94, 132–40, 142, 151–2, 154
Sperber, Dan 42, 49, 68, 92, 160
Spinks, Bryan D. 16
Staal, Frits 65, 101
Stausberg, Michael 26, 30, 55, 62, 73, 114
Stegemann, Ekkehard 145
Stegemann, Wolfgang 145
Stephenson, Barry 8, 28, 30$n$, 35, 41, 62
Stepper, Sabine 161
Sterelny, Kim 136
Stewart, Eric C. 19, 43
Still, Todd D. 140
Stoller, Paul 106
Stommel, Eduard 175
Stowers, Stanley K. 22, 81, 141, 142, 146–9, 153
Strack, Fritz 161

Strecker, Christian 16, 24, 102, 104, 111–12, 146
Stringer, Martin D. 16, 17
Sun, Ron 61
Swedberg, Richard 54–5
Symons, Cynthia S. 91

Taft, Robert F. 15, 17, 27
Tambiah, Stanley J. 100
Tappenden, Frederick S. 159
Taussig, Hal 7, 16, 146, 147
Taylor, Joan E. 72, 82–5, 88–9, 93
Theissen, Gerd 18, 20–1, 102, 104, 105, 110, 111–14, 119, 140
Tom, Gail 161
Tomasello, Michael 133, 155, 167
Tooby, John 47, 48, 160$n$
Tremlin, Todd 45, 160
Troelsch, Ernst 9
Tucker, Brian J. 180$n$
Turcotte, Paul-André 19
Turley, Stephen Richard 7, 145, 146
Turner, Léon 36, 45–6, 59
Turner, Mark 159
Turner, Victor 17, 20, 24, 36, 145–7, 154
Twelftree, Graham H. 102, 104, 112–13, 121$n$

Uller, Tobias 136
Unger, Domini J. 121
Uro, Ilkka 106$n$
Uro, Risto 3$n$, 12, 17$n$, 19, 32, 37, 42, 45, 61, 68, 71, 81, 87, 89, 92, 98, 111, 134, 143, 155, 172$n$, 180$n$

Vaage, Leif. E. 71$n$
van Aarde, Andries 107
van Baaren, Rick B. 151
van Gennep, Arnold 20, 145
van Knibbenberg, Ad 151
Van Slyke, James A. 56
Várhelyi, Zsuzsanna 81$n$
Vegge, Tor 16
Vermes, Geza 102
Vial, Theodore M 59
Vielhauer, Philipp 91
Visala, Aku 47, 48, 52, 53, 56
von Dobbeler, Stephanie 83$n$, 89
Vyse, Stuart A. 106

Wahlen, Clinton 118
Wallace, Daniel B. 83$n$

Wassen, Cecilia 117, 118
Webb, Robert L. 71–2, 80, 83–4, 89, 93
Wedderburn, A. J. M. 12, 144, 146
Weimer, Jade Brooklyn 152, 163
Weinhold, Jan 35, 41, 66
Weiss, Johannes 9
Werline, Rodney A. 81
West, Fritz 15
White, Michael L. 168$n$, 169$n$
Whitehouse, Harvey 32, 35–7, 39, 42–5, 59–61, 68, 76–8, 83, 90, 119, 156, 163, 171–2
Willard, Ayana K. 48, 156
Williams, Ritva H. 19
Wilson, Margaret 51, 172–3
Wilson, Robert A. 158$n$, 171
Wiltermuth, Scott S. 152

Winkelman, Michael 103, 115, 149
Winkielman, Piotr 150
Winkler, Gabriele 15
Wise, Michael O. 111$n$
Wrede, William 9
Wright, N. T. 80

Xygalatas, Dimitris 60, 137, 152

Yarbro Collins, Adela 83, 94, 104, 110$n$
Ylikoski, Petri 55

Zahavi, Amotz 39, 138
Zahavi, Avishag 39, 138
Zimmer, Hubert D. 162
Znamenski, Andrei A. 104, 115$n$

# General Index

action representation 33n, 39, 86, 129
altered state of consciousness (ASC) 97, 101, 103, 109, 149
Amma (Ammachi) 78–80, 84, 86
  ritual hugging of 84, 86
*Apocryphal Acts* 120
*Apostolic Tradition* 122, 123–6, 173
ascetic practices 98, 143, 163, 166, 182
Athanasius of Alexandria 120, 166n
*awan* (Mali Baining dance) 77

baptisteries 174
baptism (Christian) 11, 12, 16, 20–1, 27, 33, 34, 68, 69, 72n, 75, 84, 99, 123–4, 144, 145, 146, 150, 154, 163–7, 168–9, 172–5, 181, 182
baptism (immersion) of John 71–3, 75, 80–9, 92–8, 99–100, 122
  of Jesus 71n, 97, 102, 173–4
baptismal fonts 174
behavioural ecology 39, 49–50, 61, 134, 136
biocultural theory of religion 51

canonical messages (Rappaport) 131, 163n
Catechumenate 124, 172, 182
Charismatic Signalling 50, 93, 96–7, 133
circumcision 144, 169
Clement (First Epistle of) 153
co-evolutionary (dual inheritance) theory 48, 49–51, 132
cognitive attraction 49n, 177
cognitive modules 47–8, *see also* mental tools
  language module 58, 85, *see also* universal grammar
cognitive science 32, 39, 43, 45, 46, 51, 56n, 63, 68, 157–8, 172, 175–6, 177
Cognitive Science of Religion (CSR) 26n, 32, 37n, 38, 40, 41–70, 85, 115, 134, 155, 156, 158, 175, 176
  adaptationist vs. by-product debate 46, 134–5
  broadly defined 39, 45, 70, 134

'standard' model 46–50, 56, 58, 61, 70, 75, 175
cognitive tools (M. Wilson) 51, 165n, 172, 174, 182
Commitment (Honest) Signalling 33, 38–9, 50, 61, 67, 69, 92–6, 133–9, 141, 143–7, 152–3, 181
*communitas* (Victor Turner) 36, 59, 145–6
Comparative Liturgy 14–15, 25
computational modelling 26n, 60, 179n
conceptual blending 159
confession of sins 81, 91, 94–6, 122
Corinthians (Epistles to) 140, 141, 143, 150, 151
Corinthians (Corinthian assembly) 22, 118, 129, 139n, 141–2, 145, 147–50, 153, 165
Costly Signalling 33, 38, 50, 67, 92, 133, 135–6
  *see also* Commitment Signalling
credibility enhancing display (CRED) 49, 90–1, 108
cultural anthropology 18–19, 20, 22, 103
cultural evolution 15, 48–9, 61, 68, 91, 115, 141n, 166n, 177, 181n
cultural learning 48–50, 60
CPS- agents (culturally postulated superhuman agents) 33–4, 63, 65–6, 86, 114, 127

dance 77, 127, 133, 149, 152
*darshan* 79–80
Database of Religious History (DRH) 141n
dual process (of mind) 45

embodied cognition 51, 68, 157–60, 163, 166n, 170, 173–4, 176, 182
embodied states 161–2
embodiment 29, 157, 159, 161–2, 175, 177
emotional contagion 150–1
emotions (as costly or honest signals) 138, 147, 151–3

evolutionary approaches 45, 47, 136n, 139
Evolutionary Cognitive Science of Religion (ECSR) 45
evolutionary psychology 39, 44, 47–50, 125, 160n
evolutionary sciences 31, 40–1, 44, 136, 177, 180
  see also evolutionary approaches
Excerpts of Theodotus 123–4
exorcism 101–4, 109–12, 114, 117, 120–2
  liturgical 123–5, 172
  modern 105–6
explanation (theory of) 26n, 52–6, 58, 62
explanatory mechanism 31, 53, 55, 62
explanatory pluralism 56–7, 61, 70, 176
extended cognition 51–2, 68, 131

family-resemblance concept 1n, 28, 62, 73, 155
firewalking 74, 152
functionalism 18, 20, 21, 38, 54, 136, 145–7
fuzzy-set concept, see family-resemblance concept

genealogical approach 12–14
Generative Historiography of Religion Project (GEHIR) 179n
glossolalia, see tongue speaking
Gospel of Thomas 126, 142
Greek Magical Papyri 102, 121

Handicap Principle 39, 138
Hazard-Precaution System 38n, 83n, 125
History of Religion School 8, 9–13, 20, 24, 40
house churches (early Christian) 67, 181
hypersensitive agent detective device (HADD) 45, 47

iconic signs (in Peirce's theory) 132
Ignatius of Antioch 166
immersion, see baptism of John
indexical signs 132–3, 138, 151, 163n
International Association for the Cognitive Science of Religion (IACSR) 41n, 44
Irenaeus of Lyons 121

James (epistle of) 113, 121–3, 125
Jesus
  as healer 100, 102–8, 109, 111–14, 118
  as magico-religious practitioner 102–3, 107, 115
  as shamanic figure 102–3, 107, 109, 112, 115
  as teacher of kingdom 100, 103, 108
John (First Epistle of) 95–6, 122
John the Baptist 35, 59, 66–98, 100, 108, 113, 164, 169, 173
  and Jesus 72, 98, 100
  disciples of 75, 93, 98
  movement of 72, 78, 83–5, 87–8, 93, 95–6, 99
  as teacher 89
Josephus 72, 75, 82, 83, 89, 90, 92, 93, 118
Justin Martyr 120, 173

liturgical history 13–18, 40, 175
Liturgical Studies 8, 9, 13, 17
liturgy of Sarapion 12
Lord's Supper 11, 12–13, 20, 144–5, 148
Luke (Gospel of) 71, 75, 111, 151

magic 35, 66, 69, 99–100, 103, 106, 113–14, 120, 121, 128–9
  antagonistic 111
  contagious 110
  sympathetic 110
Mark (Gospel of) 71, 82–3, 94, 97, 104, 111–12
Martyrdom of Justin 169n
Matthew (Gospel of) 71, 93, 111
maturational vs. practiced naturalness 75–6, 156
meal (early Christian) 3n, 11–12, 16, 22, 28, 129, 147–8, 180
medical anthropology 101, 126
memory 14, 36–7, 39, 44, 45n, 58, 60, 68, 90, 92, 155, 161, 163, 167, 171–2, 177
  episodic 36, 60, 90, 171
  long-term 90, 92, 162, 172n
  procedural 162n
  semantic 36, 60, 90, 171
mental tools 44, 47, 51n
  see also cognitive modules
'Mickey Mouse problem' 48, 156

## General Index

middle-range theory 54–5, 59, 62, 65, 67, 137, 139
minimal counterintuitiveness 44, 46n, 49
*miqveh* 83, 86, 169n
model-dependent realism 64
 *see also* theory-dependent realism
Modes of Religiosity Theory 33, 35, 37, 43, 44n, 45n, 58–60, 68, 90, 171
 imagistic mode 36–7, 60, 90
 doctrinal mode 36–7, 60, 78, 90, 119
modularity (of the mind) 33, 47–8, 58, 158, 160
 *see also* cognitive modules
Montanism 119
multilevel analysis 52, 53, 56–7, 61, 62, 70, 180
music 25–6, 97, 110, 119n, 133, 144, 148, 149, 152, 163, 172, 182
myth and ritual theory 22, 69, 154

naturalism 52, 56

*Odes of Solomon* 119

*Passio Sancti Justini et socii* 169n
Paul (apostle) 11, 12, 13, 19–20, 22, 24, 67, 103, 107, 118, 119n, 129, 140–53, 165
Pauline Christianity 18, 19–20, 69, 139–47, 152–3, 179
performance theory 30, 31, 147n
phenomenological approach (to religion) 46
Philippians (Epistle to) 143
polyphasic vs. monophasic culture 105, 107
Pomio Kivung 35–6, 43, 77–8, 163, 172n
practice theory 17, 29–30, 31, 159
Principle of Superhuman Agency 33–4
prophecy 118–19, 148–50, 152
proselyte baptism (Jewish) 84n
prosociality 92, 151
proximate and ultimate causes 136–7
purification, *see* purity
purity 19, 32, 82–3, 84n, 86, 88, 109, 124–5, 164, 180

'Q' (Sayings Source) 71
Qumran 94, 118

rabbinic Judaism 59, 84n
recursion 167

redescribing Early Christianity 21–2
Religionsgeschichliche Schule, *see* History of Religion School
religious experience 23, 32, 36, 46, 56, 119n, 149, 174
Religious Studies 1n, 22, 32, 41, 43, 57, 85, 155
Revelation (Book of) 119, 144
ring ceremony 77–8
rite, *see* ritual
ritual
 as action 33, 35, 65–6, 67, 69, 70, 74, 85–6, 88, 100, 152
 agent 33–4, 67, 77, 85–7, 91, 99, 164–5, 175, 182
 archetypal quality of 65, 74–5
 bathing (Jewish) 80, 83, 85–6, 89
 and belief 24, 91, 108, 154
 cognitive theories of 8, 31, 39, 40, 41–2, 58–62, 68, 69, 70, 73, 87, 99
 as communication 38, 65, 67, 92, 126, 131, 133, 134, 138
 and cooperation 38, 50, 65, 66–7, 69, 70, 92–3, 96, 128–53, 154, 167
 as costly (commitment) signal 38, 67, 92, 93, 95–7, 132n, 134, 138
 definition of 1n, 28–9, 35, 63–4, 65, 67, 100–1, 108, 114, 125, 126, 130, 137
 doctrinal 68, 90, 171, 172
 effervescence 11, 128, 147, 151, 167
 efficacy 33, 35, 66, 69, 74, 75, 111, 114n, 129, 168–9
 failure 101, 111, 112
 frame 30, 175
 'grammar' 92, 129
  *see also* ritual structure
 as hard-to-fake signal, *see* as costly signal
 healing 34, 66, 69, 98, 100–1, 111, 113–14, 121–3, 126, 181
 high-arousal 78, 90, 92, 147–52
 imagistic 68, 78, 90, 150, 171–2
 initiation 16, 17, 83–4, 87, 98, 123, 124, 146, 172
 innovation 59, 72, 73–6, 78–80, 88, 92, 98, 99, 109, 151, 152, 164, 180
 invention, *see* ritual innovation
 knowledge 69, 155, 157, 165
  *see also* religious knowledge

ritual (cont.)
  patient 33–4, 63, 65–7, 70, 85–8, 91, 94, 97, 99, 100, 114, 122, 127, 129, 164–5
  in Pauline assemblies 19–20, 69, 141, 144–52
  performance-centred 108, 122, 125, 126
  of repentance 81
  special agent 33–4, 66, 77, 85–8, 91, 99, 113, 114, 123, 164
  special instrument 33–4, 67, 86, 114, 164, 166$n$
  special patient 33–4, 114, 123, 164
  spontaneous exegesis of 60, 78, 90, 171–2
  structure 34, 85, 86, 88, 91, 92, 98, 114, 164
  transmission 32, 37, 39, 60, 61, 68, 85, 89–91, 131, 154, 159
  *see also* magic
Ritual and the Emergence of Early Christian Religion (REECR) project 3$n$
Ritual Competence Theory 33, 35, 42, 44, 58–61, 69, 85–6, 114, 129, 164, 180, 182
Ritual Dynamics (Collaborative Research Centre) 25–6
Ritualdynamik, *see* Ritual Dynamics
Ritual Form Theory, *see* Ritual Competence Theory
ritualization 22, 28, 29, 35, 66, 74, 108$n$, 137, 139, 159, 180, 181
Ritual Studies 1$n$, 8, 17, 23–6, 30, 40, 41, 63, 67, 68, 73, 101, 127, 159, 161

sacrifice (early Judaism) 80–1
sacrificial cult 21, 82, 142–3
self-referential messages 131–2, 138, 163$n$

shamanism 101, 105, 115
  neoshamanism 115
Signalling Theory 35, 39, 50, 67, 92–4, 96, 132–4, 138, 141, 181
situated cognition 51, 69, 158$n$, 170–2, 175, 177, 182, *see also* embodied cognition
social anthropology 17, 128
social constructionism 43$n$
Social-Scientific Criticism (SSC) 7, 18, 22, 40
socio-cognitive approach 31, 42, 61, 67, 70, 129, 131, 180, 182
sociology of knowledge 18, 20, 43$n$
spirit possession 69, 71$n$, 97, 101–7, 112, 114, 115–20, 123, 125–7, 149–50, 181
  executive 116–19, 125, 126
  pathogenic 116–18, 123, 125, 126
  peripheral 103
  positive 118–20
*Stargate* (science fiction) 106$n$
structural approach (to liturgy) 14
symbolic anthropology 43, 61, 67–8
symbolic signs 132, 163$n$ (in Peirce's theory)
*symposium*, *see* meal
synchrony 96–7, 149–53
syncretism 11–12
Synoptic Gospels 109, 117, 118, 142

Tertullian 168$n$
theological incorrectness 44
theoretical pluralism 29, 42, 55, 62–4, 70, 158
theories and models 26$n$
theory-dependent realism 28, 64, 126
tongue speaking 118, 144, 148–53

universal grammar 33, 58, 85, 176$n$

volitional religiosity 119, 149

The manufacturer's authorised representative in the EU for product safety is Oxford University Press España S.A. of el Parque Empresarial San Fernando de Henares, Avenida de Castilla, 2 – 28830 Madrid (www.oup.es/en or product. safety@oup.com). OUP España S.A. also acts as importer into Spain of products made by the manufacturer.

www.ingramcontent.com/pod-product-compliance
Lightning Source LLC
Chambersburg PA
CBHW061920200126
38499CB00019B/557